PAUL D. WOLFOWITZ

PAUL D. WOLFOWITZ

Visionary Intellectual, Policymaker,
and Strategist

Lewis D. Solomon

PRAEGER SECURITY INTERNATIONAL
Westport, Connecticut • London

Library of Congress Cataloging-in-Publication Data

Solomon, Lewis D.
   Paul D. Wolfowitz : visionary intellectual, policymaker, and strategist / Lewis D.
Solomon.
      p. cm.
   Includes bibliographical references and index.
   ISBN 978-0-275-99587-4 (alk. paper)
   1. Wolfowitz, Paul. 2. Wolfowitz, Paul—Political and social views. 3. Wolfowitz,
Paul—Influence. 4. Statesmen—United States—Biography. 5. Intellectuals—United
States—Biography. 6. United States—Foreign relations—Iraq. 7. Iraq—Foreign
relations—United States. 8. United States—Foreign relations—1989– 9. Conservatism—
United States. 10. World Bank—Officials and employees—Biography. I. Title.
   E840.8.W65S65 2007
   327.730092—dc22   2007008470
   [B]

British Library Cataloguing in Publication Data is available.

Library of Congress Catalog Card Number: 2007008470
ISBN-13: 978-0-275-99587-4
ISBN-10: 0-275-99587-9

First published in 2007

Praeger Security International, 88 Post Road West, Westport, CT 06881
An imprint of Greenwood Publishing Group, Inc.
www.praeger.com

Printed in the United States of America

∞

The paper used in this book complies with the
Permanent Paper Standard issued by the National
Information Standards Organization (Z39.48-1984).

10 9 8 7 6 5 4 3 2 1

Contents

Chapter 1

Introduction

This book seeks to go behind the overabundance of negative media stories and the caricature of Paul Wolfowitz: his being branded an American imperialist and called "Wolfowitz of Arabia,"[1] or suggestions that he is a follower of Leo Strauss, a noted twentieth-century political philosopher. Conspiracy theories abound, with some placing him at the center of a neoconservative, predominantly Jewish cabal, which sought to run the world.

Prior to his becoming an international civil servant as head of the World Bank Group, Wolfowitz spent most of his public-service career thinking about America's power—political, economic, and military—in the world, representing the United States abroad, and lobbying to enlarge its unipolar position. Ultimately, he sought to use American military might to build a new political order in the Middle East.

In the wake of September 11, America proceeded to redefine its relationship with the rest of the world. Wolfowitz offered a well-articulated global vision, developed over nearly thirty years of U.S. governmental service. He combined a hard-nosed assessment of America's national security interests with an expansive sense of idealism.

His vision focused on four major elements. First, he coupled his idealism, particularly his longstanding quest to promote democracy overseas, with a searching assessment of U.S. strategic national-security and geopolitical interests. Second, he saw a unipolar world in which the United States had become the global custodian by virtue of its military superiority. Although not a veteran, he evidenced a belief in the efficacy of U.S. military power. He looked to the military as a key American tool in dealing with other nations. Third, he manifested an optimistic assessment of U.S. capabilities in terms of money and commitment. He sought to use America's military and diplomatic positions to promote U.S. interests, keep the United States on the initiative and not simply react to the world as America found it. Given its preeminence in global affairs, Wolfowitz believed the United States could preempt perceived threats to its security, domestically and overseas.

The power of Wolfowitz's ideas found a key patron. After 9/11, President George W. Bush implemented Wolfowitz's concepts of a hegemonic foreign policy, based on using military power to spreading democracy and a belief in America's omnipotence. A proponent of American exceptionalism—its unique destiny and superiority—and a believer in the United States as a beneficent force for good throughout the world that lacks predatory instincts, Bush sought to create a world order based on democratic capitalism with the United States as the world's sheriff: the guarantor of order and stability as well as the enforcer of norms. Through its military deployment and diplomatic efforts to buttress the global economy, the United States would provide the basic governance mechanism to keep the world stable and on track.

OVERVIEW OF THE BOOK

Instead of pursuing Wolfowitz's personal and career steps in dogged detail, I want to capture him at key points in his life. I trace the road to Baghdad based on his interventionistic, practical but idealistic worldview, which is less sensitive to diplomatic alliances. He rose to greater prominence than any previous deputy defense secretary, the number two in the civilian leadership of Pentagon, drawing controversy not only for the invasion of Iraq and its aftermath but also for his vision of a democratic transformation of the Middle East, a deeply troubled, autocratic region. His current position, as president of the World Band, provides us with a way to analyze the bank's efforts to alleviate global poverty.

In brief, Wolfowitz's career progressed through eighteen steps as follows:[2]

1. June 1966 to September 1966: Management Intern, U.S. Bureau of the Budget

2. September 1970 to June 1973: Assistant Professor of Political Science, Yale University

3. September 1973 to March 1977: various positions at the U.S. Arms Control and Disarmament Agency (the Agency): including 1973–74, staff member, Evaluation and Policy Division of the Plans and Analysis Bureau; 1974–75, Special Assistant to the Agency's Director; 1975–76, Deputy Assistant Director for the Agency's Verification and Analysis Bureau; 1976–77, Special Assistant for Strategic Arms Limitation Talks in the Office of the Director of the Agency

4. June 1976 to December 1976: member of Team B, which provided an intelligence and foreign-policy critique

5. March 1977 to September 1980: Deputy Assistant Secretary of Defense for Regional Programs, U.S. Department of Defense

6. September 1980 to December 1980: Visiting Associate Professor, School of Advanced International Studies, Johns Hopkins University

7. January 1981 to December 1982: Director of Policy Planning, U.S. Department of State

8. December 1982 to March 1986: Assistant Secretary of State for East Asia and the Pacific, U.S. Department of State

9. April 1986 to May 1989: U.S. Ambassador to Indonesia

10. May 1989 to January 1993: Undersecretary of Defense for Policy, U.S. Department of Defense

11. January 1993 to December 1993: George F. Kennan Professor of National Security Strategy, National Defense University

12. January 1994 to March 2001: Dean, Paul H. Nitze School of Advanced International Studies, Johns Hopkins University

13. 1996: chief foreign policy advisor to the presidential campaign of Robert Dole

14. January 1998 to September 1998: member, Commission to Assess the Ballistic Threat to the United States

15. June 1998 to February 2001: member, U.S. Defense Policy Board, an adjunct advisory group to the U.S. Secretary of Defense

16. 1999 to 2000: a foreign policy advisor to the presidential campaign of George W. Bush

17. February 2001 to May 2005: Deputy Secretary of Defense, U.S. Department of Defense

18. June 2005 to date: President, The World Bank Group

Chapter 2 considers Wolfowitz's personal and intellectual roots. His worldview goes back to three sources: his father, Jacob Wolfowitz, who provided an atmosphere of intellectual and moral seriousness; his undergraduate days at Cornell University, particularly the intellectual hothouse of the Telluride Association residence; and his graduate mentor, Albert Wohlstetter, at the University of Chicago. Starting with his association with Wohlstetter, Wolfowitz began a long series of key professional relationships with his mentors and then his students. He was always loyal and unthreatening. The chapter concludes with a description of two lucky breaks that marked his career in the federal bureaucracy.

Chapter 3 discusses Wolfowitz's development as a practical idealist. He coupled his idealism, particularly his longstanding vision of democracy, with a hardheaded assessment of strategic U.S. interests. His experience with the 1985–86 "people power" uprising against the Filipino dictator Ferdinand Marcos propelled Wolfowitz's passion for spreading democracy through the globe. Based on the premise that people everywhere seek political freedom and self-government, he believed universal ideals could be used to achieve a practical, twenty-first-century goal of curtailing terrorism and creating as he put it, "a world that will be very congenial for American interests."[3] Beginning with his 1976 service on Team B, which critically analyzed Soviet strategic aims, he also pressed the need for the United States to develop more accurate intelligence. His efforts in 2002, this time with respect to al Qaeda's ties to Iraq, are examined in chapter 3. Wolfowitz also sought to ground American foreign and national-security policies in the need to protect and advance U.S. interests as well as in a rigorous analysis of global and regional situations and their geopolitical implications, particularly with regard to the importance of petroleum resources and the precariousness of the Persian Gulf region. Spotting Iraq as a regional menace in 1977, he viewed that nation as a threat to strategic U.S. interests in the Middle East. He saw that the energy-rich world of the Middle East eclipsed everything else on the list of U.S. geopolitical concerns.

Chapter 4 analyzes Wolfowitz's belief, going back to his service in the State Department in the 1980s and the Defense Department in the early 1990s, that the United States could (and should) assert its military and diplomatic power, especially in a post–cold war world. The 1992 Defense Planning Guidance, which reflected Wolfowitz's views, examined the implications of the United States as the world's sole superpower. Wolfowitz had a longstanding belief in the efficacy of U.S. military power, despite the debacle in Vietnam, believing that the buildup of U.S. military strength would make it fruitless and financially disastrous for any nation (or group of nations) to compete with the United States in the global arena. As a corollary, he thought that the United States ought to be reluctant to enter into agreements or make accommodations with other nations, such as China. He evidenced concern that making deals would constrain U.S. freedom of action overseas. Based on an optimistic assessment of U.S. capabilities in terms of money and commitment, he wanted the United States to embrace its unipolar status and take steps to protect and enhance that status whether or not other nations agreed with the United States.

Wolfowitz doubted whether the old multilateral institutions and the cold war containment strategies would continue to remain viable. No longer could national goals be pursued exclusively though a network of alliances and multilateral institutions. His skepticism that other nations shared American interests or values led him to favor acting alone, with only a few allies, and the formation of ad hoc coalitions, looking to multilateral institutions only when it served U.S. interests.

With the United States as the sole superpower, he concluded that many nations would look to America for leadership. If the United States did not provide leadership on key matters, others lacked the capacity or the will to do so.

In tracing three wars, the 1991 Gulf War (chapter 5), the 2001 campaign in Afghanistan (chapter 6), and the 2003 liberation of Iraq (chapter 7), the book examines the efforts of the United States to reverse Iraq's invasion of Kuwait, root out al Qaeda from Afghanistan, and bring down a tyrant and strive to create a stable democracy in Iraq.

In 1989, Wolfowitz became Undersecretary of Defense for Policy. He established an enduring bond with his boss, Secretary of Defense Richard B. (Dick) Cheney. As discussed in chapter 5, Wolfowitz participated in the Bush 41 administration's deliberations, before, during, and after the Gulf War. In these discussions, Wolfowitz repeatedly warned Cheney, among others, against attempting a strategy based on containing Saddam Hussein.

The Gulf War of early 1991 started with an intensive air campaign followed by a flanking maneuver advocated by Cheney and Wolfowitz and the quick defeat of Iraq. The United States asserted its leadership in mounting an extensive international coalition and by its willingness to use military force.

Wolfowitz long believed that the sudden end to the 1991 Desert Storm ground campaign, which left Saddam in power, was a mistake. By the late 1990s, he came to support a policy of regime change in Iraq.

Chapter 6 analyzes how the events of 9/11 upended conventional thinking and strategies, providing an opening for Wolfowitz on September 15, 2001, at a key Camp David meeting with President Bush, and thereafter. In an era of weapons of mass destruction—biological, chemical, nuclear—monstrous dictators in the Middle East, leading rogue nations, threatened not only their beleaguered countries and nearby nations, but the West as well. Amorphous, stateless groups, such as al Qaeda, a terrorist network that circles the globe, posed an ever growing threat. Combating religiously motivated terrorism unconstrained by any limits on violence, particularly the targeting of civilians by unconventional means, became for Wolfowitz America's first priority overseas and at home.

Following 9/11, Bush needed a vision, a way of looking at America and its place in the world. Based on his years of study and his governmental experience, Wolfowitz readily supplied that a vision. Bush came to reject America's former policy of treating terrorism as a legal, not a military, problem. Declaring that the United States would call to account not only terrorist groups but also nations that harbored and sponsored them, Bush took the battle to the enemy, beginning with draining one swamp where the terrorists trained. The 2001 war in Afghanistan represented the initial military steps by the United States in an ongoing war against any terrorist group or nation that could threaten American supremacy.

From early 2001 up to the beginning of the war of March 2003, as described in chapter 7, the Bush White House faced the question of what to do about Saddam Hussein's regime. Deterrence and defensive operations came into disfavor. The White House gravitated toward strategies focused on an offensive military action.

The terrorist attacks of 9/11, as part of a campaign of violence aimed at total victory, represented by the establishment of a theocratic Islamic caliphate from Spain to Indonesia, were (and are) not something that could be wished away or dealt with after the fact as a law-enforcement matter. Terrorists and the regimes that sponsor them are not legal matters; rather, they represent a national-security issue.

The enemy could not be answered by understanding, aid, or in the hardest cases, legal action.

The combination of terrorism and weapons of mass destruction presented a threat of an entirely new and different magnitude. As described in chapter 7, the Bush Doctrine, which basically reflects the 1992 Defense Planning Guidance, recognizes that the United States could not wait for terrorists or rogue states to strike and then retaliate. This formed the basis for Wolfowitz's advocacy of regime change in Iraq. Both Bush and Wolfowitz saw real evil in the world and sought to confront and destroy it. Where small groups of fanatical individuals could, without warning, unleash violence against the civilized world, the traditional system of reactive, multilateral cooperation and institutions had to give way to a proactive, preventive approach.

Wolfowitz served as the chief idea man and policy expert, the preeminent intellectual force in the Defense Department, during Bush 43's first term. As a leading architect of the 2003 invasion of Iraq, perhaps more than any other Pentagon official, he became identified with the Iraq war and the campaign to implement democracy there.

After 9/11, Wolfowitz focused on the need to transport democratic ideals to the Middle East as a wedge against America's new enemy, terrorist groups and rogue nations. As an outspoken advocate of removing Saddam, he held firm to his belief about Iraq's and, more generally, the Middle East's democratic potential and the possibility of building an ever increasing number of regimes friendly to the United States. Changing the political culture by creating a functioning democracy in one country, he assumed, could shift a whole region in a chain reaction. A democratic Iraq would serve as the new pillar of the Middle East. It would harbor neither terrorists nor evil designs on neighboring nations.

As described in chapter 8, the American venture in Iraq represented a roll of the dice, a high-stakes gamble. Wolfowitz sought to shake up the status quo, traditionally centered on keeping reliable autocrats in place and oil flowing, not only in Iraq but also in the whole Middle East.

Wolfowitz did not view the 2003 conflict in terms of the use of American military power. Noting that he saw the debate instead in terms of overturning the status quo in the Middle East, he asserted: "I see it as a debate over the acceptability of the status quo—whether you go back to containment; living with the Soviet Union; living with Marcos, Korean dictators, Suharto; living with Saddam; or even today living with Iranians. There is a constant bias toward inaction, because the risks are less obvious. . . . The point is, this has something to do, I think, with the morality of what we did. But it also has a lot to do with the nature of the enemy we are still fighting. The use of force to liberate people is very different from the use of force to suppress or control them, or even to defeat them."[4]

He saw the futility and danger of foreign and national-security policies centered on the notion of equilibrium. Instead of opting for the illusion of stability and risk avoidance, Wolfowitz sought change, which would lead to freedom and democracy. He hoped that the liberation of Iraq, creating the opportunity to build a freer, more open society there, would serve as a beacon of hope in the Middle East. It represented one of the most ambitious programs to transform a region in U.S. history.

However, the Bush Administration, including Wolfowitz, underestimated the price of regime change in Iraq, a nation marked by sectarian rivalries, ethnic feuds, and ancient grudges as well as significant al Qaeda operations. The constant, prolonged, day-to-day peacekeeping activities in Iraq proved costly in human and financial terms. The security, political, and economic mistakes made by the United States in Iraq are analyzed in chapter 8, along with the planning for postwar Iraq, the players, and their assumptions that have proved faulty, at least in hindsight.

The insurgents, including al Qaeda and Sunni Baathists, realize how much is at stake. Forcing a premature withdrawal of U.S. troops, thereby destroying any chance for a democratic Iraq, would represent a huge defeat for the United States, demonstrate American vulnerability, and force a reexamination of U.S. foreign and national-security policies. Iraq has thus become the central front in the global war on terrorism.

The security, political, and economic challenges in Iraq, although great, are not insurmountable. At present, however, it is uncertain whether it is possible to plant a relatively stable, religiously based, decentralized democracy in Iraq and if so, whether this transformation in one nation will spur the democratization of the Middle East. Also, it is unclear whether America's foray into Iraq will be followed by withdrawal and disengagement.

Wolfowitz saw the 2003 invasion of Iraq as part of the larger war against terrorism, with the fight against Islamic fascism as America's ongoing battle against totalitarianism, the twenty-first century's successor to its previously successful struggles against Nazism and Soviet Communism. For Wolfowitz, there was a basic similarity in these three struggles. In an interview, he noted, "[W]e're dealings with a fundamental existential threat to our way of life, to our values." "The main parallel," he continued, is "the nature of the challenge it presents to us. That is, it really does require mobilization of a major effort on our part. It requires contemplating a long-term struggle."[5] Iraq is one piece, albeit an important piece, in a global war against terrorists and their state sponsors, which has been described as World War IV (with the cold war as World War III),[6] involving billions of people and dozens of nations.

The broader struggle to overcome nihilistic Islamic fascism—those who follow the cult of death and the politics of slaughter—in Iraq and elsewhere throughout the world will take hard work, sacrifice, and time, probably decades, perhaps with no end in sight. This new global war faces, however, the radical pacifism and a disdain, to put it mildly, for George W. Bush, of a pampered American elite and many of those overseas.

Wolfowitz continues to be an optimistic believer about human nature and the possibility for progress. Chapter 9 examines Wolfowitz's role as head of the World Bank Group, where he continued most, but not all, of his predecessor's policies for economic development. Seeking to build a peaceful, prosperous world, the bank presidency serves as a logical extension of his longtime goal to foster a political economy based on free-market democracies as the key tool for economic development. He believes in the ineluctable triumph of a free market in goods and services and political democracy.

Long before taking the bank presidency, in November 1989, Wolfowitz sketched two basic ideas he sought to implement at the World Bank:

> One is that the route to economic development lies not through government control of economic activity but through freeing the creative energies of individuals. The second idea is that democracy and openness are not obstacles to economic development, but often necessary for it. Those countries that gave up fundamental freedoms in the belief that they would develop faster most often ended up with neither freedom nor prosperity. When the government controls the economy and is not open to criticism, the economy does not work.[7]

Many are pessimistic about the possibilities for economic growth and development in sub-Saharan Africa, a part of the continent filled with tribal conflict, corrupt dictatorships, and widespread disease and hunger. Not Wolfowitz, who wants the World Bank to move Africa to prosperity, political stability, and peace as a top priority, along with rooting out corruption in nations receiving the bank's assistance.

Emphasizing the need to expand microenterprise lending and unleash the forces of entrepreneurial capitalism, the chapter concludes with an analysis of public-sector international efforts to alleviate poverty in the third world, focusing on policy prescriptions for the World Bank.

Although free-market economics and political democracy remain appealing throughout most of the world, not everyone views them favorably. The radical strain within Islam hates America for what it is and what it represents—a country that is democratic, pluralistic, tolerant, materialistic, open to talent, providing opportunity. Free-market critics, who oppose policies aimed at globalization, economic growth, wealth creation and accumulation, likewise dislike America's culture. Some view the United States as having a long history as a predatory nation.[8] Only time will evaluate the viability of the claim of American exceptionalism—its unique destiny and the universality of its values—as well as an optimistic belief in the possibility of progress based on the spread of a political economy oriented to democratic capitalism throughout the globe. Paul Wolfowitz's career provides a lens to examine whether America's highest ideals are achievable in practice.

Chapter 2

The Personal
and Intellectual
Roots of Paul
Wolfowitz's Worldview

The roots of Paul Wolfowitz's worldview go back to three sources: the influence of his strong-willed father, Jacob Wolfowitz, who provided an atmosphere of intellectual and moral seriousness; the four years he spent at the Cornell University, particularly at the intellectual hothouse of the Telluride Association residence; and the influence of his dissertation advisor and mentor, Albert Wohlstetter, at the University of Chicago.[1] The chapter concludes by describing two lucky breaks that marked his career in the federal bureaucracy.

THE INFLUENCE OF HIS FATHER,
JACOB WOLFOWITZ

Wolfowitz's father, Jacob, was born in Warsaw in 1910.[2] Jacob's family immigrated to the United States in 1920 and settled in New York City when he was ten years old. Family members who remained behind in Poland perished in the Holocaust. After graduating from the College of the City of New York in 1931 with a bachelor of science degree, during the Depression, he taught high school math and obtained a Ph.D. in mathematics from New York University in 1942.

Jacob Wolfowitz, a Jew, was a 1930s FDR liberal and an interventionist in global matters. He brooded over the Holocaust throughout his life. Paul subsequently reflected, "The history of World War II had a big impact on me."[3] Jacob often told his children how fortunate they were to have escaped totalitarian Europe and to have grown up in American's benign security. Jacob was also passionate about the need to defend Israel. Later in life, he became a staunch anti-Communist, organizing protests against the repression of dissidents, intellectuals, and minorities in the then-Soviet Union. The world's perils and America's moral responsibility were repeated topics at the Wolfowitz dinner table. Jacob believed in the power of the United States to do good works and vanquish totalitarianism.

Beginning his rise to one of America's leading experts in the theory of statistics, Jacob joined the Statistical Research Group at Columbia University in 1942. There, he conducted war-related research for the U.S. military. In 1945, he became an associate professor of statistics at the University of North Carolina and in 1946 joined the newly formed Department of Mathematical Statistics at Columbia University.

In 1934, he married Lillian Dundes. On December 22, 1943, Paul Dundes Wolfowitz was born, the second of the Wolfowitzes' children. Laura Mary, Paul's older sister, had been born two years earlier, in 1941. Laura married an Israeli and lives in Israel.

Jacob Wolfowitz left Columbia's statistics department following the 1950 death of his friend and principal collaborator, Abraham Wald. He joined the faculty of Cornell University in 1951. Although Jacob taught semesters at the University of California at Los Angeles and the University of Illinois in 1952 and 1953, respectively, he then settled in an upper-middle-class enclave of Cornell faculty families.

Paul Wolfowitz grew up in Ithaca, New York, enjoying a well-rounded upbringing typical for a precocious child in the Eisenhower era of innocence. He was a spelling-bee champion and an Eagle Scout; he played tennis and basketball, excelled on the Ithaca High School debate team, and was the features editor for the school newspaper.

Jacob served as a visiting professor at Technion in Haifa, Israel in 1957 and brought his family along. Paul prepared for the trip by bringing Arabic-language books with him to swimming practice in Ithaca.

Paul and his friends treated Cornell University as their personal playground, using the university's indoor basketball courts for pickup games. Once, when a member of the maintenance staff tried to kick the tenth-graders off the basketball courts, Paul marched into the office of the university's athletic director and obtained a permission note.

Paul quickly outgrew Ithaca High School. During his senior year, he attended a freshman honors calculus class at Cornell every morning, before returning to high school for the rest of his classes. Even in a class with the cream of the freshmen, Paul dominated the college students.

THE IMPACT OF HIS UNDERGRADUATE YEARS
AT CORNELL UNIVERSITY

After winning a full academic scholarship at Cornell, he matriculated there. Initially majoring in mathematics and then chemistry, he seemed destined to follow his father into math or the sciences. By his senior year, his interests had branched out into other fields. Sharing his father's fascination with history and global politics, he spent his free time reading books on those subjects. He later recalled, "I was a Cuban Missile Crisis kid. I was a sophomore in college when all that happened. There were other things in it as well. It was a kind of passion for history and politics even though I was good in math and science. But it is amazing to me to realize how remote the idea of nuclear war is to my kids' generation. We lived with it as a reality. I suppose that was one of the things that motivated me originally."[4] Profoundly moved by John Hersey's *Hiroshima*,[5] he shifted his focus toward political science and the prevention of nuclear war.

On entering Cornell, Paul had become a member of the Telluride Association, an elite group of Cornell undergraduates who received free room and board at a large campus residence, the Telluride House.[6] There, these students lived, studied, and absorbed the intellectual atmosphere. The selected students learned democracy in practice; they ran the house, hired and supervised the staff, and organized various intellectual exchanges such as speakers. Paul excelled at the mundane duties of Telluride self-governance. It was at Telluride that he met his future wife, Clare Selgin, whom he married in 1968 and divorced in 2002, and with whom he would have three children.

In 1963, Allan Bloom (1930–92), a professor of political philosophy, arrived at Cornell and served as a faculty resident at the Telluride House. Bloom, who published his bestseller, *The Closing of the American Mind*, in 1987,[7] preached the importance of great books and traditional values and ideals. The charismatic Bloom quickly developed a network of undergraduate students. At dinner or in the basement kitchen of the Telluride House, the young professor conducted hours-long, informal Socratic dialogues, mixing debate with jokes and gossip. Bloom was spellbinding; he was Socrates incarnate.

Bloom rhapsodized about the students he encountered at Cornell. Paul was among them. Others included intelligence specialist Abram N. Shulsky, a Telluride member, 1963 Cornell graduate, and graduate student who preceded Paul at the University of Chicago. Wolfowitz subsequently hired Shulsky onto his staff at the State and then the Defense Departments.

Wolfowitz now downplays the impact Bloom and his ideals had on his views. As he later reflected, "[Bloom] had a lot to do with my coming to appreciate that the study of politics could be serious business, even though it wasn't science in the sense that I understood science to be. That was an important eye-opener. But I never, for better and for worse, took the political theory [course] . . . most of his other students did."[8]

Despite his intellectual devotion to Bloom, Wolfowitz was never a blind follower. An independent thinker, "[h]e always thought for himself," according to Charles Fairbanks Jr., a 1965 Cornell graduate, fellow Telluride member, and now the director of the Central Asia Institute at the Johns Hopkins University Nitze School of Advanced International Studies. Fairbanks noted, "The effect of Allen Bloom's teaching was to liberate his natural interest or bent toward public affairs."[9]

As Wolfowitz recalled, his father and Bloom regarded each other with admiration, but with a degree of wariness. Although "somewhat disdainful of hard science

in general because it left out the philosophical dimension," Bloom, who believed that
the life of the mind served as the highest form of human activity, was "in some awe"
of the way Jacob would pace around the campus deep in thought, without a pencil
or paper.[10] However, Jacob did not hold the social sciences and humanities or those
engaged in them, including Bloom, in high regard. Thus, a wide gulf separated
Jacob, the mathematician, and Bloom, the political theorist and protégé of Leo
Strauss, with whom he had studied at the University of Chicago.

Besides Bloom, Telluride had another faculty guest, Frances Perkins, the former
Secretary of Labor under FDR and the first woman to hold a U.S. cabinet-level
position. When she moved to Telluride in 1960, Perkins was in her late seventies
and teaching as a visiting lecturer at Cornell's School of Industrial and Labor
Relations. She served as a living link to the interventionist Democratic Party that
Jacob Wolfowitz admired. Paul was deeply impressed by her noblesse oblige
and sense of duty to society. The two forged a special bond. He served as one of
her pallbearers after her death at age eighty-three in May 1965.

In late August 1963, Paul and Fred Baumann, another Cornell undergraduate,
were cleaning the Telluride attic, when Paul suggested that the two of them join
some Ithaca church groups taking buses to Washington for a civil rights demonstration. Baumann agreed, and the two joined some 250,000 people who heard Rev.
Martin Luther King Jr. deliver his "I Have a Dream" speech on August 28, 1963.

Years later, Wolfowitz indicated that he remained a proponent of civil liberties and a "bleeding heart" on social issues.[11] A JFK Democrat while in high
school, Paul switched parties during the Reagan administration.

In May of his senior year at Cornell, Paul, a solid anti-Communist, participated in a minuscule three-person demonstration in support of U.S. involvement
in the Vietnam War. He joined the Committee for Critical Support of the United
States in Vietnam, which staged a silent counterprotest to a vastly larger antiwar
demonstration on the Cornell campus.

Although student deferments kept him out of the draft during the Vietnam
War, he looked on that war with scholarly detachment and later seemed ambivalent about the war and the desirability of fighting it. Paul remembered that in
the 1960s he was sympathetic to the war. Vietnam appeared to be a noble cause.
Following the lead of Singapore's Lee Kuan Yew, he believed that the United
States saved Southeast Asia by delaying and ultimately postponing the Communist march in the region.[12] Wolfowitz subsequently questioned whether the war
was worth its "horrendous" costs in American lives and the resulting polariza-
tion of U.S. society. Although it seemed to him an "overexpenditure of American
power,"[13] he reflected, "[b]ut we don't know what that part of the world would
have looked like today if it hadn't been."[14]

Wolfowitz's subsequent, rather ambivalent, reflections mirror the views of
his graduate school mentor, Albert Wohlstetter, who was not a strong supporter
of the Vietnam War. According to Wohlstetter:

In Vietnam, the United States entered a conflict in which the chances were poor
to start with for affecting events in the direction of basic United States interests

and aims for the political and economic self-development of the "third world." The skillful communist leadership benefitted from its success in the long struggle against the French. They had built up a formidable apparatus of cadres in the south. The heritage of French colonialism left the noncommunist alternative for leadership weak and badly divided.[15]

Wohlstetter viewed the U.S. military effort in Vietnam as a "distraction, a rather misguided venture" that drained America's energies and diverted its attention from its paramount objective: success in its long-term competition with the Soviet Union.[16]

In his senior year at Cornell, Paul applied to graduate schools in both political science and international relations. Jacob's efforts to direct Paul to economics, the social science most closely related to mathematics, proved futile. Admitted to graduate programs at Harvard and the University of Chicago, Paul chose the latter. One of the key factors was the presence there of Leo Strauss (1899–1973), a German-Jewish refugee from Nazism, who taught political philosophy at the University of Chicago beginning in 1949. Wolfowitz recalled Strauss as "pretty remarkable."[17] He thought him "a unique figure, an irreplaceable asset."[18]

ALBERT WOHLSTETTER: A MENTOR
AT THE UNIVERSITY OF CHICAGO

After arriving at the University of Chicago, Paul did not become close to Strauss. He took two of Strauss's courses, one on Plato and another on Montesquieu. The latter course helped him better understand the U.S. Constitution. Strauss left Chicago in 1967 before Paul completed his graduate work.

Despite Paul's continuing emphasis on stopping tyranny and condemning evil, as his career unfolded, he sought to distance himself from Strauss. He told an interviewer, "I don't particularly like the [Straussian] label, because I don't like labels that much."[19] He dismissed talk of a Straussian conspiracy and the idea that Strauss's ideas could be linked to the 2003 Iraq war as "a product of fevered minds who seem incapable of understanding that September 11th changed a lot of things and changed the way we need to approach the world."[20]

At the University of Chicago, Wolfowitz gravitated to a new field, nuclear strategy, and a key mentor, Albert Wohlstetter.[21] Wohlstetter, who combined mathematics, science, and public policy, might have been someone Jacob approved of. Growing up in New York City, he had graduated from the College of the City of New York and received his Ph.D. from Columbia University.

In 1951, Wohlstetter became a senior policy analyst at the RAND Corporation, a California-based think tank devoted to research and development. Emerging as one of America's preeminent theorists and strategists on nuclear war, he became the godfather of the anti-detente school during the cold war. He also focused on the vulnerability of the bombers of the U.S. Air Force at bases overseas to a surprise Soviet attack, which could knock out the America's retaliatory capacity.

His conclusions led the Strategic Air Command to base its bombers far from the U.S.S.R., which would have enabled the United States to strike back after receiving a first attack by the Soviets.

In 1964, Wohlstetter started teaching political science at the University of Chicago. He attracted a number of students, including Wolfowitz, who wanted to combine theory and practical application together with a technical and technological approach to military strategy, weapons, and war.

Returning from a trip to Israel in the late 1960s, Wohlstetter became concerned about the spread of nuclear weapons in the Middle East, particularly the possibility that nuclear-powered desalination stations near Israel's borders with Egypt and Jordan could produce plutonium that could be used in nuclear weapons programs. A U.S.-based firm, Kaiser Engineers–Catalytic Construction Co., proposed a nuclear desalination project in Israel. Wohlstetter brought back written materials on the project and the general subject. These materials became the basis of Paul's doctoral dissertation.

Wolfowitz's dissertation argued against building nuclear-power desalting stations.[22] He maintained that the benefits were vastly overestimated and the risks of nuclear proliferation too great. He focused on the difficulties of conducting effective, international nuclear inspections and the risks of a secret diversion of nuclear materials to weapons production. He also opposed an Israeli nuclear weapons program that, he asserted, would lead one or more Arab nations to match it "if not from the Soviet Union, then at a later date from China or on their own."[23]

Throughout the late 1960s, Wolfowitz maintained a student deferment, exempting him from military service. Although he considered volunteering to serve in the military, he did not. He noted: "[B]ut sort of [my father's] view was if they aren't drafting you, and I had a student deferment, you should stay in school, and I'd already had enough of an argument over switching out of mathematics which he considered divine, and going into political science which he considered something low."[24]

In the summer of 1969, while still a graduate student, Paul served as an intern, working for expenses, at the Committee to Maintain a Prudent Defense Policy.[25] At the committee's office in Washington, D.C., Dean Acheson and Paul H. Nitze passed along their tough-minded views of American foreign policy to Wolfowitz. Serving in the Truman administration at the beginning of the cold war, Acheson, as Secretary of State, and Nitze, as the Director of Policy Planning at the State Department, advocated uncompromising policies toward the Soviet Union. They took a dark view of Soviet intentions, viewing the Kremlin as seeking world hegemony.

Acheson and Nitze created the committee to lobby Congress to continue to support America's antiballistic missile (ABM) system, designed to destroy incoming Soviet missiles in midair. In the midst of the ever-increasing unpopularity of the Vietnam War, the defensive ABM system, an expensive budgetary item, faced extensive senatorial opposition.

Acheson and Nitze sought to counter scientists, including experts from Harvard and MIT, who raised questions about the cost of the ABM system, whether it would work to intercept a sufficient number of incoming missiles, and whether it would stimulate an arms race. They turned to Wohlstetter as the principal theoretician, and he, in turn, recruited Wolfowitz among others.

Under the supervision of Acheson and Nitze, a team of graduate students, including Wolfowitz, wrote research papers and prepared fact sheets and charts for senators in support of the ABM system. They generated materials for Senator Henry M. (Scoop) Jackson, a fierce anti-Soviet advocate and a key proponent of funding the ABM system. Jackson maintained that the system was cost effective, technologically feasible, and needed as a U.S. deterrent. As Wolfowitz later observed:

> [Senator Stuart] Symington got hold of a Pentagon chart proving the ABM would not work. I talked with Albert Wohlstetter about how easy it was to make a chart that refuted Symington's. We came up with charts and delivered them to Senator Jackson. It was the first time in my life I met a U.S. Senator. What impressed me was that he insisted on understanding the results we got on the graphs. He sat on the ground in shirtsleeves with a twenty-[five] year old graduate student to master them. He then called Senators John Tower and Peter Dominick and went through it with them. It was clear from the reaction after the secret session that Jackson had scored a big win. When it came down to it, it was not the intellectual argument, but who you believed. . . . He spoke with such authority that when he really believed something on a defense issue, few members of the Senate were comfortable challenging him.[26]

Nitze subsequently praised the committee's team of graduate students. In his memoirs, he wrote, "The papers they helped us produce ran rings around the misinformed and illogical papers produced by [the] polemical and pompous scientists."[27]

On August 6, 1969, the Senate defeated an amendment to the 1970 fiscal-year military authorization bill that would have halted the Safeguard antiballistic missile system and prohibited anything but research and development on other "advanced" ABM programs by one vote, 51–50.[28] Under the Senate rules, a tie vote defeated an amendment, with Vice President Spiro T. Agnew casting an unnecessary vote against the amendment. The Senate vote gave President Richard M. Nixon a bargaining chip in his negotiations with the Soviet Union. The United States would limit the development of its ABM system in return for similar Soviet concessions. In 1972, Nixon signed the Anti-Ballistic Missile Treaty between the United States and the Soviet Union,[29] restricting the development of ABM defensive weapons for three decades. Although the 1972 ABM treaty allowed the United States and Soviet Union to build an antimissile system at a single land-based site, it prohibited more extensive, nationwide systems. It also barred the development, testing, or deployment of space-located defenses against long-range missiles.

The summer of 1969 proved to be a turning point for Wolfowitz. Discovering that he enjoyed "hands on" public-policy work, he began to focus on a possible future career in the federal government. He became a defense and foreign policy hawk and developed a skepticism toward arms control with the Soviet Union. He gravitated to the view that United States ought to challenge the Soviet Union on all fronts rather than merely containing that nation through detente.

SUBSEQUENT DEVELOPMENTS

After Paul graduated from Cornell in 1965, his father's isolation grew, accelerated by disputes over the Vietnam War and the retirement of older colleagues. Jacob Wolfowitz took a series of visiting professorships, first at University of Paris and Technion in 1967, and then at the University of Heidelberg in 1969. After nineteen years in Ithaca, in 1970 he left for the University of Illinois. Subsequently, at the University of South Florida in Tampa, where he taught from 1978 until his death in 1981, he often spoke with pride about Paul's accomplishments as a policymaker. He seemed reconciled to the career choice his son had made.

Bloom also left Cornell in 1970 in dismay over what was, in his view, the university president's failure to confront armed black students in April 1969. He saw the incident as Cornell's surrender to an assault on academic freedom and viewed the concessions from Cornell administrators on curriculum matters as marking the start of the end of great American universities.

After completing his course work at Chicago in 1970, Paul secured a tenure-track faculty position as an assistant professor in Yale's Political Science Department. Then, in 1973, Wolfowitz accepted a job at the U.S. Arms Control and Disarmament Agency, where he worked until 1977, serving as Special Assistant for Strategic Arms Limitation Talks in 1976–77.

In 1973, President Nixon appointed Fred C. Iklé, a RAND strategist who had worked with Wohlstettler, to head the arms control agency. Iklé, who was less enthusiastic about the benefits of arms control than other previous heads, brought a new team with him to the agency. One of the new recruits was Wolfowitz, whom Wohlstetter had recommended to Iklé. Paul quickly became one of Iklé's most trusted colleagues. He wrote policy papers on the problems of missile launches and early-warning systems; he delved into strategic-arms limitation talks and various arms-control negotiations. In 1974 and 1975, he was closely involved with the successful U.S. campaign to block South Korea from reprocessing plutonium, which could have produced fuel for nuclear weapons.

While at the arms control agency, Paul also volunteered at the New Alternatives Workshop, a group that Wohlstetter, who advocated limited, small-scale wars fought with precision-guided bombs, put together. Its mission, noted Wolfowitz, was "[t]o look at the implications of new technology," particularly "the ones that promised great improvements in accuracy." Wohlstetter recognized that the

Tomahawk cruise missile being developed by the Navy mainly to deliver nuclear weapons was "much more significant as a conventional delivery system because it could give you very accurate weapons with ranges of what we have now, 600 miles or more." Wohlstetter and Wolfowitz persuaded Iklé that the United States "should oppose giving up the [T]omahawk on arms control grounds because it had the potential to substitute conventional for nuclear weapons and that was a good thing from the point of view of arms control." For Wolfowitz, it was "a matter of considerable personal satisfaction to watch those missiles turning right angle corners in the 1991 Gulf War and demonstrating that this stuff really could do what Albert Wohlstetter had envisioned 15 years before it might be able to do."[30] By 2001, as discussed in chapter 6, in Afghanistan the American military's pinpoint targeting ability had advanced far beyond its achievements ten years earlier.

WOLFOWITZ'S TWO LUCKY BREAKS

Two lucky breaks marked Wolfowitz's federal-government career. First, with the coming of the Reagan administration in 1981, Wolfowitz rose in prominence and came to head the State Department's Policy Planning Staff. Richard N. Perle, a member of the State Department transition team, spoke to Richard V. Allen, a Reagan talent scout and National Security Advisor-designate, about Perle's friend from the Committee to Maintain a Prudent Defense Policy, Paul Wolfowitz.[31]

Although the job did not require Senate confirmation, Republicans on the Senate Foreign Relations Committee cleared new Reagan State Department appointees. Senator Jesse Helms, a powerful member of the committee, initially recoiled at Wolfowitz's name, thinking he might be a liberal Democrat because he had worked in the Carter administration from 1977 to 1980 as the Deputy Assistant Secretary of Defense for Regional Programs.[32]

Wolfowitz met with John E. Carbaugh Jr., then Helms's staff aide and foreign policy advisor. Setting forth his beliefs and credentials and promising to appoint Alan Keyes, a leading African American conservative, as part of his State Department team, Wolfowitz convinced Carbaugh that he was fit for the position.[33]

Second, beginning in 1996 Wolfowitz forged a bond with Donald H. Rumsfeld. When he was Assistant Secretary of State for East Asian Affairs in the Reagan administration and the State Department helped put together a U.S.-Japan "wise man's group" chaired on the American side by David Packard, Wolfowitz had met Rumsfeld. Rumsfeld was one of eight Americans in the group.[34]

The 1996 presidential campaign of Robert (Bob) Dole, served as a tryout for the Rumsfeld-Wolfowitz duo. Rumsfeld became Dole's national campaign chairman, taking over the languishing presidential bid. Serving as the principal advisor on foreign-policy matters, Wolfowitz played a key role in formulating Dole's foreign-policy positions. Rumsfeld and Wolfowitz found themselves compatible on foreign policy and national security issues. Both were confrontational hawks on foreign policy; both favored a strong national defense.[35]

In 1997, Congress created a new commission to examine available intelligence regarding the threat ballistic missiles posed to the United States and prod the Clinton administration toward funding and deploying a missile defense system.[36] Rumsfeld served as chairman of the Commission to Assess the Ballistic Missile Threat to the United States and Wolfowitz became one of the nine commission members. In its July 1998 report, the commission concluded that the danger to the United States from a missile attack was greater than the American intelligence community had reported. With the spread of ballistic missile technology, rogue nations could deploy missiles for an attack against the United States with little or no warning. The report listed three nations—Iran, Iraq, and North Korea—as the most worrisome for the United States.[37]

In July 1998, George W. Bush, then Texas governor, invited Wolfowitz to visit him in Austin, along with Dick Cheney, then head of the Halliburton Corporation, and a group of Hoover Institution scholars, including President Reagan's former Secretary of State George P. Shultz, Stanford Provost Condoleezza Rice, and Martin Anderson, an advisor to Presidents Nixon and Reagan, whom Bush had met previously in Palo Alto, California in April 1998. Bush told his guests he was thinking of a presidential run and asked for their help.[38]

In the fall of 1998, Bush added Wolfowitz as a second foreign-policy advisor in addition to Rice. Having functioned as Dole's foreign-policy advisor in 1996, Wolfowitz picked up where he had left off two years earlier. Along with Rice, who was the primary advisor, he served as one of Bush's two main advisors on international matters, preparing position papers, holding telephone conference calls with the presidential candidate, and coordinating daily events.[39] To compensate for his lack of experience in foreign affairs, Bush relied heavily on his advisors.

In early 1999, Rice and Wolfowitz started to assemble a team of foreign-policy advisors for the Bush campaign. Locking up the best people before any other Republican candidate could sign them up, they quickly secured a topflight team.

Rumsfeld played an important, behind-the-scenes role in the Bush campaign. During 1999 and 2000, he headed a separate, more secret, campaign group focused on missile defense. Rice and Wolfowitz took part in discussions with Rumsfeld's group.[40]

With his election, Bush tapped Rumsfeld to be Secretary of Defense. Although Wolfowitz was not Rumsfeld's first choice, Rumsfeld then offered Wolfowitz the job of becoming the number two at the Pentagon as Deputy Defense Secretary.[41] Wolfowitz did not think twice about it. He recalled, "It was very much what I wanted to do."[42]

Beginning with Wohlstetter, Wolfowitz began a long series of key professional relationships with his mentors. Throughout his long public service career, one academic or governmental leader groomed and promoted him. As a loyal and unthreatening protégé, he never rebelled against or abandoned any of them.

An exceptionally bright, hardworking, low-key, soft-spoken, and innovative intellectual, Wolfowitz bridged the academic and governmental worlds. For his governmental mentors, including Cheney and Rumsfeld, he consistently offered a conceptual framework for policy formulation and decision making.

Wolfowitz enjoyed toiling inside the federal government. A bureaucratic survivor, he was viewed as a policy wonk, happily engaged in writing analytical papers and struggling within the bureaucracy on behalf of his ideas. He returned to ever-higher-level governmental roles, over and over again. By working inside the federal government, Wolfowitz sought to influence decisions before they became final. As a hyperrational insider, he could challenge a proposed policy's underlying rationale or seek to expand or narrow the scope of projected governmental position or action. From his years of federal governmental service evolved his vision of practical idealism.

Chapter 3

Wolfowitz, the Practical Idealist

Beginning in the mid-1980s and throughout his federal-government career thereafter, Wolfowitz effectively shaped the idealistic policy path George W. Bush's administration sought to follow in Iraq and more generally, the Middle East. Wolfowitz's experience with the 1985–86 "people power" uprising against Ferdinand Marcos, the Filipino dictator, propelled the passion for democratization that animated his thinking. Often overlooked, however, is the practical dimension to Wolfowitz's views. He long pressed the need for the United States to develop more accurate intelligence. This chapter examines his efforts on Team B in 1976 and his 2002 attempt to link al Qaeda and Iraq. He also sought to ground U.S. foreign and national-security policies in a hardheaded analysis of the global and regional geopolitical situation, particularly stressing the importance of energy security and the precariousness of the Persian Gulf region. As early as 1977, while the United States was primarily concerned with the Soviet menace, Wolfowitz viewed Iraq as a threat to strategic U.S. interests in the Middle East. His efforts through the years shaped American foreign policy to protect these interests.

WOLFOWITZ AND THE NEED FOR MORE ACCURATE INTELLIGENCE

For decades, Wolfowitz evidenced skepticism of governmental intelligence, believing it generally underrated problems and let many things go undetected. In June 1976, George H. W. Bush, the new Central Intelligence Agency (CIA) director who had recently been called back from his role as head of the U.S. liaison office in Beijing, appointed a team of outside experts (Team B) to review classified materials and prepare its own report on the Soviet Union and its intentions.

Team B was created at the recommendation of President Gerald R. Ford's Foreign Intelligence Advisory Board and consisted of the heads of American intelligence agencies and intelligence-oriented departments. Allegations that the CIA (Team A) consistently underrated Soviet military programs disturbed the Board, which requested a comprehensive analysis by an outside group with access to secret U.S. materials. Richard Pipes, a Harvard professor of Russian history, headed the ten-member Team B. Wolfowitz, then at the U.S. Arms Control and Disarmament Agency, became one of the team's members on Richard Perle's recommendation. The team also included another of Wolfowitz's mentors, Paul H. Nitze.[1]

The report, delivered in December 1976, analyzed Soviet strategic aims differently from the way CIA had in its 1976 National Intelligence Estimate, which represented the written consensus of the U.S. intelligence community. Wolfowitz played a minor role in Team B, contributing an analysis of the role of medium-range missiles in the Soviet military strategy.[2] Based on available intelligence data, Team B concluded that the Soviet Union sought military superiority over the United States, viewing detente only as a strategic means to achieve this goal. The first paragraphs of the report stated that U.S. intelligence estimates through 1975 "substantially misperceived the motivation behind Soviet strategic programs, and thereby tended consistently to underestimate their intensity, scope, and implicit threat." Expressing alarm, the report declared that "all evidence points to an undeviating Soviet commitment to what is euphemistically called the 'the worldwide triumph of socialism,' but in fact connotes global Soviet hegemony."[3] Wolfowitz believed that if the Soviet Union ever achieved nuclear superiority, it would use its military power to wage a conventional war, such as it did in Angola, rather than starting a nuclear war with the United States.[4] The report criticized the CIA for: offering too complacent a view of Soviet leadership; relying too heavily on technology, such as satellite photographs; and failing to consider what Soviet leaders were saying both privately and publicly.

As part of Team B, Wolfowitz focused for the first time on the underpinnings of U.S. foreign and national-security policies and the assumptions on which intelligence studies were based. Wolfowitz concluded that the CIA often propounded unsupported conclusions. Years later, he noted:

> The B-Team demonstrated that it was possible to construct a sharply different view of Soviet motivation from the consensus view of the [intelligence] analysts and one that provided a much closer fit to the Soviets' observed behavior (and also provided a much better forecast of subsequent behavior up to and through the invasion of Afghanistan). The formal presentation of the competing views in a session out at [the CIA headquarters in] Langley [, Virginia] also made clear that the enormous experience and expertise of B-Team as a group were formidable.[5]

Wolfowitz frequently returned to the theme of U.S. intelligence inadequacies. He felt intelligence analysts in general were insufficiently skeptical; they were too satisfied with information that merely confirmed their preconceptions. He characterized "mirror imaging" as a source of error. "People," noted Wolfowitz, "will be rational according to our [the American] definition of what rational is."[6] American analysts often fell victim to the "rational person syndrome," that is, they tended to analyze foreign leaders as rational decision makers by attributing to them types of behavior expected from their U.S. counterparts in similar circumstances.

Subsequent to the formation of and the report by Team B, whenever members of Congress believed the CIA had minimized the gravity of a foreign-policy or national-security question, calls would arise for a new Team B–type group to review the intelligence data and come up with its own analyses and conclusions. For example, as noted in chapter 2, in 1997 the Republican-led House and Senate set up a special commission, modeled after Team B, to analyze the threat the United States faced from ballistic missiles. After reviewing intelligence materials, the Missile Defense Commission, which had Donald H. Rumsfeld as its head and Wolfowitz serving as one of its leading members, concluded that the United States faced a far greater danger from missile attacks launched by rogue nations than the CIA had reported.

As Deputy Defense Secretary, Wolfowitz again became concerned about intelligence inadequacy in the wake of 9/11. He not only feared that such an attack would reoccur if al Qaeda's ties to nation-states were not discovered and extinguished, but also that America's intelligence capabilities were unequal to the task of fully unearthing such ties. Consequently, he pushed hard for the CIA and the Pentagon's main intelligence office, the Defense Intelligence Agency (DIA), to develop stronger information on Iraq's ties to terrorist organizations.

Douglas J. Feith, the Pentagon's Under Secretary of Defense for Policy, created a special team, with Rumsfeld's and Wolfowitz's approval, called the Policy Counterterrorism Evaluation Group (PCTEG), as a counterweight to the CIA.[7] Feith brought in two outside consultants to constitute the PCTEG in October 2001. These two consultants looked at intelligence information regarding terrorist groups, the network of ties between and among such groups, and the roles performed by state sponsors in terrorist activity.[8]

After the consultants left the project in December 2001 and January 2002, two naval reserve officers assigned to the PCTEG constituted the group. These officers' inquiry focused on the al Qaeda network, and targeted, to some degree, information concerning al Qaeda's relationship with Iraq, using a software program called Analyst Notebook to show links between pieces of information. They prepared a report based on both the intelligence community's raw and finished analyses of data as well as the officers' own analysis based on the intelligence community's products.[9]

An intelligence analyst on detail from the Defense Intelligence Agency assisted the team by reviewing DIA and CIA intelligence assessments. The detailee found some facts from previous intelligence reports that she believed had been inadequately analyzed and insufficiently incorporated into the agencies' finished analyses. Her work with PCTEG included preparing her own report on the data, which strongly criticized the CIA's own conclusions, asserting that "the CIA report should be read for content only—and [the] CIA's interpretation ought to be ignored."[10]

Incorporating the detailee's work and the analysis prepared by the two naval reserve officers, a special assistant from Wolfowitz's office created briefing slides of the PCTEG's conclusions in the summer of 2002. In addition to criticizing the American intelligence community for underestimating the relationship between Iraq and al Qaeda, the slides presented Secretary of Defense Rumsfeld's conclusions that Iraq and al Qaeda were much more closely linked than the U.S. intelligence community believed.[11]

One of the naval officers and the DIA detailee presented the briefing to Rumsfeld and Wolfowitz in early August 2002. Both men were impressed by the team's work product. Wolfowitz afterwards sent a note to both Feith and the PCTEG members, suggesting that an opportunity be found to present PCTEG's conclusions to the CIA, with a goal not of reaching a consensus on the facts, but of "scrub[bing] one another's arguments."[12]

Feith and one of the naval officers and the DIA detailee, among others, then briefed the CIA Director, George J. Tenet, along with other CIA officials, on August 15. The DIA detailee subsequently briefed senior White House officials, including Stephen J. Hadley, Deputy National Security Advisor, and I. Lewis (Scooter) Libby, Vice President Dick Cheney's Chief of Staff, on September 16. Libby became interested in the likelihood of a meeting in Prague between Mohammed Atta, who led the 9/11 attacks, with the head of Iraqi intelligence, which the CIA maintained never occurred.

Wolfowitz was apparently pleased with both the methodology that the PCTEG used and the conclusions that it reached, prior to the unit being disbanded in September 2002. However, his ultimate goal in pushing for the PCTEG exercise does not seem to have been arriving at a correct conclusion as such. Characterizing the project as "data mining," he described the team's work as helping to "sift through enormous amounts of incredibly valuable data that our many intelligence resources have vacuumed up," emphasizing that "[t]hey are not making independent intelligence assessments." He further illuminated his view of PCTEG's purpose by describing "a phenomenon in intelligence work, that people who are pursuing a certain hypothesis will see certain facts others won't, and not see other facts that others will. The lens through which you're looking for facts affects what you look for." Such a statement is ironic given that Feith had specifically directed the team to report on the connections between Iraq and al Qaeda, but sensible if made under the view that the PCTEG's purpose was to expose the American intelligence community to facts that Rumsfeld, Wolfowitz, and Feith believed had been insufficiently explored. The intelligence process, Wolfowitz concluded, "should not permit you to create or deny facts. The correct process is one that surfaces as many facts as possible."[13]

The CIA briefly reversed its position on the al Qaeda–Iraq relationship after it was confronted with the team's report. Previously, the CIA had reported its conclusion that al Qaeda and Iraq were only tenuously linked, at best. John E. McLaughlin, the CIA deputy director, then stated in an October 7, 2002 letter to the Senate Intelligence Committee that the CIA had "solid evidence of senior level contacts between Iraq and al-Qa'ida going back a decade." McLaughlin further informed the committee that these "growing indications on a relationship with al-Qa'ida suggest that Baghdad's link to terrorists will increase, even absent U.S. military action."[14] Shortly thereafter, the CIA returned to its former position that the Iraq–al Qaeda relationship was limited to a few instances of contact and offers of safe haven, but that no joint operational activity was ever planned or undertaken.

WOLFOWITZ, THE PRACTICAL, HARDHEADED ANALYST

Early on in his career, Wolfowitz had urged the United States to look at the Middle East from a different angle, outside the traditional anti-Soviet framework. In so doing, he began to conceptualize foreign policy and national security issues that would arise after the collapse of the Soviet Union.

Wolfowitz first studied the Persian Gulf in 1977. Originally concerned about the possibility of a Soviet drive toward Middle East oil fields, Wolfowitz subsequently would change the focus to the prospect that Iraq under Saddam Hussein's dictatorship might try to dominate these resources by invading its neighbors. This change of focus was the first step in delineating a post–cold war U.S. Middle East policy and an idea to which Wolfowitz would return again and again. But his late 1970s focus on the region arose from concerns about petroleum reserves and global geopolitics.

In 1977, as Deputy Assistant Secretary of Defense for Regional Programs, Wolfowitz was responsible for contemplating the Pentagon's future problems, not its day-to-day crises. He began work on a new project, the Limited Contingency Study, which would break new ground in transforming U.S. military policy toward the Persian Gulf in coming decades. President James Earl (Jimmy) Carter's Secretary of Defense, Harold Brown, had asked Wolfowitz to analyze possible threats that the U.S. military might face in the third world. Wolfowitz began his inquiry by focusing on the Persian Gulf's petroleum resources.

By 1977, the United States had already experienced an Arab oil embargo and dramatic increase in the price of petroleum following the 1973 Yom Kippur War. In December 1973, the Shah of Iran persuaded OPEC to raise the price of oil to four times what it had been just three months earlier. It was hoped that any similar situation could be avoided in the future. The possibility that the United States might resort to military force to break any future oil embargo led Wolfowitz to ask whether American military forces could defend Saudi Arabia's oil fields and if the United States would be able to deploy troops to do so in a timely manner.

Earlier in 1977, Wolfowitz had attended a seminar given by Professor Geoffrey Kemp, a Middle East specialist at Tufts University's Fletcher School of Law and Diplomacy. Kemp asserted that the U.S. military was too preoccupied with defending Europe against a Soviet invasion and was not paying sufficient attention to the possibility of the Soviets moving into the Persian Gulf. Finding the theory interesting, Wolfowitz soon hired Kemp to serve as a consultant on the Limited Contingency Study. Wolfowitz also recruited Dennis B. Ross, a Soviet specialist who later achieved fame as the Clinton administration's Middle East peace negotiator.[15]

The Limited Contingency Study, more specifically entitled "Capabilities for Limited Contingencies in the Persian Gulf," marked the Pentagon's first far-reaching examination of the U.S. military's need to defend the Persian Gulf and its oil resources. The study began, "We and our major industrialized allies have a vital and growing stake in the Persian Gulf region because of our need for Persian Gulf oil and because events in the Persian Gulf affect the Arab-Israeli conflict. The importance of Persian Gulf oil cannot easily be exaggerated." If the Soviet Union were to control Persian Gulf oil, its impact would "probably destroy NATO and the U.S.-Japanese alliance without recourse to war by the Soviets."[16] This concern represented a significant change from the Pentagon's former assessments, one more in line with Kemp's criticisms of the U.S. military's Eurocentric strategy, and followed the Team B thesis that the American intelligence community had underestimated the Soviet threat.

Wolfowitz expanded the Limited Contingency Study's scope beyond assessing the possibility of the Soviets' seizing oil fields in the Persian Gulf. Seeing Iraq as a growing menace, he raised the question of what would happen if Iraq were to invade Kuwait or Saudi Arabia. In considering not only the likelihood of this contingency but its consequences, particularly its disastrous impact on the United States, the study concluded:

> Iraq has become militarily pre-eminent in the Persian Gulf, a worrisome development because of Iraq's radical-Arab stance, its anti-Western attitudes, its dependence on Soviet arms sales, and its willingness to foment trouble in other local nations. . . . The emerging Iraqi threat has two dimensions. On the one hand, Iraq may in the future use her military forces against such states as Kuwait or Saudi Arabia (as in the 1961 Kuwait crisis that was resolved by timely British intervention with force). On the other hand, the more serious problem may be that Iraq's implicit power will cause currently moderate local powers to accommodate themselves to Iraq without being overtly coerced. The latter problem suggests that we must not only be able to defend the interests of Kuwait, Saudi Arabia and ourselves against an Iraqi invasion or show of force, we should also make manifest our capabilities and commitments to balance Iraq's power—and this may require an increased visibility for U.S. power.[17]

For Secretary of Defense Brown, planning for the possibility of an Iraqi invasion of one or more of its neighbors and an American response by military force proved to be too much. He also feared that if the study leaked, the United States might be forced to explain to an Iraqi government, increasingly controlled by

Saddam Hussein, why the United States considered Iraq a military threat. But because the study was never leaked, this worry proved groundless.[18]

The study's military implications were clear. The United States needed to take steps to be able to bring American forces quickly into the Persian Gulf region should any crisis arise. Recognizing that the United States faced a long lead time in getting any significant military forces into the area, the report recommended creating new U.S. bases in the region, improving runways and airlift capabilities for American troops, and constructing new storage facilities to hold military equipment and supplies.

However, as a study by midlevel Defense Department civilians, it had little immediate impact on the U.S. military's practices.[19] Senior American military leaders resisted suggestions that they change the U.S. armed forces' structure to reflect the importance of the Persian Gulf. As Wolfowitz later put it, the Pentagon said, "Well, we don't plan forces for the Persian Gulf. The Shah [of] Iran takes care of the Persian Gulf for us."[20] In 1977, President Jimmy Carter issued a directive asking the Defense Department to establish a U.S. rapid deployment force to go into the Persian Gulf. But bureaucratic inertia prevailed and the deployment effort stalled.[21]

The change was catalyzed, however, two years later in 1979, with a revolution in Iran that removed the Shah from power and the Soviet invasion of Afghanistan. As a result of these two events, the Carter administration quickly increased America's military presence in the Persian Gulf. The easing of the resistance from U.S. military services allowed the Pentagon to create a Persian Gulf rapid-deployment force. Attention was now shifting toward the Middle East.[22]

In his January 23, 1980 State of the Union Address, the president announced the Carter Doctrine. The doctrine specified that "an attempt by any outside force to gain control of the Persian Gulf region will be regarded as an assault on the vital interests of the United States of America, and such an assault will be repelled by any means necessary, including military force."[23] By an "outside force," Carter was referring to the Soviet Union, meaning the United States was still unwilling to shift all of its attention away from its Communist adversary. However, by declaring the Persian Gulf as vital to America's national interests, the Carter Doctrine logically applied to nations both outside and inside the region that might try to control vital petroleum resources.

American interests in the Persian Gulf and its oil resources had thus come to be viewed as too critical to be left in the hands of any one leader, such as the Shah of Iran. In developing its own capabilities to protect the Persian Gulf nations and their oil supplies, the United States decided to rely on its own military forces, in addition to diplomacy, to obtain cooperation from Middle Eastern nations in support of American interests.

Over time, the United States started to give the Persian Gulf the same attention it accorded to Western Europe and East Asia.[24] U.S. officials sought air and naval bases near the Persian Gulf in various countries, such as Oman. These officials encouraged friendly Middle Eastern nations to build bigger airfields and storage facilities that U.S. military forces could use. The Defense Department began to develop speedy ships that could transport American troops from the eastern United States to the Suez Canal within ten days. Continuing the trend, the Reagan administration created the U.S. Central Command (CENTCOM), a new military command for the Middle East. Wolfowitz, with the help of others, had successfully shifted a focus of American foreign and national security policies toward the region.

In 1989, Wolfowitz returned to Washington as Undersecretary of Defense for Policy in George H. W. Bush's administration. He assumed responsibility for arms control, the Middle East, and the Persian Gulf. Working under Dick Cheney, then Secretary of Defense, Wolfowitz carried out a review of U.S. defense policy toward the Soviet Union. Because it was too early to know if the Soviet Union was really changing, the study concluded that the United States should proceed cautiously in its dealings with President Mikhail S. Gorbachev.

But Wolfowitz also returned to an old theme, again shifting the Pentagon away from a myopic focus on the Soviet Union. In fall of 1989, he ordered a review of U.S. policy toward the Persian Gulf, with an emphasis on defending the Saudi oil fields. Unlike the late 1970s review, this study did not have a premise based on the defense of the Persian Gulf against a Soviet invasion. Rather, the study focused on protecting the oil fields from seizure by a Persian Gulf nation, such as Iraq.[25] Again, Wolfowitz sought to increase American awareness of the geopolitical importance of the Persian Gulf region.

WOLFOWITZ, THE PRACTICAL IDEALIST: THE IMPORTANCE OF DEMOCRACY AND DEMOCRATIC NATIONS

In characterizing himself as a "practical idealist," Wolfowitz noted, "I don't like the caricature Wilsonian view that says we're going to impose something on the world regardless of whether it can take in the real world. . . . I consider myself pragmatic but I don't like the kind of pragmatism that sort of stares at people who hold principles very strongly and thinks that it's all just a matter of doing business and being sensible."[26] In other words, Wolfowitz saw himself as pursuing a world that falls in line with his democratic ideals, but not to the point that he lost sight of reality.

WOLFOWITZ AT THE STATE DEPARTMENT

In the mid-1980s, Wolfowitz, Richard L. Armitage, and Gaston J. Sigur Jr. formed a troika that sought to be in charge of the Reagan foreign and national-security policies in Asia. Wolfowitz, the passionate conceptualizer, represented the State Department as the Assistant Secretary for East Asia and the Pacific;

Armitage, a nonideological Vietnam combat veteran, spoke for the Defense Department as Deputy Assistant Secretary of Defense for Asia; and Sigur brought his views to the table as senior director of Asian affairs at the National Security Council. Generally, their weekly Monday afternoon meetings in Wolfowitz's State Department Office were not secret.[27] Touchy subjects, however, necessitated more clandestine gatherings.

In reaching their goals, the trio often had to overcome the attitudes of their bureaucratic superiors. George P. Shultz, the Secretary of State, and Caspar W. Weinberger, the Secretary of Defense, personally disliked each other and were often at loggerheads. Weinberger was an implacable foe of the then Soviet Union; while Shultz favored arms-control negotiations with Moscow. None of Reagan's national-security advisors lasted long in the position, causing more instability. Because of the Shultz-Weinberger friction and the weakness of Reagan's national-security advisors, the triumvirate concluded that many policy issues would result in a stalemate at the top and that lower-level discussions would be more productive.[28]

But another barrier stood in the way of the trio's pro-moral stance. The Reagan White House team viewed the preceding Carter administration's push for political liberalization under the Shah in Iran as propelling a revolution that eventually harmed U.S. interests by removing an American ally. In turn, the Reagan administration saw international human rights as mainly an issue favoring the Democratic Party. Reagan's actions in South Korea were in keeping with this stance.

The South Korean president, Chun Doo Hwan, a military leader, had seized power in a May 1980 coup after the 1979 assassination of President Park Chung Hee. Because Chun Doo Hwan imposed martial law upon his country, the Carter administration had frozen U.S. relations with South Korea. In February 1981, however, the Reagan administration restored U.S.–South Korean ties and welcomed Chun to the White House, seeming to turn a blind eye on the way in which he chose to run his country.

But the new administration was not entirely oblivious to human rights and moral issues in South Korea. Before agreeing to Chun's visit, the Reagan team, in conjunction with the outgoing Carter group, obtained a commitment from Chun that Kim Dae Jung, an imprisoned dissident, would not be executed. Perhaps in hopes of further securing the visit, Chun also ended martial law, at least in name, in South Korea.[29]

Reagan's invitation to Chun marked a turn in U.S. foreign policy. Unlike Carter, it was clear the new administration would not criticize U.S. allies, regardless of the manner by which these regimes governed internally. Reagan would denounce Communist oppression but generally remain quiet regarding repressive actions by American allies. Concerns over national-security realities took precedence over those about human rights.[30]

Instead of publicly criticizing nations allied with or not hostile to the United States, the Reagan administration sought to solve human rights problems through diplomatic channels.[31] This willingness to overlook moral issues served as a countercurrent to Wolfowitz's actions. But Wolfowitz had a strange bedfellow in his attempts to refocus Reagan's foreign policy—Communism. Though willing to brush undemocratic issues aside for allies, Reagan did not hold a similar view for enemies.

In his June 8, 1982 speech to the British members of Parliament, Reagan proclaimed the promotion of democracy in Eastern Europe and the Soviet Union as a key goal of American foreign policy. He called for the promotion of democracy as a fundamental global security imperative. As a Reagan biographer put it, "The Westminster speech expressed more cogently than any other address of his presidency Reagan's belief that the forces of freedom would triumph over communism."[32]

Reagan proposed new efforts "to foster the infrastructure of democracy," including a free press, labor unions, political parties, and academic freedom, "which allows a people to choose their own way, to develop their own culture, to reconcile their own differences through peaceful means." He continued, "This is not cultural imperialism, it is providing the means for genuine self-determination and protection for diversity. Democracy already flourishes in countries with very different cultures and historical experiences. It would be cultural condescension, or worse, to say that any people prefer dictatorship to democracy." He concluded by stating, "Let us now begin a major effort to secure the best—a crusade for freedom that will engage the faith and fortitude of the next generation. For the sake of peace and justice, let us move toward a world in which all people are at least free to determine their own destiny."[33]

Reagan's speech led to the creation in November 1983 of a nonprofit, nongovernmental organization, the National Endowment for Democracy (NED), which provides funds to assist in building democratic institutions overseas. Still in existence today, the NED, funded by congressional appropriations and the private sector, strives to assist democratic movements across the globe. Awarding over three hundred grants annually, NED's supported projects have included those promoting political and economic freedom, a strong civil society, an independent media, and the rule of law and impartial administration of justice.[34]

Some believed Reagan's new belief in spreading democracy could go beyond just Communist nations. In the State Department, Secretary of State Shultz and Elliott Abrams, Assistant Secretary of State for Human Rights,[35] began pushing Chilean general Augusto Pinochet to open his dictatorship to democratic change, at least to some degree. But the State Department's actions did not represent the Reagan White House, which still stood by its unwillingness to criticize American allies. Shultz admitted, "[T]o them, Pinochet was a friend of the United States and a bulwark against communism. Pinochet made everyone uneasy, but he was on our side."[36]

Some members of the Reagan team, such as Abrams, then began to have second thoughts about the desirability of an unquestioning embrace of pro-American dictators. When Wolfowitz was first named to be Assistant Secretary of State for

East Asian and Pacific Affairs in December 1982, he received a call from Abrams, who said, "I hope you're going to stop this policy of coddling Ferdinand Marcos." As Wolfowitz recalled, "He was the first person, but by no means the last, who made that suggestion to me."[37] With respect to the Philippines, it was Wolfowitz, among others, who helped develop the idea that the United States should support democracy in both adversary and allied nations.

THE PHILIPPINES: AN EXAMPLE OF AMERICAN SUPPORT FOR DEMOCRACY

Before focusing on the crisis of 1985–86, some background on the Filipino-American relationship is appropriate.[38] In reality, the U.S. acquisition of the Philippines began with Cuba. The Spanish-American War of 1898 was kindled by an effort to aid Cuban rebels in their liberation from Spanish rule. An American presence in the conflict was guaranteed when the *Maine,* an American warship, exploded in Havana's harbor on February 15, 1898. As a strategic ploy, Commodore George Dewey led U.S. naval ships to the Philippines, also a Spanish territory, in April of that year.

Dewey entered Manila's bay on May 1 and quickly conquered the aging Spanish naval presence stationed there. Filipino rebels, led by Emilio Aguinaldo, then surrounded Manila and declared their independence on June 12. But the Americans took Manila as their own, fearful that other powerful nations with navies in the Pacific, such as Japan or Germany, would gain control of the Philippines if the United States did not colonize the entire island. The rebels felt betrayed, a sentiment furthered when they were excluded from negotiations for the Treaty of Peace,[39] signed on December 10, 1898, in which the United States acquired the Philippines from the Spanish for $20 million.

The Filipino insurgents and the Americans then prepared for war. The fighting began on February 4, 1899, two days prior to the Senate's ratification of the treaty, and lasted until President Theodore Roosevelt declared the war over on July 4, 1902.[40] However, a stubborn Filipino resistance operated until several years beyond Roosevelt's declaration. Ultimately, the Americans prevailed after losing more lives there than in the 1898 war against Spain and committing numerous atrocities.

Despite its ignominious beginning, the American colonization of the Philippines was different from those colonies established by European nations in that its eventual goal was the territory's independence and the creation of a functioning democracy. President William McKinley established two commissions with such an outcome in mind. The latter one, led by William Howard Taft, took over civil authority from the military in the new colony and assumed legislative functions. The Philippine Organic Act of 1902, also known as the Lodge Act,[41] provided for general elections for the lower house of the Philippine legislature, with the commission serving as the upper house. The first Philippine Assembly was elected in 1907 and the commission was replaced by the elected Senate, pursuant to the Philippine Autonomy Act of 1916, also known as the Jones Act.[42]

The 1934 Philippine Independence Act, also known Tydings-McDuffie Act,[43] which inaugurated the commonwealth period, started a ten-year countdown to self-governance for the Philippines, at the end of which the archipelago was to be granted its independence. The islands were governed by a Commonwealth Constitution, designed along the American model but placing greater power in the hands of an elected president, who could declare an emergency and tempo-rarily exercise near-dictatorial powers. World War II interrupted the transition to self-governance, with the Philippines finally achieving independence on July 4, 1946. Despite the apparent separation, the United States maintained a strong military presence in the islands, most importantly, the Subic Bay Naval Station and Clark Air Force Base. In return, the Americans provided military and eco-nomic aid to the islands, which became a "military protectorate of the United States."[44] In the cold war, the Philippines became a strategic U.S. asset and a bulwark against the spread of Communism in Asia.

Ferdinand Marcos became president of the Philippines in 1965 and, after imposing martial law in 1972, held unchallenged power there.[45] In the late 1970s and early 1980s, Marcos faced a growing challenge from a Communist insur-gency and its military arm, the New People's Army (NPA). Coupled with this threat was an emerging economic crisis, which only worked to fuel membership in the Communist movement. Some American officials became concerned that a revolution would threaten access to Clark Air Force Base and Subic Bay Naval Station, both still key to the U.S. strategic presence in Asia.

AMERICAN ATTEMPTS TO REFORM THE PHILIPPINES UNDER MARCOS

In September 1982, Marcos and his wife visited Washington for the first time in sixteen years. They were given a lavish welcome and feted at a White House state dinner. Initially, Reagan and other administration leaders supported the Marcos government wholeheartedly.[46]

But after the assassination of opposition leader Benigno S. Aquino Jr. on August 21, 1983, Reagan's approach of unconditional support came into question among his aides. Recognizing its major stake in safeguarding the military bases and help-ing Southeast Asia avoid falling under leftist control, the White House began to place itself in a position from which it could be disassociated from Marcos and the predicted public upheaval that would result if he were tied to the assassina-tion. The administration continued to embrace Marcos as an ally against Commu-nism but, hoping to better secure the strategic U.S. military bases, began to look for new tactics to deal with both the strength and boldness of the Communist insurgency and the nation's underlying economic and political problems. The continued strengthening of the NPA only catalyzed Reagan's policy shift.

In 1984, the White House initiated a new policy in the hope of spurring political, economic, and military reform under Marcos's leadership. The United States started to push for fair elections, a free press, the breaking up of economic monopolies granted to Marcos's cronies, and bringing new leadership into the military.

In September 1984, in testimony before the Subcommittee on East Asian and Pacific Affairs of the Senate Foreign Relations Committee, Wolfowitz, as the State Department's top Asian expert, gave reasons why "the United States has a deep concern with the future of the Philippines and the health of its economy and political institutions." He pointed to an inflation rate running at 50 percent and an economy projected to contract three to 6 percent in 1984. He spoke of the successes of the NPA. He noted:

> The United States has used both public and private diplomacy to express our support for institutional reform. We have spoken out clearly on such questions as the need for a credible investigation of the Aquino assassination, the need for a new Presidential succession formula, and the importance of rebuilding democratic institutions to get the country through the current period of political transition.[47]

Wolfowitz chaired an administration strategic-planning group that looked at ways to push Marcos to implement democratic changes. The group recognized that it was "difficult for the U.S. to design a bridge from dictatorship to democracy and harder still to get Mr. Marcos to cross it."[48]

Wolfowitz visited the Philippines in January 1985, delivering a letter from Reagan to Marcos, stating U.S. concerns and assessing that nation's condition. His visit also served as a basis for him to make recommendations regarding future U.S. aid levels and other policies. Wolfowitz indicated that future American aid programs for the Philippines would seek to strengthen democratic institutions and encourage economic, social, and military reforms, such as dismantling crony capitalism and replacing overstaying generals who held their positions through favoritism to stem the root causes of the insurgency. He also met with opposition leaders and human rights monitors. He optimistically declared, "We have been encouraged by the progress of democratic institutions in the Philippines and note with pleasure the desire for further progress."[49]

On his return, he briefed Shultz on the Philippine situation. Wolfowitz urged that the U.S. approach to "quiet diplomacy" ought to focus on urging Marcos to reform, developing procedures for an orderly succession to Marcos, and restructuring of the nation's foreign debt.[50]

Shultz then met with CIA director William J. Casey; Defense Secretary Weinberger; Admiral William J. Crowe, the U.S. navy commander for the Pacific; and Robert C. (Bud) McFarlane, National Security Advisor, to discuss the Philippine situation. A rough consensus emerged from the meeting. They agreed on the need to strengthen Philippine political, military and economic institutions and expressed the wish that Marcos would reform his regime. Shultz notified Reagan, who agreed with the group's assessment and hoped that Marcos would work with the United States on reform.[51]

According to the administration's new policy, although Marcos was "part of the problem, he is also necessarily part of the solution."[52] As formulated in a February 1985 National Security Decision Directive, designed to provide essential guidelines for American foreign and national security policies, the United States sought to encourage a peaceful and democratic transformation via diplomatic and economic tools. The immediate goal was not to remove Marcos from power, but to strengthen the underlying democratic institutions in the Philippines and encourage economic and social reforms designed to stem the root causes of the Communist insurgency.

On February 22, 1985, Wolfowitz, in a speech to the National Defense University, publicly urged the Marcos government to speed its progress on political, military, and economic issues. Declaring that military abuse against civilians "was one of the most commonly-cited factors in explaining the alarming growth of the Communist insurgency throughout the islands," he added that a U.S. proposal for an extra $15 million in military assistance would be "premised on the full expectation that the incipient reforms we have just seen will continue and expand."[53]

In March 1985 testimony before the House Foreign Affairs Subcommittee on Asian and Pacific Affairs, Wolfowitz stated, "[T]he Philippines cannot afford a business as usual approach to the [Communist] insurgency or the urgent need to deal with its root problems." Referring to the dismissal of Foreign Minister Arturo Tolentino and the resignation of Labor Minister Blas Ople, he remarked, "Forcing moderates out of the government are not steps in the right direction."[54]

These negative comments were balanced by Wolfowitz's positive statements about Marcos and his regime. For example, in February 1985 testimony before the same House subcommittee, he noted that there was "broad press freedom" and there had been "important progress towards the revitalization of political institutions."[55] In reality, Filipino political institutions "only had the life that Marcos allowed them."[56]

In August 1985, more than sixty foreign-policy analysts and officials from the State Department, the Pentagon, the CIA, and the National Security Council, as well from academia, gathered at the National War College in Washington, D.C. to discuss the situation. Some still maintained that only Marcos could defeat the NPA. Others, seemingly with the concurrence of Wolfowitz, argued for continued pressure on Marcos to reinstate democratic processes, but doubted whether he would implement significant reforms.[57]

To underscore the message that it was time for Marcos to change his dictatorial ways, Reagan sent Senator Paul Laxalt, his close friend, to Manila in mid-October 1985. Laxalt carried a personal, handwritten letter from the president, which stated his views on the severity of the Communist threat and the need for Marcos to undertake reforms. Despite his pledges, Marcos did not affect any major changes.[58]

The Democratic-controlled House of Representatives demanded a much stronger position from the Reagan administration and a break from Marcos.[59] But the White House and congressional Republicans believed this would have unintended consequences, and so turned aside the House's demands. Fearing that a decline in American military support would only work to aid the Communist effort in the Philippines, Wolfowitz, among others, struggled to prevent the Congress from freezing U.S. military aid to the Philippines.

But the key piece of the U.S. policy centered on whether Marcos would act on America's suggestions via "quiet diplomacy." Unfortunately, despite efforts by Wolfowitz and other State Department officials, including Undersecretary of State Michael H. Armacost and U.S. Ambassador to the Philippines Stephen W. Bosworth, Marcos failed to respond. Marcos seemed to believe that Reagan would continue to give him unqualified support regardless of his actions, which was not illogical given the administration's avowed stance toward its non-Communist allies.

THE U.S. REACTION TO MARCOS'S FRAUDULENT ELECTION

Working to reassert his leadership, on November 3, 1985, Marcos ordered a "snap" presidential election be conducted in February 1986, more than a year ahead of schedule. His moderate opponents and the Roman Catholic Church supported Corazon C. Aquino, Benigno Aquino's widow.

Between October 1985 and January 1986, Wolfowitz testified several times before the Senate Foreign Relations Committee and the Asian and Pacific Affairs Subcommittee of the House Foreign Affairs Committee. In October, Wolfowitz cited the clear signals the United States had sent Marcos on the need for early and dramatic progress toward fundamental political, military, and economic reforms. He advised that the survival of the American military bases was "ancillary" to the survival of Filipino democracy and that the failure to reform the government would result in the United States losing the bases.[60] The next month, Wolfowitz reiterated that U.S. policy sought to promote peace through institutional changes that would allow the Philippines to deal with economic and political crises on its own. The American objective was to secure a "strong, stable democratically oriented Philippines" through fundamental political, economic, and military reforms implemented by that nation itself. He predicted that a fraudulent election would result in "a complete collapse of political confidence" in the Marcos government and a "disaster of large and indefinable proportions."[61] In January 1986, Wolfowitz reiterated the fear that a corrupt election would result in "deepening the disillusionment with the present system" and the Filipinos turning their support elsewhere, "specifically to the Communists."[62]

One week before the February presidential election, Leslie Gelb, a *New York Times* national-security correspondent who had served in the Carter State

Department, wrote that most U.S. officials "hoped that Marcos would win [an] election that was not too unfair and then quickly step aside in favor of his vice presidential candidate, Arturo Tolentino."[63] The article also outlined efforts by U.S. subcabinet officials, including Wolfowitz, to turn Reagan, Weinberger, and Casey away from their continued support of Marcos. Gelb's article angered Wolfowitz because it presented him together with Carterites as attempting to tilt U.S. policy in a more "liberal" direction, away from Marcos.[64]

By late January 1986, continuing his carrot-and-stick policy, President Reagan publicly offered to increase military and economic aid significantly if the election were free and fair and the resulting government worked toward political, economic, and military reforms.[65]

The February 7 election was filled with claims of fraud and violence. The Marcos-controlled National Assembly then declared Marcos the winner. Despite the appearance of election fraud carried out on Marcos's behalf, and as Aquino supporters took to the streets, official U.S. policy withheld judgment on who won the election, once again standing by its hands-off policy. Publicly, the administration maintained its stance that the selection of their government was the business of the Philippine people.

But policy debate within the Administration continued. Shultz, whom his staff had finally won over, and Reagan engaged in intense exchanges about the appropriate method for handling Marcos. Reagan balked at Shultz's insistence that the United States detach from Marcos, holding strong to his tenet that the United States must support its allies, even dictators, as a bulwark against the Soviet Union. By continuing to support Marcos, Shultz countered, the United States might enhance the insurgents and pave the way for a Communist take-over in the Philippines. Shultz gradually convinced Reagan that remaining silent about Marcos's actions did not represent the best policy.[66] On February 15, the White House released a statement acknowledging the widespread electoral fraud and violence, largely perpetrated by Marcos and his supporters, which called into question the credibility of the election.[67] But the White House still thought an anti-Marcos stance was premature, fearful that ending U.S. aid to the Marcos government would only work to radicalize both political sides.

Soon after Reagan placed the blame on Marcos, Wolfowitz appeared privately before the Council on Foreign Relations. Admitting that Marcos had engaged in election fraud, he urged caution, maintaining that Marcos was still the government. Asserting that "everything was happening too fast,"[68] he worried that the Philippines could become another Iran.

Just days later, in the midst of massive pro-Aquino demonstrations in Manila that became known as the "people power" revolution, external circumstances again forced the United States to show its hand and move further away from its traditional pro-Marcos stance. Two of Marcos's leading military officers, Lt. Gen. Fidel V. Ramos, Chief of Staff of the Armed Forces, and Juan Ponce Enrile, Minister of National Defense and one of Marcos's closest aides, resigned from the government, called for Marcos's resignation, and joined Aquino's opposition.

Though still seeking a political resolution, the White House issued a statement in support of Ramos and Enrile, declaring that the fraud within the Marcos government was so widespread that it impaired the Philippines' ability to control the Communist insurgency and revitalize a faltering economy.[69] This statement was a clear message that American support for Marcos was waning.

On February 23, as rumors of a potential strike against Ramos's and Enrile's breakaway military forces reached the United States, the White House released another statement threatening to cut off military aid if such a use of force occurred. The administration also unequivocally stated: "We cannot continue our existing military assistance if the government uses that aid against other elements of the Philippine military which enjoy substantial popular backing."[70]

Despite this strong signal to Marcos, the administration refrained from publicly demanding his resignation. But as a U.S. envoy, Philip C. Habib, returned from Manila to report that Marcos was finished, talk turned to how to encourage a peaceful change of leadership. Having lost confidence in Marcos's ability to manage the military, Reagan reversed course, issuing a statement urging Marcos to resign,[71] thereby "taking responsibility for removing an ally from power."[72]

Ultimately, on February 25, after weeks of street demonstrations, Marcos gave up power and was flown out of the Philippines on a U.S. Air Force plane. Shultz then pushed for the United States to give formal recognition to the Aquino government. Reagan remained dubious. "The president objected. . . . We argued," Shultz recalled. Shultz warned the president that equivocation by the United States "can turn a triumph of democracy into a catastrophe." Reagan "nodded his agreement."[73]

In moving to support a democratic government in the Philippines, the Reagan administration, motivated by a desire to protect American military bases and prevent Communist control of Southeast Asia, developed policy in a crisis-driven way. However, the White House demonstrated that the United States could withdraw its support from a dictator-ally and favor democratic change without producing another Iran. As Shultz later wrote:

> The rise to power of Corazon Aquino and the fall of Ferdinand Marcos marked an important shift in American official thinking: support for authoritarian governments that opposed communism could not be taken for granted. The United States supported people who were themselves standing up for freedom and democracy, whether against communism or against another form of repressive government.[74]

Wolfowitz saw Marcos as a liability in the U.S. battle for democratic ideals. He believed Reagan's abandonment of Marcos in 1986 followed logically from his 1982 decision to encourage democracy in Eastern Europe and to support the cause of freedom against Communist regimes worldwide. Wolfowitz later explained, "You can't use democracy, as you appropriately should, as a battle with the Soviet Union, and then turn around and be completely hypocritical about it when it's on your side of the line."[75]

Wolfowitz maintained that the Reagan administration's sense of timing in the Philippines was better than that of the Carter administration's in Iran. To avoid destabilizing a dictatorial regime and strengthening anti-American forces, the Reagan team waited patiently. It encouraged Marcos to reform and avoided more drastic steps until there was both a viable non-Communist alternative and reason to expect that Marcos would listen to American advice. Years later Wolfowitz stated, "If we had said, 'We are enemies of the Marcos regime; we want to see its demise rather than reform,' we would have lost all influence in Manila and would have created a situation highly polarized between a regime that had hunkered down and was prepared to do anything to survive and a population at loose ends."[76]

He also saw a significant difference between Marcos in the Philippines and the Shah in Iran. In contrast to the situation in Iran, when Marcos declared martial law in 1972, the Philippines possessed well-established democratic institutions. Wolfowitz maintained, "When we went to work on Marcos, it was not to dismantle the institutions of the Philippines; it was actually to get him to stop dismantling them himself. Military reform, economic reform, getting rid of crony capitalism, relying on the church, political reform. It [the Reagan policy] was very institutionally oriented."[77] In a reflection of his evolving viewpoint in the mid-1980s, Wolfowitz wrote during the Philippine crisis, "The best antidote to communism is democracy."[78] Subsequently, he noted, "Political change did indeed jeopardize American bases in the Philippines but it seemed more important to have a healthy ally without American bases than a sick ally with them."[79]

THE AFTERMATH OF U.S. POLICY IN
THE PHILIPPINES

America's encouragement of democracy in the Philippines influenced other Asian countries, notably South Korea and Taiwan. After the Philippines, promoting democracy overseas became a Republican cause. With the precedent set, the White House found it easier to embrace the new approach. In 1986–87, after South Koreans turned to massive street demonstrations against Chun Doo Hwan's government, the Reagan administration sent Sigur, now Assistant Secretary of State for East Asian and Pacific Affairs, to tell Chun that he should open the way to electoral reform. Chun accepted proposals for democratic change, including direct presidential elections.[80] Likewise, Taiwan's ruler, Chiang Ching-Kuo, prepared his nation for an open political process in 1988 and was succeeded by the democratically elected Lee Teng-hui.

This support for democracy carried over into the next decade as well when the United States respected the Philippine government's requests that it withdraw from the Clark and Subic Bay bases. The agreement between the United States and the Philippines regarding American military bases was set to expire in September 1991. In May 1990, Wolfowitz, now Undersecretary of Defense for

Policy, indicated, "We hope to retain our military presence in the Philippines at least over the mid-term." He added, however, that "the Philippine Government could require us to withdraw."[81] To many Filipinos, the installations were viewed as lingering symbols of America's colonial occupation.

This view, combined with instability in the Aquino government in the face of continued armed insurgencies and its inability to deal with the poverty and corruption that plagued the nation, forced the United States to prepare to turn over the bases under the assumption a new deal could not be struck. The end of the cold war and the disintegration of the Soviet Union made it possible to consider closing the bases altogether, especially Clark Air Force Base, which lacked Subic Bay's unique advantages for America's naval repair, training, and supply needs. With the United States acknowledging that American military presence in the Philippines would come to an end, the real question turned on the timing of the withdrawal, with both the U.S. and the Philippines seeking an appropriate transition period.[82]

Ultimately, a natural disaster helped settle the issue. In June 1991, the volcanic Mount Pinatubo erupted, burying Clark in ash. In an era of long-range military aircraft and air-to-air refueling, the U.S. Air Force decided that the cleanup costs were not worth the now-diminished strategic value of the base.[83] But the United States still believed that some strategic rationale for a military presence in the Philippines remained valid and hoped to retain a naval presence at Subic Bay.

After the Philippine Senate rejected a new military bases treaty that would have allowed the United States to keep Subic Bay for another ten years,[84] negotiations on a three-year time frame stumbled when the United States was unwilling to set a clear schedule for withdrawal or guarantee that nuclear weapons would not pass through the naval base. Seeing the writing on the wall and standing by its statements that it would respect any decision by the Philippine people to remove the American presence, the United States accelerated its withdrawal plans when Manila gave a formal notice of eviction.[85] In November 1992, the American military pulled out of the Philippines, leaving the islands in the position of strategic insignificance. The U.S. Navy found other nations to take over most of Subic Bay's functions.

Despite Wolfowitz's high hopes, an American political culture never took hold deeply in the Philippines. President Joseph Estrada was driven from office in 2001 as a result of allegations of corruption. After Estrada was impeached by the Filipino congress and the armed forces withdrew their support of him, the Supreme Court declared the presidency vacant. Following brief "people power" anti-Estrada demonstrations, Gloria Macapagal Arroyo, then the vice president, was sworn in by the Supreme Court. President Arroyo, in turn, was called to step down in 2005 due to charges of fraud in the 2004 national elections, governmental corruption, and human-rights abuses. After a failed impeachment attempt in the fall of 2005, part of the military withdrew its support of Arroyo; however, following her declaration of a state of emergency in February 2006, she prevailed and continued in power.[86]

In addition to the continuance of a corrosive political culture and a legacy of corruption, patronage, and abuse of power in the military and society generally, the Philippines today faces stagnation in the midst of its economic and social problems, rampant poverty, and a middle-class exodus. The democracy that Wolfowitz sought to bring to the Philippines remains insecure.

SEEKING DEMOCRACY IN INDONESIA AS UNITED STATES AMBASSADOR

From 1986 to 1989, Wolfowitz served as the American ambassador to Indonesia, a country with more Muslims than any other nation in the world. There, his charge was to carry out the U.S. policy of supporting Indonesia, a cold war ally and an emerging market for American products. In addition, Wolfowitz broke new ground in his advocacy of democracy. He sought to promote human rights by publicizing abuses committed in East Timor and throughout Indonesia. He gave U.S.-government financial aid to environmental, labor-rights, and Islamic groups. He argued to Washington that the Suharto regime exceeded global "norms" because of its human-rights abuses.[87]

In 1989, Wolfowitz privately told Suharto that his record of rapid economic growth was an insufficient basis for continued American support. "If greater openness is a key to economic success, I believe there is increasingly a need for openness in the political sphere as well,"[88] he said in May 1989 at farewell remarks delivered at Jakarta's American Cultural Center as he prepared to leave Indonesia after three years as ambassador. This single sentence, in line with Wolfowitz's quiet pursuit of political and economic reforms in Indonesia, stunned some of Suharto's inner circle. While his criticism angered Suharto, Wolfowitz's frankness seemed to endear him to the Indonesian people.

Unlike the Philippines, democratic political institutions seem to have taken better root in Indonesian soil. Following the fall of Suharto in 1998, Indonesia made remarkable progress in developing a creditable democracy. It held its first presidential election in 1999 and its first parliamentary elections in 2003. The second presidential election in 2004 was the first direct general election in the nation's history.

However, corruption still exists at the local level. Poverty is widespread and may increase. The country faces a jihadist threat.

GEORGE W. BUSH ADVOCATES DEMOCRACY

During the early months of the Bush administration in 2001, the White House became increasingly willing to base American foreign policy on moral judgments, such as whether a regime or its leader was repressive or undemocratic. This was the view of Bush himself, who interrupted one foreign-policy discussion by commenting about one regime, "We're talking about them as though they were members of the Chevy Chase Country Club. What are they really like? . . . How brutal are these people?"[89] Wolfowitz was very much pleased with this direction.

For Wolfowitz, the questions raised by Bush's comments offered an important perspective that was all too rare in Washington, and one in which he believed strongly, namely, that moral judgments should play a part in foreign-policy decision making.

In June 2002, the White House embraced Wolfowitz's vision of promoting democratic institutions in the Middle East. On June 24, President Bush delivered a long-awaited speech that indicated American policy toward Israel and the Palestinians had been reshaped. He called "on the Palestinian people to elect new leaders, not compromised by terror," explicitly abandoning Yassar Arafat. Bush promised the United States would support the creation of a Palestinian state if it had new, democratic leaders in place. He also called for the Palestinians "to build a practicing democracy, based on tolerance and liberty." Any Palestinian state, said the president, should have a "new constitution which separates the powers of government," a legislature with "full authority," and "a truly independent judiciary."[90] For the first time, Bush had applied to the Middle East the democratic ideals that Wolfowitz, among others, brought to the forefront of American foreign policy beginning in the mid-1980s.

Bush took a similar stance less than a year later. In February 2003, prior the invasion of Iraq, he voiced the hope that liberating that nation would transform not just Iraq, but the entire region. The president broadened the ideas he had articulated regarding Palestinian leadership in 2002, applying them to all governments in the Middle East, even those such as Egypt that were generally pro-American. Noting, "A new regime in Iraq would serve as a dramatic and inspiring example of freedom for other nations in the region," he continued, "It is presumptuous and insulting to suggest that a whole region of the world, or the one-fifth of humanity that is Muslim, is somehow untouched by the most basic assumptions of life."[91]

As discussed in chapter 7, Wolfowitz similarly hoped that regime change in Iraq brought about by U.S. military action could turn the nation into a model for democracy that would alter Middle Eastern politics and transform the region's political culture.

Although his ideals may not have been completely absorbed and were not successful in all cases, Wolfowitz has had a large hand in preparing, if not shifting, American foreign policy from a Russo-centric, anti-Communist stance to one centered on building democratic nations throughout the globe. At the same time, he has always kept in mind U.S. strategic interests, focusing attention on the Middle Eastern nations' geopolitical importance, and used these strategic interests as a practical platform from which to promote changes in American foreign and national-security policies. In his dealings with the Philippines and Indonesia, Wolfowitz helped to demonstrate his notion that democratic allies are much more strategically helpful to the United States than allied countries run by dictators, and so had a hand in setting George W. Bush's foreign policy toward a key goal, namely, the worldwide promotion of democratic ideals.

Chapter 4

Wolfowitz Views the United States as the World's Sole Superpower

The 1990s witnessed the fall of Soviet Communism, the continued globalization of the world's economy, and the spread of democracy, as well as a revolution of high technology. These developments left the United States as the world's sole economic, political, and military superpower.

After leaving the Pentagon at the end of the Bush 41 administration, Wolfowitz often spoke and wrote about America's preeminent world role. Recognizing the existence of a one-superpower world, he talked of preserving America's global hegemony and its strategic military depth. In 1996, he stated in testimony before the House National Security Committee that "American dominance gives us an opportunity to lead the world in building a peaceful relationship among the emerging great powers of the next century, a relationship that will bring security to our children and our grandchildren. If we are unwilling to pay this price now, it will be like failing to buy insurance. There will be a much higher price to be paid later."[1]

At the State Department in the 1980s and Defense Department in early 1990s, Wolfowitz focused on longer-term, broader foreign-policy and national-security themes and goals, trying to relate issues one to another. In view of America's military superiority, he believed the United States no longer needed to accommodate other world powers. For example, he urged the United States to take a unilateral stance in its dealings with China. The 1992 Defense Planning Guidance, which reflected Wolfowitz's views, presenting a vision of the United States as the world's sole superpower. Wolfowitz's critique of multilateralism is relevant at least in the military sphere where America's overwhelming power generally permits unilateral action as a realistic policy option.

ENCOURAGING A MORE UNILATERAL
PERSPECTIVE AT THE STATE DEPARTMENT

As head of the State Department's policy-planning staff, Wolfowitz focused on the Reagan administration's efforts to define its relations with the rest of the world. In the spring of 1981, Wolfowitz replaced nearly all of the twenty-five professional members of the policy-planning staff working under him. Over the next twenty-five years, some members of Wolfowitz's new team would become leading players in the neoconservative network within the U.S. foreign policy bureaucracy. Wolfowitz's department became a training ground for a new group of national-security and foreign-policy experts, most of whom shared Wolfowitz's ideas and assumptions.

From Cornell, Wolfowitz brought in Alan Keyes, an African American conservative and a future political candidate, as well as Francis Fukuyama, a political theorist. Fukuyama, a Cornell undergraduate (B.A. 1974) who received his Ph.D. from Harvard, became a noted author and scholar. His writings include *The End of History*.[2]

From the University of Chicago, he brought in Zalmay M. Khalilzad, an Afghan American student of the nuclear theorist Albert Wohlstetter, who received his Ph.D. in 1979 before teaching political science at Columbia University.[3] Later, Khalilzad would serve as the U.S. ambassador first to Afghanistan and then to Iraq.

From the Department of Defense, Wolfowitz imported Navy Captain James Roche, who became Secretary of the Air Force and then Secretary of the Army in the administration of George W. Bush. Wolfowitz and Roche met when both worked at the Defense Department during the Carter administration. Roche also served on the staff of Senator Henry M. Jackson.

Developing a probing and questioning approach as the Director of Policy Planning, Wolfowitz challenged some of the key tenets of American foreign policy soon after his appointment. Not unexpectedly, he proved to be one of Israel's most steadfast supporters in the Reagan administration. He questioned the desirability of selling the American-manufactured Airborne Warning and Control System (AWACS) aircraft to Saudi Arabia. He sought to slow down the momentum at the State Department toward doing business with the Palestine Liberation Organization.[4] He maintained that the United States did not need an arms-control agreement with the Soviet Union. Rather, he felt the United States would be better off without one.

His anti-détente position bore fruit two decades later, when in 2002 the United States abandoned the Anti-Ballistic Missile (ABM) Treaty, which prohibited the development and deployment of nationwide defenses against long-range ballistic missiles. The U.S. withdrawal from the ABM treaty culminated in efforts for a national-defense system, the Strategic Defense Initiative, designed to create a defensive umbrella to protect the United States from missile attack, proposed by President Reagan. These efforts gained momentum in the late 1990s, under Donald Rumsfeld's leadership. As discussed in chapter 2, Rumsfeld headed a congressional commission, with Wolfowitz as one of the members, that warned in 1998 of the possibility of missile attacks on American soil. Rumsfeld, an outspoken critic of the 1972 treaty and proponent of an effective nationwide shield against long-range missiles, also headed an informal missile-defense group during the 2000 Bush presidential campaign.

In May 2001, in its drive for a missile-defense system to provide limited but effective protection for the United States, its deployed forces, and its friends and allies, the Bush administration announced its hope to move beyond the constraints of the ABM treaty. The White House regarded the treaty as ill suited to a world in which Russia was no longer a hostile power. The treaty, the president asserted, no longer served its initial objective, namely, to protect the United States from the former Soviet Union. However, it did not protect the United States from missile attacks by current threats: rogue nations and terrorists with access to nuclear weapons. In a speech of the National Defense University on May 1, Bush noted:

> This Treaty does not recognize the present or point us to the future; it enshrines the past. No treaty that prevents us from addressing today's threats, that prohibits us from pursuing promising technology to defend ourselves, our friends and our allies, is in our interests or in the interests of world peace. . . .
>
> We should leave behind the constraints of an ABM Treaty that perpetuates a relationship based on distinct and mutual vulnerability. This Treaty ignores the fundamental breakthroughs and technology during the past 30 years. It prohibits us from exploring all options for defending against the threats that face us, our allies and other countries.
>
> That's why we should work together to replace this Treaty with a new framework that reflects a clear and clean break from the past, and especially from the adversarial legacy of the cold war.[5]

However, the president stopped short of saying the United States would withdraw from the treaty.

Later that month, Wolfowitz, now the Deputy Defense Secretary, asserted that the ABM treaty, negotiated by the Nixon White House, no longer made sense. "The world of 2001 is fundamentally different from that of 1972," Wolfowitz, as the head of one of three White House teams fanning out across the globe, asserted. Now, rather than the Soviet threat, the United States faced challenges from the proliferation of missiles and weapons of mass destruction in the hands of rogue nations and terrorist groups. Twelve years after the fall of the Berlin Wall, he questioned why "we are still in some ways . . . wedded to old Cold War notions of deterrence."[6]

In July, Wolfowitz gave Congress its first detailed description of Bush's missile-defense plan, which went well beyond Clinton's ground-based interceptor system. Bush's plan included ship-launched missiles and jet-mounted lasers, both of which were prohibited by the ABM treaty. He outlined a strategy for negotiating with Russia to amend the treaty, while aggressively testing antimissile technologies. "We will not conduct tests solely for the purpose of exceeding the constraints of the Treaty," he told the Senate Armed Services Committee, "but neither will we design our program to avoid doing so. . . . Such an event is likely to occur in months rather than in years."[7] He indicated that the administration would withdraw from the ABM treaty if the Russians did not agree to modify its terms so as to allow these tests.

Then, in December 2001, unable to bridge differences with Russia regarding the development of a new missile-defense system and under post-9/11 pressure to increase national security, the White House announced that the United States would withdraw from the ABM treaty in six months. The treaty, Bush noted in a speech on the future of the American military at the Citadel, "was written in a different era for a different enemy. America and our allies must not be bound to the past. We must be able to build the defenses we need against the enemies of the 21st century."[8] The withdrawal freed the Pentagon to test and deploy a missile-defense system designed to shoot down incoming missiles, especially longer-range missiles, without restrictions.

Because the White House had previously supported Russian President Vladimir V. Putin on a number of issues, from Russia's admission into the World Trade Organization to intergovernmental cooperation on antiterrorism, the Russian reaction to the U.S. withdrawal was muted. Avoiding any hint of his feeling slighted, Putin made it clear that he did not feel that the move threatened Russia. However, he called the American decision "an erroneous one."[9]

UNITED STATES–CHINA RELATIONS

Wolfowitz's 1980s policy planning occurred during a period when the Reagan team quickly emphasized the importance of American military power in foreign policy making. Within weeks after the inauguration, Caspar W. Weinberger, Secretary of Defense, recommended that Congress raise the Pentagon appropriation by $32.8 billion for fiscal years 1981 and 1982. He sought an 11 percent ($25.8 billion) increase in the Carter administration's defense budget for fiscal year 1982. He also sought an immediate $6.8 billion for the second half of fiscal year 1981.[10]

Wolfowitz soon advocated that the United States could take a more unilateral foreign-policy stance. He believed that the United States need not reflexively seek to reach an accommodation with any other world power. For instance, as America's military position became increasingly stronger, it would cease to require China's help in the cold war with the Soviet Union. Wolfowitz argued against cultivating a relationship with China, foreseeing the time when the United States would not view China as a strategic ally against the Soviet Union.

In reaching this conclusion, Wolfowitz challenged the established order, namely, the Nixon-Kissinger opening to Beijing in 1972. Since the early 1970s, American foreign policy had moved from the premise that the United States needed China's cooperation in the cold war against the Soviet Union. Under this assumption, American policymakers accommodated the Chinese government and its leaders.

After the United States ended diplomatic relations with Taiwan on January 1, 1979, diplomatic recognition shifted to Beijing. The 1979 Taiwan Relations Act provides a framework for the unofficial relationship between the United States and Taiwan.[11] The act requires the United States to provide Taiwan with sufficient articles and services for the island to maintain its self-defense capability. The act states, "It is the policy of the United States . . . to maintain the capacity of the United States to resist any resort to force or other forms of coercion that would jeopardize the security, or the social or economic system, of the people on Taiwan."[12]

In 1981 and 1982, China, claiming sovereignty over Taiwan, consistently sought a promise from the Reagan administration that the United States would cut off American military sales to the island. In the administration's discussions about China's demands, Alexander M. Haig Jr., Secretary of State (who previously served as National Security Advisor Henry A. Kissinger's deputy), invoked China's strategic importance in the cold war struggle. Recommending placing limits on arms sales to Taiwan, Haig asserted that the United States should not antagonize China.[13]

In addition to questioning the need to end American arms sales to Taiwan, Wolfowitz challenged the existing U.S. foreign-policy assumptions about China. He reasoned that the U.S. defense buildup under President Reagan, together with the weakness of the outdated conventional Chinese military force, meant that China, though important in East Asia, could not provide much assistance to the United States in any war with the Soviet Union. Wolfowitz maintained that China feared a Soviet invasion and thus needed help from the United States more than America needed China's assistance. As such, America underestimated its bargaining power in its dealings with China.[14]

Wolfowitz soon found himself at odds with Haig. Although the two men had previous contacts while Wolfowitz was at the arms-control agency and Haig was head of NATO forces, in 1981 the two antagonized each other almost immediately. Wolfowitz's memos questioning China's strategic importance seemed to infuriate Haig. In the spring of 1982, one Wolfowitz memo lambasted the State Department for making unnecessary concessions to China with respect to Taiwan arms sales.[15] In view of the growing friction between the two, the Secretary of State snubbed other proposals for Wolfowitz's policy-planning staff and attempted to cut them out of the communication loop.

The Haig-Wolfowitz acrimony reached a peak in the spring of 1982, when the *New York Times* reported that Haig had "notified Paul D. Wolfowitz, the director of policy planning, that he will be replaced. . . . Associates reported that Mr. Haig found Mr. Wolfowitz too theoretical."[16] Haig later denied the story.

Whether or not Haig meant to fire Wolfowitz soon became moot, however. Haig's own job security worsened as he fell out of favor with the White House. To Reagan's increasing irritation, Haig fought a series of losing battles with the White House staff about his (Haig's) authority over American foreign policy.

He eventually became a target of open mockery within the administration. On June 25, 1982, President Reagan announced that Haig was stepping down, although he actually was forced out. In his autobiography, Haig candidly states: "The President was accepting a letter of resignation that I had not submitted."[17]

Marking one more step away from the Nixon-Kissinger approach to diplomacy, Reagan nominated as Secretary of State George P. Shultz, who was sworn in on July 16, 1982. Shultz appointed Wolfowitz Assistant Secretary of State for East Asia and the Pacific, replacing the pro-China John Holdridge, who had served with Haig on Kissinger's National Security Council staff.

Wolfowitz's appointment represented a triumph of the pan-Asian faction at the State Department, which had emphasized building diplomatic ties to Taiwan and Japan. For the first time in his career, Wolfowitz's scope extended beyond exploring ideas and writing memos, to implementing the policies that he had formulated. Perhaps having some reservations about nominating Wolfowitz to the post, Shultz first asked Wolfowitz if he was ready for a managerial position. "Paul, this is an administrative job," Shultz told Wolfowitz. "It's not just thinking. It's a big area. You've got to get around, get to see a lot of people."[18]

Throughout his long public service career, Wolfowitz consistently had to overcome the perception that he was basically a theorist, not an administrator. Because rapid economic growth marked many East Asian nations, Wolfowitz found his new position refreshing. He recalled, "When I went from policy planning, where I was doing mostly Middle East stuff, to East Asia, it was like walking out of some oppressive, stuffy room into sunlight and fresh air. At the time, I felt that I was going from a part of the world where people only knew how to create problems to part of the world where people solve problems."[19]

In contrast to Haig, Shultz soon embraced Wolfowitz's ideas about America's policy toward China. Shultz concluded that the United States had overvalued China's strategic importance, thereby weakening its bargaining position with China. Shultz later described his approach as "a marked departure from the so-called China-card policy: the idea that the United States could maneuver back and forth, playing one big Communist power off against another." He continued:

> When the geostrategic importance of China became the conceptual prism through which Sino-American relations were viewed, it was almost inevitable that American policymakers became overly solicitous of Chinese interests, concerns, and sensitivities. Indeed, while President Nixon's historic opening to China in 1972 gave both countries some leverage with the Soviets, it is also true that the opening gave the Chinese leverage against us. As a result, much of the history of Sino-American relations since normalization of relations in 1978 could be described as a series of Chinese-defined "obstacles"—such as Taiwan, technology transfers, and trade—that the United States had been tasked to overcome in order to preserve the overall relationship.
>
> On the basis of my own experience, I knew it would be a mistake to place too much emphasis on a relationship for its own sake. A good relationship should emerge from the ability to solve substantive problems of interest to both countries. . . .

> When problems are not addressed, the relationship unfailingly deteriorates. I am
> convinced that in international relations . . . the road to a bad relationship is to
> place too much emphasis on the relationship for its own sake.[20]

In reorienting American foreign policy, Shultz began to view China not as a counterweight to the Soviet Union, as Wolfowitz had urged. Shultz also focused on Japan, not China, as the centerpiece of U.S. policy in Asia.[21]

British Prime Minister Margaret Thatcher signed the Hong Kong agreement with China in December, 1984, Deng Xiaoping considered the time ripe to reach an agreement with the United States about Taiwan. Hoping to apply the "one county, two systems" approach to Taiwan, Deng asked Thatcher to deliver a message to the White House. Deng hoped that Thatcher would use her influence with Reagan convince the United States to reopen the topic of Taiwan. Although Thatcher never delivered Deng's message, Wolfowitz discovered there had been quiet lobbying at high levels by friends of China to persuade Shultz to consider Deng's proposal. Kissinger was among those who weighed in on China's offer as worth considering.

Shultz supported Wolfowitz in rejecting Deng's offer. Wolfowitz, who opposed bargaining with China over Taiwan, feared that future Chinese leaders might be less willing than Deng to uphold such an agreement.[22] The White House remained resolute in refusing to open talks with Beijing on a Hong Kong–type deal for Taiwan.

Over the years, U.S. policy toward Taiwan, specifically regarding the question of arms sales, continued to be a thorny issue in America's dealings with China. Reagan's refusal to end American arms sales to Taiwan resulted in the joint August 17, 1982 United States–China communiqué, permitting the United States to continue to provide weapons to Taiwan on a limited scale to help maintain the island's defensive capabilities. The 1982 communiqué was followed by the 1985 Indigenous Defense Fighter project, in which Taiwan embarked on a program to build its own fighter plane, and the U.S. sale of F-16s to Taiwan in 1992. But for years, Washington crossed items off Taiwan's military shopping list for fear of angering Beijing.

In and out of government, Wolfowitz remained skeptical of engagement with China and a staunch proponent of defending Taiwan. In August 1999, the Heritage Foundation and the Project for the New American Century organized a joint statement calling for an end of America's policy of strategic and moral "ambiguity" toward Taiwan, based on U.S. recognition of the "One-China" principle, which holds that Taiwan is part of China, and opposition to a unilateral declaration of independence by Taiwan. The statement called on the United States to "declare unambiguously that it will come to Taiwan's defense in the event of an attack or a blockade against Taiwan."[23] Wolfowitz, now dean of the Nitze School of Advanced International Studies at John Hopkins University, was one of twenty-three signers of the statement calling for revising U.S. policy to remove any ambiguity about the American response should China use force to resolve the

Taiwan issue. According to Wolfowitz, "I don't believe that in the case of Taiwan today [November 1999] that anything is gained by leaving any doubt in the minds of Communist China that the use of force against Taiwan would be met with a strong American response." Rejecting the notion that defending Taiwan would depend on the circumstances of the attack, he asserted, "If we leave any ambiguity about that, all we are doing is encouraging Chinese actions that could get both of us in trouble."[24]

George W. Bush, who as a presidential candidate saw China as a "strategic competitor,"[25] openly supported Taiwan, now, as noted in chapter 3, a flourishing democracy. His support erased the 22-year-old U.S. policy of ambiguity on one major issue with China. The controversy surrounding the April 2001 collision of a U.S. surveillance plane and a Chinese fighter jet over the South China Sea, followed by the detention of the American crew, strengthened the position of those in the administration advocating a tougher stance toward China. One of the foremost advocates was Wolfowitz, who continued to assert that the United States exaggerated Beijing's strategic value to Washington.

Later in April 2001, an interviewer asked Bush whether the United States had an obligation to defend Taiwan if attached by China. He replied, "Yes, we do. And the Chinese must understand that." "With the full force for the American military?" came a follow-up question. "Whatever it took to help Taiwan defend herself," the president replied.[26] Although supporting the One-China policy, Bush's "whatever it takes" statement, put the United States unequivocally on the side of a self-governing, democratic Taiwan. The Bush administration then offered Taiwan a $4 billion arms package, its biggest since 1992.

The Bush administration balanced these steps toward Taiwan with various pro-China measures. For example, in December 2003, Bush rebuked the Taiwanese leader for taking actions that implied the Taiwanese president could change the status quo in cross-straits relations. When the Chinese government quelled the movement for direct elections in Hong Kong, the White House offered no strong objection. The president continued to emphasize the importance of maintaining good relations between the United States and the world's strongest nations, including China.

However, on his November 2005 trip to the Far East, Bush asserted the universality of the principles of individual liberty. "In the 21st century," he stated, "freedom is an Asian value because it is a universal value." If the principles of liberty have come to Japan, South Korea, and Taiwan, why not China? Bush held up Taiwan as a "free and democratic Chinese society," an exemplar for mainland China. He asserted, "As China reforms its economy, its leaders are finding that once the door to freedom is opened even a crack, it cannot be closed."[27] However, President Bush failed to bridge the gap between the One-China policy and the White House's pro-democracy doctrine.

Wolfowitz also offered his thoughts on China's broader role in the world. During the 2000 presidential campaign, Wolfowitz, one of George Bush's two key foreign-policy advisors, said he thought that China would be "probably the single most important foreign policy challenge of the coming decades." Although China's power was increasing, Wolfowitz continued, "I think it would be a mistake to treat China like the old Soviet Union during the Cold War, restricting trade in order to deliberately weaken it or to use its human rights leverage." Unlike the former Soviet Union, Wolfowitz indicated that China has "a substantial private sector whose scope and sphere [are] growing."[28] With China increasingly tied to the global economy, Wolfowitz favored continued American trade with China.

In recent years, the question of Taiwan as a source of U.S.-China irritation has faded somewhat, despite China's expenditure of billions of dollars on hundreds of short-range ballistic missiles and a fleet of diesel submarines designed to stymie U.S. efforts to protect Taiwan. Whether China's growing economic pains and its burgeoning economic might, coupled with its boundless thirst for new sources of petroleum and other raw materials, will hurt the United States in the future remains, however, an open question. China is both a formidable competitor seeking regional domination, and a trading partner concerned about maintaining access to both the U.S. export market and American high technology. Strategic issues, not only geopolitical questions but also economic ones, as China is a major international investor with a heavy concentration of U.S. bonds and it accounts for about 25 percent of the U.S. trade deficit,[29] will continue to be a focus of America's foreign-policy considerations, if not consternation, at least until China becomes a functioning democracy and likely for many decades thereafter. However, it is far from certain whether economic liberalization will lead to opening a petrified, single-party political system. At best, the United States must learn to deal with China's economic and military might and through dialogue and negotiation to solve contentious issues and hopefully realize the huge potential of a Sino-American partnership.

FORMULATING A STRATEGY TO GUIDE
U.S. MILITARY THINKING

When the Soviet Union disintegrated in the fall of 1991, the Pentagon needed a new strategy to guide post-cold-war U.S. military thinking. The task of formulating such a plan fell to Wolfowitz as Undersecretary of Defense for Policy in the Defense Department headed by Dick Cheney.

In May 1990, before the Soviet Union imploded, Wolfowitz had given a briefing to Secretary of Defense Cheney and the Defense Resources Board on a post-cold-war defense strategy.[30] The briefing focused on two issues: first, the shifting from a military strategy designed to fight a global war to focusing on two possible major regional conflicts, including the Iraqi threat to the Arabian Peninsula; and second, America's need to retain its capability to deal with two major regional conflicts simultaneously, for instance, one against Iraq in the Persian Gulf and another against North Korea, despite a 40 percent reduction in U.S. defense spending.

In November 1991, after the end of the Gulf War, Wolfowitz argued in favor of preserving American military power. He saw the continuing problem of access to Middle East oil reserves. He foresaw a danger from Iran or a rebuilt Iraq, perhaps by end of the decade. He also expressed concern that North Korea appeared to be developing nuclear weapons.

In 1992, the Defense Department, under Wolfowitz's leadership, produced a new version of the Defense Planning Guidance, which in its original draft form and a subsequently sanitized version, outlined many ideas and policies subsequently pursued by George W. Bush. This document, which describes America's military strategy, is distributed to U.S. military leaders and civilian Defense Department officials to instruct them on how to prepare their forces and provides the basis for future defense budgets.

Wolfowitz delegated the task of preparing the 1992 Defense Planning Guidance to I. Lewis (Scooter) Libby, who, as his top assistant, held the title of Principal Deputy Undersecretary of Defense for Strategy and Resources. Libby, a student of Wolfowitz's at Yale's political science department in the early 1970s, then assigned the task of writing the document to Khalilzad, a member of Libby's staff and a longtime aide to Wolfowitz. In writing the draft, Khalilzad worked from briefing papers Wolfowitz had prepared. He held a series of meetings, some of which included Wolfowitz and Libby. He also looked to various Pentagon insiders as well as outsiders, including Wohlstetter, Wolfowitz's mentor at the University of Chicago.

When he finished a draft, Khalilzad obtained Libby's permission to circulate the draft inside the Pentagon. Neither Libby nor Wolfowitz read the draft, which was leaked to the *New York Times*.

The March draft set forth a new vision of a world dominated by the United States, which would ward off potential rivals and forcefully make certain no nation or group of nations could emerge to challenge its preeminent position. The document spoke of America's need to actively work to block the emergence of any rival superpower to the point of preventing currently friendly powers from presenting new, future threats, and "convincing potential competitors that they need not aspire to a greater role or pursue a more aggressive posture to protect their legitimate interests."[31] As with Wolfowitz's view of China ten years earlier, the new strategy implicitly proposed that the United States need not and should not reach a disadvantageous accommodation with any other nation. Rather, the United States must make certain that no future adversary would arise with whom it might need to pursue détente. The United States would discourage other nations from challenging the American position through its superior military strength and its constructive behavior, including taking these nations' interests into account, thereby discouraging "them from challenging [American] leadership or seeking to overturn the established political and economic order." The draft stated that the goal of American policy should be "to prevent any hostile power from dominating a region whose resources would, under consolidated control, be sufficient to generate global power."

Although noting that the United States could not become the world's "'police-man,' by assuming responsibility for righting every wrong," it would "retain the pre-eminent responsibility for addressing selectively those wrongs which threaten not only" its interests and those of its allies or friends, but also those "which could seriously unsettle international relations. Various types of U.S. interests may be involved in such instances: access to vital raw materials, pri-marily Persian Gulf oil; proliferation of weapons of mass destruction and ballistic missiles; threats to U.S. citizens from terrorism in regional or local conflicts."

The draft asserted the central U.S. interest in promoting increased respect for international law and "the spread of democratic forms of government and open economic system." It spoke of the need to maintain and nurture U.S. alli-ance commitments and indicated that coalitions hold the promise for promoting collective action. However, it warned that future coalitions could be "ad hoc assemblies, often not lasting beyond the crisis being confronted," rather than permanent, formal alliances. For that reason, the United States must retain the power to act unilaterally.

The draft also focused on the potential threat to the United States from the spread of weapons of mass destruction—nuclear, chemical, and biological. In dealing with this threat, the United States should contemplate not merely containment but the possibility of a preemptive military action.

To calm the furor that arose from the image of a United States desirous of keeping its allies weak and blocking countries, such as Japan and Germany, that might aspire to regional leadership, the White House distanced itself from the leaked draft.[32] Wolfowitz seemingly did not want to be associated with it. How-ever, Cheney read the draft and praised it.[33]

Wolfowitz turned the task of rewriting the leaked document over to Libby. The final version of this Pentagon document was issued under Cheney's name in January 1993, after Wolfowitz urged him to make it public. Although Cheney took ownership of the document, it reflected Wolfowitz's longstanding views.

Libby had a threefold aim in rewriting the draft. His first goal was to tone down the proposal contained in the March version to keep U.S. allies weak, as that section made the White House particularly uneasy. The final version said instead that the United States must "preclude any hostile power from dominat-ing a region critical to our interests."[34] Any nation that rose to rival American power would be deemed potentially hostile if its policies did not parallel those of the United States. Furthermore, America would preserve its "strategic depth," namely, its advantageous global position, built around its network of bases, weapons, and advanced military technology. Second, in emphasizing the need to preserve and make permanent America's superiority over other nations with respect to its military and technological capabilities, the revision spoke about "shaping the future security environment."[35] In other words, America would not wait for threats or rivals to emerge. Third, although the revision referred to the importance of alliances and the need for collective security, it questioned whether collective action would work and left open the possibility of unilateral action by the United States. The final version stated: "We will, therefore, not ignore the need to be prepared to protect our critical interests and honor our commitments with only limited additional help, or even alone, if necessary. A future President will need options allowing him to lead and, where the international reaction proves sluggish or inadequate, to act independently to protect our critical interests."[36] It noted, "[N]either can we allow our critical interests to depend solely on international mechanisms that can be blocked by countries whose interests may be very different from our own."[37]

The incoming Clinton administration set aside Cheney's vision. However, it did not repudiate the intellectual blueprint for a world dominated by American military power.

In an article published in 2000, Wolfowitz, with perhaps a slight exaggeration, asserted that the 1992 document formed a consensus view of America's post-cold-war military strategy. He stated:

> Just seven years later, many of these same critics seem quite comfortable with the idea of a Pax Americana. They have supported or urged America military intervention in places like Haiti and Rwanda and East Timor, places never envisaged in my 1992 memorandum. Moreover, they seem very comfortable that all of this can be accomplished, and our commitments to our European and Asian allies maintained, with a greatly reduced defense burden and without risking the "basic health of our economy." Today the criticism of Pax Americana comes mainly from the isolationist right, from Patrick Buchanan, who complains that "containment, a defensive strategy, had given way to a breathtaking ambitious offensive strategy—to 'establish and protect a new order.'"
>
> One would like to think that this new consensus—Buchanan apart—reflects recognition that the United States cannot afford to allow a hostile power to dominate Europe or Asia or the Persian Gulf; that the safest, and in the long run the cheapest, way to prevent this is to preserve the U.S.-led alliances that have been so successful . . . at keeping Americans engaged, allies reassured, and aggressors deterred. But in reality today's consensus is facile and complacent, reflecting a lack of concern about the possibility of another major war, let along agreement about how to prevent one. . . .
>
> Perhaps, indeed, we have seen the last of the Napoleons and the Kaisers and Hitlers and Stalins and Tojos. In a world where American primacy seems so overwhelming, it is hard to imagine how threats of that magnitude could come about. But if we contemplate the last century we find abundant evidence that even a decade can bring about enormous transformations in world affairs. (Consider the changes from 1905 to 1915, or from 1929 to 1939, or from 1981 to 1991.) And if that was true in earlier decades, how much truer is it today when the tempo of change has increased so dramatically? Further, even if the chances of another assault on world peace are remote, what is at stake is too great to permit complacency or neglect of America's responsibility as the world's dominant power.[38]

In formulating U.S. foreign and national-security policies, American policy-makers could not assume the rest of the globe would be filled with disinterested internationalists, ready to join an American-led military coalition. This became apparent in 2003. However, in the 1991 Gulf War, President George H. W. Bush assembled a broad-based coalition to overturn Iraq's invasion of Kuwait.

Chapter 5

The Road to Baghdad, Part One: Operation Desert Storm

In August 1990 Iraqi forces annexed Kuwait. The United States and its allies thereafter used a U.N.-mandated force to liberate Kuwait in early 1991, relying on military power in a region where nonintervention had previously been the rule for fear of a cold war confrontation with the Soviet Union. The U.S. thus asserted its leadership and its willingness to use military force when circumstances demanded it.

Wolfowitz was intimately involved in the planning and execution of both the political and strategic military aspects of this campaign, participating in the Bush 41 administration's deliberations, before, during, and after the Gulf War. In 1989, Wolfowitz became Undersecretary of Defense for Policy, where he established an enduring bond with his boss Secretary of Defense Dick Cheney. Throughout his career, Wolfowitz had been concerned with preserving U.S. access to Persian Gulf oil. As discussed in chapter 3, in the late 1970s, Wolfowitz foresaw that Iraq could pose a military threat to the oil fields of Kuwait and Saudi Arabia. Saddam's 1990 invasion confirmed his earlier fears. Wolfowitz repeatedly warned Cheney, among others, against attempting a strategy of containing Saddam Hussein. He believed that the United States needed to undo the Iraqi invasion of Kuwait. By 1997, Wolfowitz came to advocate U.S. encouragement of an internal coup against Saddam, so that, among other reasons, Iraq would not militarily threaten its neighbors.

BEFORE IRAQ'S INVASION OF KUWAIT

Iraq long coveted Kuwait,[1] which had received independence from Britain in July 1961. Abdul al-Karin Quassim, Iraq's strongman at the time, immediately claimed sovereignty over Kuwait, regarding it as artificially separated by the British from what had historically been Iraq. He also sought Kuwait for its oil fields and its coastline. Kuwait quickly obtained British military protection. An Arab peacekeeping force took over from the British and stayed until 1962. In an effort to assuage Baghdad, the Kuwaitis made multibillion-dollar loans to Iraq, which were never repaid. The dispute over the boundaries and islands off Kuwait as well as the loan repayments remained ongoing.

In July 1990, Iraq began threatening Kuwait and the United Arab Emirates (U.A.E.) for overproducing oil and thus driving down prices. Iraq viewed the production of oil in excess of OPEC quotas as tantamount to "military aggression."[2]

The U.A.E. asked the United States to supply two KC-135 aerial-refueling tankers, which would enable the Emirates to keep its patrol planes continuously in the air.[3] This action would help fend off an air attack. Colin L. Powell, the Chairman of the Joint Chiefs of Staff, Cheney, and Wolfowitz recommended that the United States agree to the Emirates' request.[4]

The State Department's Bureau of Near Eastern and South Asian Affairs initially opposed the request, arguing that the U.A.E. should work with the Saudis. However, in a telephone conversation on July 21 between Robert M. Kimmitt, the Undersecretary of State for Political Affairs, and Wolfowitz, the Near Eastern Bureau was overruled. The White House gave its final approval.[5]

A short-notice U.S. Navy exercise with the U.A.E. was announced. The naval exercise served as the cover for the transfer of the KC-135s. Signaling U.S. support for the U.A.E., Peter (Pete) Williams, the Defense Department spokesman, publicly confirmed the naval exercise.[6]

Then on July 27, Kimmitt called a meeting of the Deputies Committee, consisting of the second-highest-ranking officials from the State and Defense Departments and other federal agencies. Middle East specialists at the State Department and the White House's National Security Council staff presented a draft of a restrained cable to be sent to Saddam Hussein. It assured Saddam that the United States was interested in a diplomatic solution and that Iraq should work with the United States. Wolfowitz objected, arguing that if a stronger message could not be sent, it would be better to send nothing.[7]

At the meeting, the general feeling was that Saddam would not cross Egyptian President Hosni Mubarak, who had sent Bush 41 a personal message forecasting no immediate difficulties and recommending allowing the Arab nations to handle it. The Egyptians were not concerned. Arab nations did not invade other Arab countries. Bush's restrained message was sent.[8]

In response, Wolfowitz tried to figure how the United States could indirectly influence the situation.[9] Following the recommendations of his 1979 study, discussed in chapter 3, he proposed relocating the Navy's Maritime Pre-Positioned Ships (MPSs) based in Diego Garcia, to the Persian Gulf, 3,000 miles away. These ships held enough tanks, artillery, and other heavy weapons to equip a Marine unit of more than 16,000 men, and enough food and ammunition to supply them for thirty days.

Powell opposed this show of force. He did not want a civilian's idea to result in the commitment of U.S. military forces without a clear objective. The deployment of MPSs would signal the commitment of ground forces, an option that had not been discussed.[10]

Powell was a "reluctant warrior." Defining victory in terms of destroying Iraq's ground forces, Powell opposed using U.S. military forces to send a diplomatic signal. Furthermore, the KC-135s sent to the U.A.E. had been relatively ineffective, and Powell now felt this move to have been a mistake. If news of the deployment of the MPSs leaked, the Bush administration would need to provide an explanation.[11]

In hindsight, Powell's reluctance to deploy the MPSs deprived the Bush administration of one of the tools it needed to hedge its bets. Wolfowitz thought Powell's mindset undervalued the diplomatic impact that a show of U.S. military force would bring to the equation. He believed that ambiguity had its benefits. Powell countered with the fact that Kuwait had not requested any help from the United States. Furthermore, finding a suitable landing zone for the MPSs would be a logistical nightmare. Wolfowitz conceded these points, and no MPSs were deployed.[12]

The Kuwaiti ambassador to the United States had visited Wolfowitz in the Pentagon earlier that week to discuss his worries. Although Wolfowitz gave him every opportunity to ask for assistance, the ambassador declined the opening.

AFTER THE INVASION

On August 1, Iraq invaded Kuwait. Brent Scowcroft, National Security Advisor, called an emergency meeting of the Deputies Committee that night and chaired it by video link from the White House. Scowcroft proposed offering twenty-four F-15 fighters to Saudi Arabia. Wolfowitz; Admiral David Jeremiah, Vice Chairman of the Joint Chiefs of Staff; Kimmitt; and Richard Kerr, CIA Deputy Director, agreed.[13]

On August 2, the full National Security Council (NSC) gathered at the White House. The bureaucratic machinery of the NSC was established by the National Security Act of 1947,[14] but it became a true engine of foreign-policy making under Henry A. Kissinger, Nixon's National Security Advisor. The NSC includes the president; vice president; the secretaries of state, defense, and the treasury; the national security advisor; the director of the CIA; the chairman of the joint chiefs of staff; and other cabinet secretaries the president designates. Additionally, other governmental officials may attend NSC meetings for the purposes of discussing specific foreign-policy or national-security topics. The NSC also includes White House staffers, working for the national security advisor, who write policy papers and coordinate the multi-agency security apparatus.[15]

At the August 2 NSC meeting, Wolfowitz and General H. Norman Schwarzkopf, the CENTCOM Commander, were also there, while Kimmitt sat in for Baker.

The morning meeting was rambling and rather inconclusive. Wolfowitz observed the meeting in silence, fearing that the National Security Council might debate itself into paralysis. The administration would not do anything without Arab support, which was not forthcoming; therefore, nothing would be done.[16] Powell merely wanted to defend Saudi Arabia. Predicting that Saddam would withdraw his troops from Kuwait, he was wary of the civilian establishment's impulse to use the U.S. military to liberate Kuwait.[17] Later that day, Powell and Cheney met, along with their aides. Wolfowitz foresaw the difficulties of deploying a large ground force to Saudi Arabia, stating "We need nineteen days."[18]

On August 3, the National Security Council again met at the White House.[19] Scowcroft began: "We have got to examine what the long-term interests are for this country and for the Middle East if the invasion and taking of Kuwait became an accomplished fact. We have to begin our deliberations with the fact that this is unacceptable. Yes, it's hard to do much. There are lots of reasons why we can't do things but it's our job."[20] Wolfowitz thought Scowcroft's presentation had "changed the entire focus" of the meeting.[21]

They considered a CIA report concluding that the invasion posed a threat to the current world order and that the long-run impact on the world economy could be devastating. Saddam sought to turn Iraq into an Arab superpower. Between Iraq and Kuwait, he would control 20 percent of the world's oil, and would have had sufficient leverage to achieve his goal. There was also an ominous assessment of Iraqi military capability. The CIA believed that Saddam could easily swing his armies south and be in Riyadh, the Saudi capital, in three days.

Scowcroft stated the need for two tracks. First, he believed that the United States had to be willing to use military force to stop Saddam's aggression and that this had to be made clear to the world. Second, Saddam had to be toppled—covertly through the CIA—though this goal should remain hidden from the world. President Bush ordered the CIA to begin planning a covert operation to destabilize the regime and hopefully overthrow Saddam.[22] The CIA would recruit Iraqi dissidents to remove Saddam from power, without violating the ban on direct U.S. involvement in assassinations. However, because Saddam ran a police state and brutally repressed any dissent, covert action would be difficult if not impossible.

On August 3, the Saudi ambassador to United States, Prince Bandar bin Sultan, met first with Scowcroft and Bush, and then with Cheney, Powell, Wolfowitz, and National Security Council Middle East expert Richard Haass. The Saudi ambassador was told that Saddam was building up 70,000 troops near the Saudi border, requiring a massive ground presence in response, and was shown CENTCOM's military plan.[23]

After Bandar left, Wolfowitz expressed his surprise at the suddenly serious mood evinced by the ambassador. Wolfowitz then suggested that, given Bandar's apparent receptivity, the necessary forces be put on alert, especially the airborne troops who would deploy forward first.[24] "[Bandar] blows smoke," retorted Powell, "I don't think it's time to start alerting the 82nd Airborne."[25] Cheney agreed with Powell.[26]

On August 4, at Camp David, Schwartzkopf and several top CENTCOM commanders met with Bush, Cheney, Powell, Wolfowitz, Secretary of State James A. (Jim) Baker III, CIA Director William H. Webster, and Scowcroft, among others. The origins of CENTCOM went back to the Rapid Deployment Joint Task Force, a Persian Gulf intervention force created by President Carter in response to the Soviet invasion of Afghanistan in 1979. Upgraded in 1983 by President Reagan to a geographical command, CENTCOM had responsibility for U.S. military operations in most of the Middle East, except Israel, Lebanon, and Syria, which remained under the European Command. Created to coordinate and command the rapid deployment of U.S. ground forces to the Middle East, CENTCOM had no forces assigned to it. Thus, it needed to borrow forces from other geographical commands that had been earmarked for Middle East contingencies.[27]

Schwarzkopf said it would take a minimum of one month to get a capable defense of Saudi Arabia in place. The buildup of military forces necessary to liberate Kuwait would take eight to ten months.[28] Bush stated that he had given Bandar his word of honor that the United States would protect Saudi Arabia. No one opposed seeking Saudi approval for a U.S. military deployment.[29]

Returning to the White House on August 5, in a personal, emotional statement, Bush asserted, "I view very seriously our determination to reverse out this aggression. . . . This will not stand. This will not stand, this aggression against Kuwait."[30] This statement marked a change from stopping Saddam from going into Saudi Arabia, to reversing the invasion of Kuwait. He followed this up with a statement on August 8, "[W]e seek the immediate unconditional and complete withdrawal of all Iraqi forces from Kuwait."[31] The president established a limited objective for a limited campaign.

In response to King Fahd ibn Abdul Aziz's request that an American team brief him, Cheney went to Saudi Arabia with Schwarzkopf; Robert Gates, Deputy National Security Advisor; Wolfowitz; Charles W. Freeman Jr., U.S. Ambassador to Saudi Arabia; and others.[32] Wolfowitz said Cheney would be asking King Fahd to confront a decision the Saudi rulers had spent their lifetimes shying away from. It would be radical departure to accept U.S. forces of any size on Saudi soil.

On August 6, the American delegation met with Fahd and six key members of his government as well as other princes from the royal family. The delegation successfully convinced the Saudis to accept the deployment of American forces in Saudi Arabia, though Fahd asked that the United States keep the deployment secret until American troops were on the ground. The United States then deployed forty-eight F-15 jets and five airborne warning and control aircraft. Combat forces, consisting of 2,300 men from the 82nd Airborne Division, were also sent, but without logistical support, leaving them vulnerable to an Iraqi attack.

On August 25, David Ivri, director general of the Israeli Defense Ministry, led a team of Israeli officials to Washington to meet with Wolfowitz, Kimmitt, and other senior U.S. officials.[33] The Israelis adamantly maintained that in the event of a U.S.-Iraq conflict Iraq would fire Scud missiles at Israel. A Scud was an obsolete Soviet missile designed to carry a half-ton warhead about 190 miles. The Iraqis learned to increase the missile's range to 300 miles but with a warhead of 160 pounds. Wolfowitz asked Ivri how Israel would respond if it was attacked by Iraqi Scuds, which could terrorize civilian populations. Ivri indicated that Israel's response would depend on a number of factors: whether civilians were hurt and whether the United States had taken all possible action to prevent the Scud attack. Seemingly, a perception existed on Israel's part that cooperation between it and Washington was lacking.[34]

Cheney recommended that the U.S. offer to send Patriot antimissile batteries to Israel. The Pentagon wanted to ship the missiles by September 30, the end of the U.S. government's fiscal year, before the expiration of a $75 million congressional authority to cover arms transfers to Israel.[35] Secretary of State Baker resisted the move because of concern about the appearance of U.S.-Israeli cooperation. His resistance ended when Cheney reminded him of the domestic political costs if the United States failed to defend Israel. The Pentagon then offered to supply Israel with Patriot antimissile batteries, but the Israelis refused, convinced that the offer did not constitute the cooperation Israel envisioned.[36]

In a September 24 meeting at the White House with Bush, Cheney, and Wolfowitz, Powell set forth the containment strategy that he believed was working. Favoring the continued use of economic sanctions against Iraq, he was extremely cautious about the use of military force. Economic sanctions were cutting off up to 95 percent of Saddam's imports and nearly all of his exports. Powell realized, however, that sanctions left the initiative with the Iraqis. Wolfowitz argued that strangulation was a defensible position only if sanctions were maintained indefinitely. A policy that said or implied that sanctions would be in effect for a limited time period would provide Saddam with a point when he could count on relief. He could tell the Iraqi people they only needed to hold out until that time.[37]

In September 1990, Schwarzkopf began preparing an initial war plan for dislodging Iraqi troops from Kuwait. On October 6, Powell told Schwarzkopf, who was in Saudi Arabia, that Bush wanted an immediate briefing on the layout of an offensive operation in Kuwait. Schwarzkopf told Powell he had not had enough time to work on a land offensive and was not ready to present such a briefing. Powell responded that everyone understood it was a preliminary plan and gave Schwarzkopf two days to get someone ready to brief the Pentagon. Because Schwarzkopf could not leave Saudi Arabia, he sent a subordinate.[38]

On October 10, Powell received Marine Major General Robert B. Johnston, Schwarzkopf's Chief of Staff, at the Pentagon. Johnston's team presented a four-phase offense plan to Cheney, Wolfowitz, Powell, Jeremiah, and the other joint chiefs, among others. Johnston indicated that this was CENTCOM's best shot and they did not have a lot of time to think it through. The air campaign had been turned over to the U.S. Air Force. With respect to the ground offensive, it was a straight-up-the-middle plan into the strength of the Iraqi defense. Wolfowitz and Cheney had a negative reaction to the plan.[39]

On October 11, Johnston made another presentation to Bush at the White House. Bush's negative reaction was similar to Cheney's the day before. Seeing the likelihood of substantial U.S. casualties, Bush "hated" the plan. Scowcroft telephoned Cheney, indicating that the plan for a ground offensive was awful. Cheney concurred.[40]

On October 12, Cheney, Powell, and others met to review the plan. Cheney was troubled. "Colin, I have been thinking about this all night. I can't let Norm [Schwarzkopf] do this high diddle, diddle up the middle plan," stated Cheney. "I just can't let him do it."[41] Powell told Cheney he would stay on top of the situation and get back to him. Powell met with Schwarzkopf on October 22 in Saudi Arabia and told him that CENTCOM had to come up with a new offensive ground plan. At the same time, Cheney and Wolfowitz then began formulating their own plan.[42]

FORMULATING AN ALTERNATIVE PLAN

Cheney and Wolfowitz turned to Henry S. Rowen, a Stanford University Graduate School of Business professor, who had served as president of the RAND Corporation from 1967 to 1972. In 1990, Rowen, who planned to return to Stanford, was serving under Wolfowitz as Assistant Secretary of Defense for International Security Affairs. Rowen looked at how the British military put down a 1941 Iraqi revolt against the British-supported monarch.[43]

In 1941 the British quickly ended a rebellion by pro-German Iraqis by sending reinforcements eastward across the desert to Baghdad from present day Jordan. Rowen reasoned that the U.S. troops, with air superiority and mobile ground forces, could invade from the far western part of Iraq and move through that nation's vast desert regions. Transporting and sustaining troops in the far western desert would be demanding, but logistics was an American strength. Rowen discussed his ideas with Wolfowitz. He told Rowen to present them to Cheney, who preferred Rowen's concept over simply going "high diddle, diddle, right up the middle."[44]

Military planning became the province of the Pentagon's civilian bureaucracy. Wolfowitz and Scooter Libby, his civilian aide for contingency planning, created a secret team to explore Rowen's idea. The group, called Operation Scorpion, included some active and retired military officers with no connection to the Joint Chiefs of Staff. Basically, the plan called for U.S. troops to go into Iraq's western desert along the Saudi-Iraq border, some three to four hundred miles from Kuwait near the Jordanian border, and establish a base there.[45]

The plan offered three advantages: military, political, and economic. Militarily, if Iraqi troops responded to the ground assault, they would do so in a place lacking Iraqi fortifications. If Saddam withdrew troops from Kuwait to protect Baghdad, these forces would be vulnerable to air attack. If Iraqi forces did not move from Kuwait, allied forces inside Iraq could threaten Baghdad, hopefully leading to a settlement on favorable terms. Politically, the occupation of western Iraq would allow a direct attack on fixed missile sites in the region, thereby protecting Israel and hopefully keeping that nation out of the war. Economically, it would cut off the road from Amman to Baghdad, which Iraq used to get supplies despite a U.N. embargo. It would also cut the lines of communication between Jordan and Iraq. Cheney liked the detailed plan, dubbing it "the Western Excursion."[46] He quietly took it to Bush and Scowcroft.

Ultimately, the Rowen war plan was set aside. Both Powell and Schwarzkopf opposed it. In response to Powell's request to assess the Cheney plan, Schwarzkopf concluded that it would be impossible to supply troops in western Iraq. It detracted from the destruction of the Iraqi Republican Guard and was too far to take U.S. forces. The army could not logistically sustain an attack from the west and it would lack an adequate-size force. Conceptually, it was too risky for such a small reward.[47] Schwarzkopf subsequently wrote, "I wondered whether Cheney had succumbed to the phenomenon I'd observed among some secretaries of the Army: put a civilian in charge of professional military men and before long he's no longer satisfied with setting policy but he wants to outgeneral the generals."[48]

Evidencing the caution that later prevailed in March 1991, the White House viewed Rowen's plan as too politically risky. If it were successful, chaos might have resulted in Iraq, including the possible breakup of that nation.[49]

DECIDING ON A PLAN

Eventually, the military revised Schwarzkopf's initial war plan. The Western Excursion, from Cheney's view, had lit a fire under the military. Instead of a frontal assault on Iraqi troops, allied ground forces would carry out a flanking maneuver across the Saudi-Iraq border and circumvent the Iraqis' defenses situated to the east in Kuwait. In part, the revamped, left-hook plan referred to Rowen's ideas. Politically, the sweep across western Iraq enabled the military to buy off Cheney and defuse any pressure to implement the Western Excursion.[50]

On October 30, Bush met with Baker, Cheney, Scowcroft, and Powell. Powell unveiled Schwarzkopf's request to double the number of U.S. ground troops and deploy a large tank force to conduct the flanking attack on the Iraqis. At this meeting, Cheney and Scowcroft supported Schwarzkopf and Powell without conditions, and Bush gave his final approval to Schwarzkopf's request on October 31.[51]

As the military plans were being revised in October, Wolfowitz worried that the administration had transitioned to the offensive ground option without sufficient thought.[52] Alternatives and implications had not been written down so they could be analyzed. He felt that the inner circle of Bush, Baker, Cheney, Powell, and Scowcroft was perhaps a little too close-knit.[53] Wolfowitz did not get the sense that their frequent, private meetings were a forum for discussing and debating alternatives. Any kind of organized debate within the inner circle was done without the benefit of staff, even senior staffers like himself. Wolfowitz thought a third option existed: sending additional troops without indicating whether they constituted replacements or offensive reinforcements. The administration could subsequently make a decision as to their ultimate purpose. However, Wolfowitz did not manage to have this idea considered before Bush approved Schwarzkopf's request.[54]

On November 8, signaling a switch to the offensive, Bush ordered more than 150,000 additional U.S. ground, sea, and air forces to the Persian Gulf, for a total American force of about 380,000. He announced, "I have today directed the Secretary of Defense to increase the size of U.S. forces committed to Desert Shield to ensure that the coalition has an adequate offensive military option should that be necessary to achieve our common goals." In view of the ten resolutions adopted by the U.N. Security Council since the Iraqi invasion of Kuwait, he added, in response to a reporter's question, "I think Saddam Hussein should fully, without condition, comply to the U.N. resolutions. And if this movement of force is what convinces him, so much the better."[55]

The end of the cold war made cooperative action through the United Nations feasible by removing the threat of a Soviet veto. On November 29, the U.N. Security Council authorized the use of "all necessary means" to expel Saddam's forces from Kuwait if he did not pull out by the resolution's deadline of January 15, 1991.[56] The Security Council's decision, by a 12 to 2 vote, with China abstaining and Yemen and Cuba casting no votes, marked an important turning point in the Persian Gulf crisis. The world community declared its willingness to support a U.S.-led military action, if necessary, to drive Iraq from Kuwait. The resolution set a countdown for solving the crisis. Bush 41 later noted, "Although we didn't realize it at the time, it [the resolution] also changed the debate with Congress, creating a context for the use of force which helped bring it about. The Security Council had voted to go to war."[57]

On December 19, Cheney, Wolfowitz, and Powell arrived in Saudi Arabia for a detailed examination of Schwarzkopf's war plan. They spent a day and a half with Schwarzkopf. Wolfowitz, concerned about prematurely entering into a costly, casualty-producing ground campaign, wanted to make certain all the military options had been considered and addressed. During a break in the deliberations, he asked Schwarzkopf how long the air campaign should last before initiating the ground offensive. Schwarzkopf replied that he would be happy with a full year of airstrikes. When the principals reassembled, Wolfowitz pushed Schwarzkopf to make this comment to Cheney and Powell.[58] For Wolfowitz, the longer the air war lasted, the better. In contrast, Schwarzkopf feared that the politicians would cease military action before he could achieve his air or ground objectives. Wolfowitz tried to assuage these fears, noting that "the President and Cheney had said it would be politically acceptable for Schwarzkopf to take all the time the field commanders needed."[59]

The spirit of the Western Excursion lived on. Washington's pressure led Schwarzkopf and his team to look further to the west than they had earlier planned.

CENTCOM's final ground plan called for moving the Army's VII Corps—100,000 men, their equipment and supplies—several hundred miles to the west. Thereafter, it would engage in a massive tank attack in the form of a gigantic left hook.[60] However, the ultimate plan did not call for troops to move far enough west to solve the Scud problem. Baghdad was not directly threatened, thus allowing Saddam to hold onto power.

As Cheney and Powell prepared to leave Saudi Arabia, Wolfowitz received a telephone call from Ivri, who explained that Moshe Arens, the Israeli Defense Minister, wanted to meet with Cheney immediately concerning potential Scud attacks by Iraq. On the way back to the United States, Cheney agreed to send a high-level delegation to Israel before January 15. Realizing that Baker would be anxious to preserve the State Department's prerogatives, Cheney proposed sending Lawrence S. Eagleburger, the Deputy Secretary of State, and Wolfowitz to Israel with the message that the United States would do everything it could to protect Israel from Iraqi Scud attacks. Wolfowitz and Eagleburger managed to convince the Israeli government to accept Patriot antimissile batteries, though Israel refused to allow U.S. personnel to crew them.[61] The U.S. delegation also sounded out Israeli Prime Minister Yitzhak Shamir about what Israel would do if attacked by Iraq. Shamir would not disclose what action he might take, but promised to consult with the United States before acting.[62]

On January 2, Gates convened a meeting of the NSC Deputies Committee. Wolfowitz thought that a letter from Bush to Saddam might still make a difference. He found one draft prepared by the NSC staff "rather mild." He and Jeremiah were eager to make it tougher. They proposed changes that the others accepted.[63] In its final form, the brink-of-war letter stated: "We stand today at the brink of war between Iraq and the world." The future of Iraq was at stake and the failure to withdraw from Kuwait would mean "calamity," "tragedy," and "further violence" for Iraq. The final sentence read: "I hope you weigh your choice carefully and choose wisely, for much will depend on it."[64]

On January 9, Baker presented a photocopy of the letter to Tariq Aziz, Iraq's foreign minister, who refused to accept it or carry it to Saddam.[65] Baker and Aziz were unable to find common ground for discussion in their efforts to negotiate a settlement to the Persian Gulf crisis. Thereafter, the U.S. Congress granted Bush authority to go to war on January 12, 1991, along mostly partisan lines, by a slim majority in a sharply divided Senate (52 to 47) and a solid majority in the House (250 to 183).[66]

MILITARY ACTION AGAINST IRAQ

On January 17, the United States began its air attack on Iraq. The next day, Iraq started firing Scuds towards Israel. Arens called Cheney immediately after the attack and asked the United States to ship additional Patriot antimissile batteries, as well as American personnel to crew them, as soon as possible. Cheney asked

Arens to receive a U.S. team to discuss these developments, to which Arens agreed.[67] On January 19, Ivri called Wolfowitz, who sensed that the Israelis were close to a retaliatory strike against military targets in western Iraq. "You can give us any information you want," Wolfowitz indicated. "But there's been no decision on our part that we're going to get out of your way. All I can do is take down what you tell me." Wolfowitz then reported the conversation to Cheney.[68]

At a weekend meeting at Camp David, Bush agreed to a two-track plan. First, Eagleburger and Wolfowitz would return to Israel to reinforce the message that Israel should stay out of the war and let the United States respond on Israel's behalf to any Iraqi missile attacks on Israeli territory. Second, at Cheney's suggestion, Assistant Secretary of Defense Richard L. Armitage would go to Amman to meet with Jordon's King Hussein.[69]

Eagleburger and Wolfowitz, who arrived in time to welcome the U.S.-staffed Patriot crews, tried to reassure the Israelis that the U.S. military would deal with the Iraqi Scuds.[70] Schwarzkopf minimized the Scud problem, which the Israelis viewed as an expression of unconcern. Eagleburger complained to Washington, advising that if Schwarzkopf could not stop the Scuds, he should stop belittling the problem. Eagleburger and Wolfowitz were unhappy with how CENTCOM was privately dealing with the Israelis. In response, CENTCOM dispatched a two-star Air Force general to Tel Aviv, but he shared little information with the Israelis about the Scud campaign, perhaps because he had little knowledge of what CENTCOM was doing.

The Bush administration did take additional steps in support of additional U.S.-Israeli cooperation on military planning. After Eagleburger and Wolfowitz returned to Washington, the Pentagon dispatched a general, one of Powell's deputies, to Tel Aviv. The Israelis submitted a target list to the general, who forwarded it to CENTCOM via the Pentagon.

As the war progressed, CENTCOM had difficulty in hunting Scuds by air. Moreover, the Patriot antimissile batteries in Israel had mixed success in fending off Iraqi Scuds, deflecting them but leaving their warheads to fall where they might. Despite these difficulties, however, the Scuds failed to provoke an Israeli counterattack.[71]

On February 8, Cheney, Powell, and Wolfowitz arrived in Saudi Arabia for a status report on the air campaign and a final review of the ground plan. After the briefing, Schwarzkopf and the Pentagon officials gathered to talk more privately. Wolfowitz asked a key question: "What would be the effect of delaying the land war until March?" Powell was concerned that the ground forces could not sit in the desert indefinitely; they would lose their edge. Agreeing with Powell, Schwarzkopf rebuffed Wolfowitz's suggestion that the air campaign be extended into March. CENTCOM, concerned about the need to start the ground campaign in fair weather, recommended that the coalition land forces be ready to advance on February 21 or a few days thereafter. Thus, while Wolfowitz had given Schwarzkopf the opportunity to endorse an open-ended bombing campaign, the general declined to do so.[72]

At the time, Walter Boomer, the Marine Commander, had argued that the Iraq artillery, especially those pieces capable of chemical attack, needed to be neutralized before ground operations began. This proposal resonated with Wolfowitz, and on the flight home, he tried to raise the issue of prolonging the air campaign with Cheney and Powell. However, he was rebuffed again. Powell explained that the Marine attack against Iraqi defenses on the Saudi-Kuwaiti border was a "holding action," designed to pin and occupy the Iraqi forces in Kuwait. Wolfowitz asserted that the Marines did not naturally adhere to such limiting tactics, and might launch an all-out attack, potentially getting themselves into trouble. Powell replied that Schwarzkopf would make certain the Marines "did not get in over their heads."[73]

In the run-up to the commencement of the ground campaign, Moscow, at Baghdad's urging, attempted to broker a political settlement, which centered on Iraq withdrawing from Kuwait over a period of weeks, after a cease-fire.[74] The Bush administration responded with a counterproposal. At Powell's urging, the administration set a seventy-two-hour deadline for Iraq to begin an unconditional withdrawal from Kuwait, a deadline which ultimately passed on February 24 without a response from Iraq.[75] Cheney and Wolfowitz disapproved of this offer, irritated that the deadline would delay the ground war for several days.

Meanwhile, Dennis B. Ross, Baker's head of policy planning at the State Department, expressed confusion concerning Wolfowitz's new "gung ho" stance. Wolfowitz explained that he was now persuaded by intelligence that the Iraqi army's collapse was eminent and believed that humiliating Iraq in a land war had the strategic benefit of preventing Saddam from claiming he fought the United States to a standoff.[76]

THE AFTERMATH

The ground campaign, begun on February 24, 1991, lasted one hundred hours, concluding on February 28, 1991. On that day, the White House suspended combat operations against Iraq's forces, with President Bush declaring, "Kuwait is liberated. Iraq's army is defeated. Our military objectives are met." The president stated that the coalition "will suspend offensive combat operations" against the Iraqi military. He asked for a meeting of military commanders from both sides "to arrange for military aspects of the cease-fire."[77]

Even before Bush's announcement, on February 27, Schwarzkopf gave a report from Riyadh to the nation. He stated:

> [W]e were 150 miles away from Baghdad and there was nobody between us and Baghdad. If it had been our intention to take Iraq, if it had been our intention to destroy the country, if it had been our intention to overrun the country, we would have done it unopposed for all intents and purposes from this position at that time. But that was not our intention. We had never said it was our intention. Our intention

was purely to eject the Iraqis out of Kuwait and to destroy the military power that had come in here.[78]

Schwarzkopf's declaration that Baghdad was not a target for ground forces dismayed Wolfowitz. The allies could stop their advance without giving hope to Saddam's regime. He also questioned whether it was wise for the United States to announce a secession of operations. Hoping for a coup, Wolfowitz wanted to keep the pressure on Saddam.[79] He later wrote, "[S]imply by delaying the cease-fire agreement—without killing more Iraqi troops or destroying more Iraqi military assets—the United States might have bought time for opposition to Saddam to build and to act against him."[80] By telling the world that the ground war was over, the allies would give Saddam a reprieve. Cheney reminded Wolfowitz, however, that in his briefing Schwarzkopf had already let the cat out of the bag.[81]

For Powell, the cease-fire enabled the military to erase the stain of Vietnam and exit the Gulf War victorious and with its honor intact. It avoided the impression that the United States was "piling on" and killing Iraqis only for the sake of annihilating them. Scowcroft, Baker, and Cheney also felt it was best to avoid the impression that the United States was "piling [it] on."[82]

After the White House had set the timing for the suspension of combat operations, Cheney informed Wolfowitz, who was disturbed by the symbolism. The phrase "100-hour war" had a negative connotation in the Arab world, recalling the 1956 war launched by France, Great Britain, and Israel against Egypt after it nationalized the Suez Canal. For many Arabs, the phrase was synonymous with Western and Israeli aggression. Wolfowitz argued that anything would be better than 100 hours, but was overruled. The Bush administration appeared unconcerned with the historical association, seemingly confident that it was irrelevant for international public-relations purposes.[83]

Poor intelligence contributed to the White Houses decision to suspend combat operations. After the war, when intelligence imagery was carefully analyzed in greater detail, it became clear that more of the Iraqi Republican Guard survived than the administration had believed or anticipated. For example, half of the Republican Guard's equipment had not been destroyed.[84] The reconstituted Republican Guard subsequently suppressed the Shiite uprising in the south of Iraq.

During the cease-fire talks, Iraqi military officials asked Schwarzkopf for permission to fly helicopters over Iraqi air space on the pretext of transporting government officials around the country, where roads and bridges were out. Schwarzkopf magnanimously gave his consent, permitting armed Iraqi military helicopters, though not fighters or bombers, which could have threatened allied forces, to continue to fly over Iraq.[85]

In fact, the Iraqis used these helicopter gunships to attack Shiite and Kurdish forces seeking to overthrow Saddam Hussein. When he learned about Iraq's use of its helicopter gunships, Wolfowitz became concerned. He argued with Cheney that the United States should intervene militarily to stop the Iraqi helicopter attacks.

The coalition had won the war, he reasoned, and the United States should publicly announce that it was rigorously enforcing the ban on any postwar Iraqi flights.[86] He asserted that U.S. passivity was similar to "idly watching a mugging."[87]

Cheney seemed sympathetic to the idea of shooting down the Iraqi helicopters, but more wary than Wolfowitz about being drawn into the fighting in Iraq. Scowcroft saw Saddam's regime as buffer against the expansion of Iranian power. Baker was unenthusiastic about becoming involved in the fighting in Iraq. Powell did not want any additional military missions, hoping to avoid the burden of postwar objectives that would prevent the United States from later disengaging. He reasoned that stopping the helicopter assaults would not end the internal Iraqi conflict. Furthermore, he wanted to extract the U.S. military from Iraq as quickly and cleanly as possible and avoid being sucked into a Iraqi civil war.[88] Powell then complained to Wolfowitz that Pentagon civilians were telling the media that the issue of enforcing a complete ban on Iraqi helicopter flights was not yet decided.[89]

It was clear, however, that the issue had been decided. Although Bush warned Iraq against using helicopter gunships to put down insurrections by anti-government rebels,[90] the White House feared that any U.S. support of the Shiites and the Kurds might lead to Iraq's disintegration.[91] It also believed that the Iraqi Shiites were allied with Iran. The administration decided to let the fighting in Iraq run its course.

In the end, Saddam Hussein's political apparatus, with its ruthless internal controls, absorbed the battlefield defeats and remained in power. Iraqi troops suppressed the Shiite rebellion and set up a military blockade around Kirkuk to isolate the Kurds in northern Iraq.[92] The Bush administration helped the Kurds to form a separate area by launching Operation Provide Comfort in April 1991. Lightly armed U.S. and coalition forces, backed by the threat of American air power, assisted Kurdish guerillas in pushing Iraqi forces back to Kirkuk and out of northern Iraq until 1996. The White House's primary concern in this endeavor was not humanitarian, however; it feared that an influx of Kurdish refugees into Turkey would provoke a military response by Ankara into northern Iraq, further destabilizing the region. The Bush administration took the further step of patrolling the U.N.-mandated northern and southern "no fly" zones, but in general did little to upset the status quo inside Iraq.[93]

WOLFOWITZ'S FURTHER REFLECTIONS

In 1991, the allies rushed to get out of Iraq. At that time, Wolfowitz did not favor an allied military move on Baghdad. The Bush White House had pursued its original, limited war aim of removing Iraq from Kuwait. It did not seek to remake Middle Eastern political institutions. A march on Baghdad was considered militarily uncertain and politically risky. The Bush administration also believed, incorrectly, that after losing the war Saddam would be overthrown.[94]

As Bush 41 subsequently wrote, "Had we gone the invasion route, the United States could conceivably still be an occupying power in a bitterly hostile land. It would have been a dramatically different—and perhaps barren—outcome.[95]

Wolfowitz repeatedly endorsed the decision not to go to Baghdad. Prophetically, in light of events in postwar Iraq in 2003 and thereafter, he wrote:

> Nothing could have insured Saddam Hussein's removal from power short of a full-scale occupation of Iraq. Very few participants in the pre-war debate have any standing to suggest that President Bush should have done this, given the widespread opposition even to the more limited objective of liberating Kuwait. MacArthur's disastrous experience in Korea after the stunning victory at Inchon should be warning enough against the assumption that the occupation of Iraq would be as easy as the liberation of Kuwait. Even if easy initially, it is unclear how or when it would have ended.[96]

In providing a rationale for the Bush 41's unwillingness to take Baghdad, Wolfowitz subsequently stated: "A new regime [in Iraq] would have become the United States' responsibility. Conceivably, this could have led the United States into a more or less permanent occupation of a country that could not govern itself but where the rule of a foreign occupier would be increasingly resented."[97]

Wolfowitz remained troubled that the United States allowed Saddam Hussein to control Iraq, but until late 1997 he did not advocate using military force to topple Saddam. In 1993, he noted, "Saddam Hussein's continuation in power is a problem." Because some of America's Gulf War allies were "greedy for Iraqi contracts" and thus wanted to lift the U.N.-imposed postwar sanctions on Iraq, Wolfowitz predicted that it would be difficult to sustain the pressure on Saddam Hussein "indefinitely." He concluded, "The United States and the entire industrialized world have an enormous stake in the security of the Persian Gulf, not primarily in order to save a few dollars per gallon of gasoline but rather because a hostile regime in control of these resources could wreak untold damage on the world's economy, and could apply that wealth to purposes that would endanger peace globally."[98] Wolfowitz stopped short of calling for regime change in Iraq. However, in late 1995, he favored the U.S.-led NATO bombing of Serbian positions in Bosnia and the equipping and training of Bosnian nationals during the breakup of Yugoslavia.[99]

Then, during the 1996 presidential campaign, as Dole's chief foreign policy advisor, Wolfowitz began to criticize the Clinton administration for ineffectively containing Hussein. He asserted, "The U.S. has virtually abandoned its commitment to protect a besieged people from a bloodthirsty dictator."[100]

Wolfowitz outlined three possible U.S. policy options toward Iraq: containment; engagement; regime change. He maintained that the policy of containment was ineffective. Sanctions harmed the Iraqi people as much as the regime. With China, France, and Russia "lining up to lift sanctions," the coalition against Iraq would weaken. Engagement would not work because it would enhance Hussein's power and enable him to "attempt to destabilize the weak nations of the Gulf through terrorism and other means." He concluded that a new Iraqi regime was the best option, but left open the means of achieving this goal, noting only that the United States should "be prepared to seize opportunities and not merely respond to crises."[101]

By December 1997, Wolfowitz explicitly called for the use of military force to remove Hussein from power. In outlining six elements of a "new strategy that embraces the removal of Saddam's regime as our overall objective," notably aiding the Iraqi opposition, he asserted with his coauthor Zalmay Khalilzad: "[Military force] must be part of an overall political strategy that sets as its goal not merely the containment of Saddam but the liberation of Iraq from his tyranny."[102] Then in January 1998, Wolfowitz, along with Khalilzad and Rumsfeld, among others, signed an open letter to President Clinton on the subject of Iraq. It said that the threat Saddam posed was "more serious than any we have known since the end of the Cold War." Efforts to contain him were "steadily eroding." If Saddam acquired weapons of mass destruction, "as he is almost certain to do if we continue along the present course," the entire Middle East would be placed at risk. "The only acceptable strategy," the letter concluded, "is one that eliminates the possibility that Iraq will be able to use or threaten to use weapons of mass destruction. In the near term, this means a willingness to undertake military action as diplomacy is clearly failing. In the long term, it means removing Saddam Hussein and his regime from power."[103] This letter and another in February 1998[104] helped to propel the passage of the 1998 Iraq Liberation Act, signed by President Clinton, which made regime change in Iraq the official U.S. policy and allocated $97 million to support Iraqi opponents of Saddam.[105]

As Wolfowitz urged tougher action against Hussein in the late 1990s, the 1991 coalition seemed weaker. Advocating a "follower hypothesis," he wrote, "It has been correctly observed that sometimes, as the leader, the U.S. must act unilaterally. But a willingness to act unilaterally can be the most effective way of securing collective action. In the present crisis we may have to act alone at first, or almost alone, because the international consensus is weak." Noting that "we must also use action as a means to build a stronger consensus," he asserted that with a stronger U.S. policy, the 1991 coalition would revive; with U.S. action, other nations would follow.[106] As events demonstrated, however, when Wolfowitz helped put his theory into practice these predictions proved false. When the United States and its allies invaded Iraq in the spring of 2003, France, Germany, and Russia did not fall into line. Before the United States would use military force to depose Saddam, however, the nation, and by extension, Wolfowitz, had to face the consequences of September 11, 2001.

Chapter 6

The Road to Baghdad, Part Two: Operation Enduring Freedom

On Tuesday, September 11, 2001, two hijacked airplanes crashed into the World Trade Center and one into the Pentagon. Al Qaeda, a stateless, rather amorphous, terrorist organization had stunned the United States, attacking its financial and military pillars and killing nearly three thousand people.

Following 9/11, President George W. Bush needed a vision, a way of looking at America and its place in the world. Based on his years of study and governmental experience, Paul Wolfowitz readily supplied that vision, a recategorization of terrorism from a legal matter to a military problem. Bush soon declared that the United States. would call to account both terrorist groups and the nations that harbored and sponsored them. This led to Operation Enduring Freedom, a U.S.-led military operation in Afghanistan.

THE BUSH 43 ADMINISTRATION'S HANDLING OF TERRORISM PRIOR TO SEPTEMBER 11

By 1997, as noted in chapter 5, Wolfowitz had come to support a policy of regime change in Iraq. At his February 2001 confirmation hearing to be Deputy Defense Secretary, Wolfowitz asserted that sanctions could only serve as one component of an effective U.S. policy toward Iraq. He spoke about a "change of regime" in Baghdad, adding, "If there is a real option to [achieve a base from which an armed Iraqi opposition group can attack Saddam], I would certainly think it is still worthwhile." He cautioned, however, "I have not yet seen a plausible plan."[1]

Since 1998, the CIA had been authorized to disrupt and preempt Osama bin Laden's terrorist operations under directives signed by President William Jefferson

(Bill) Clinton after terrorists linked to Osama bin Laden bombed U.S. embassies in Nairobi, Kenya and Dar es Salaam, Tanzania.[2] In a further response to the bombings, the Clinton administration launched cruise missiles against sites in Afghanistan and Sudan believed to have ties to bin Laden, though the strikes proved to be largely ineffective.

Although President Bush reaffirmed the Clinton directives authorizing the CIA to engage in covert operations against al Qaeda, as discussed in chapter 4, missile defense and China, among other items, preoccupied the White House. Al Qaeda only slowly came to the fore as a major foreign or national security policy concern.

Afghanistan did surface on the administration's radar. Stephen Hadley, Deputy National Security Advisor, convened an informal Deputies Committee meeting on March 7, where proposals to aid the Northern Alliance and Uzbekistan and for unmanned Predator missions were discussed. No decisions were reached, but Hadley saw the need for a presidential national security policy directive (NSPD) on terrorism.[3] National Security Advisor Condoleezza Rice delayed a principals meeting on al Qaeda to give the deputies time to develop a new policy on terrorism.

On April 30, the full Deputies Committee met to discuss the problem of al Qaeda, ultimately approving covert aid to Uzbekistan. Seeming to be more interested in the threats posed by Iraq than in al Qaeda, Wolfowitz indicated, "Well, I just don't understand why we are beginning by talking about this one man bin Laden. . . . You give bin Laden too much credit. He could not do all these things like the 1993 attack on New York, not without a state sponsor. Just because FBI and CIA have failed to find the linkages does not mean they don't exist."[4] While no major commitments were made to the Northern Alliance at that time, the deputies considered other options for Afghanistan, including providing aid to anti-Taliban groups and the possibility of regime change. The deputies also recommended that the administration begin a comprehensive review of U.S. policy toward Pakistan.[5]

Wolfowitz's June 2 commencement address at West Point was remarkably prescient. He noted that 2001 was the sixtieth anniversary of the Japanese attack at Pearl Harbor. "Interestingly that 'surprise attack' was preceded by an astonishing number of unheeded warnings and missed signals," Wolfowitz noted. He continued, "Surprise happens so often that it's surprising that we're still surprised by it. Very few of these surprises are the product of simple blindness or simple stupidity. Almost always there have been warnings and signals that have been missed—sometimes because there were just too many warnings to pick the right one out." He asserted that America needed to overcome its sense of complacency and "replace a poverty of expectations with an anticipation of the unfamiliar and the unlikely."[6]

On June 7, Hadley circulated to the Deputies Committee a first draft of a new national security presidential policy directive setting out the administration's policy for confronting al Qaeda. The draft's goal was "to eliminate the al Qida network of terrorists groups as a threat to the Untied States and to friendly governments."

The proposed NSPD would recommend a "multi-year effort involving diplomacy, covert action, economic measures, law enforcement . . . and if necessary, military efforts." Significantly, the CIA would expand its covert operations in Afghanistan through considerable additional funding and other aid to anti-Taliban groups.[7] Moreover, the proposed NSPD directed Defense Secretary Rumsfeld to initiate the development of contingency plans to attack al Qaeda and Taliban targets in Afghanistan.[8]

By July, the Deputies Committee arrived at the consensus that the administration should make one "last effort" to convince the Taliban to shift its position concerning al Qaeda. Should that effort fail, the administration would then engage in a "significantly enlarged covert action program."[9] A redrafted NSPD was circulated that month.

In the spring of 2001, the White House had refused to deploy reconnaissance flights of unmanned aerial drone Predators until that aircraft was weapons capable. During the summer, ongoing arguments ensued concerning the Predator: should Predator reconnaissance flights over Afghanistan be resumed; should the Predator be armed; and if so, would the CIA or the Pentagon approve and operate any strikes? Finally, on August 1, the Deputies Committee met to discuss these issues. Apart from questions of feasibility, an argument ensued over money. If the CIA borrowed Predators from the Pentagon, which agency would bear the cost if one went down? Wolfowitz asserted that the CIA should pay for it; the CIA disagreed. The deputies decided to defer the panoply of questions regarding the Predator to the National Security Council Principals.[10]

The principals held their first meeting on al Qaeda on September 4, approving the draft NSPD. Wolfowitz, sitting in for Rumsfeld, advocated targeting bin Laden during a general air strike, similar to the targeting of Qaddafi during the strike against Libya in 1986. The principals came to an agreement to support the Uzbeks and the Northern Alliance in Afghanistan. They approved a plan to give the CIA from $125 to $200 million to implement this policy, but left it to the CIA and the Office of the Budget and Management to figure out how to finance the effort. Although the Predator was discussed, again no decision on its use was made.[11] A few days later, after the principals made minor changes, a final version of the draft NSPD was circulated.

On September 10, the Deputies Committee agreed on a three-phase strategy to pressure and, if necessary, overthrow the Taliban leadership.[12] First, an envoy would give the Taliban one last chance to turn over Osama bin Laden. Second, if that failed, the United States would combine continuing diplomatic pressure with the planned covert action program to encourage anti-Taliban Afghans to stalemate the Taliban in a civil war and attack al Qaeda bases, giving the United States time to develop a multilateral coalition to undermine the regime. Third, if the second phase failed, the United States would try covert action to topple the Taliban's leadership from within. The deputies agreed to revise the al Qaeda presidential directive being finalized for presidential approval to add the three-prong strategy to it.

SEPTEMBER 11 AND ITS AFTERMATH

For Wolfowitz, the memory of 9/11 was vivid. That morning he was at his Pentagon office, on the side of the building opposite where the hijacked American Airlines Flight 77 hit. Wolfowitz recalled, "We'd just had a breakfast with some congressmen in which one of the subjects had been missile defense. And [Rumsfeld and I] commented to them based on what [we] had both seen and worked on the Ballistic Missile Threat Commission, that we were in for some nasty surprises over the next ten years," but that "it's in the nature of surprise that you can't predict what it's going to be."[13]

Wolfowitz then went to a meeting in his office, where word soon came that one airplane had hit the World Trade Center. "Then we turned to the television and we started seeing the shots of the second plane hitting. . . . There didn't seem to be much to do about it immediately and we went on with whatever the meeting was," Wolfowitz reflected. A half hour later, at 9:43 a.m., a third plane hit the Pentagon. He recalled, "Then whole building shook. I have to confess my first reaction was that it was an earthquake." Rumsfeld, however, instantly made the connection between what had happened at the World Trade Center and the current commotion. Rumsfeld charged out to the impact site to survey the damage and help with the rescue effort. "[T]he next thing we heard was that there'd been a bomb and the building had to be evacuated," Wolfowitz continued. "Everyone started streaming out of the building in a quite orderly way."[14]

Returning to the building, Wolfowitz encountered a "huge fire," and "acrid smoke." He noted, "[T]hat was an experience and I won't ever forget."[15] As a result, Rumsfeld and his team went up to an isolated communications network room where the air was better.

Wolfowitz was soon whisked out of the Pentagon and then the area to prevent the Defense Secretary and his deputy from being together during an attack, thus ensuring continuity of government. Staying away only briefly, Wolfowitz quickly returned to Washington.

On the afternoon of 9/11, Rumsfeld mused about going after not only Osama bin Laden, but also Saddam Hussein. He asked one of his aides, a Pentagon attorney, to talk to Wolfowitz about Iraq's connection with bin Laden.[16] Rumsfeld's instinct was to hit Osama bin Laden and Saddam at the same time because either might have been the responsible party.[17]

In the days immediately after 9/11, Wolfowitz recalled:

> I know my thinking at that point was that the old approach to terrorism was not acceptable any longer. The old approach being you treat it as a law enforcement problem rather than a national security problem. You pursued terrorists after they've done things and bring them to justice, and to the extent states are perhaps involved, you retaliate against them but you don't really expect to get them out of the business of supporting terrorism completely.
>
> To me what September 11th meant was that we just couldn't live with terrorism any longer. . . .

And I think what September 11th to me said was this is just the beginning of what these bastards can do if they start getting access to so-called modern weapons and that it's not something you can live with any longer. So there needs to be a campaign, a strategy, a long-term effort, to root out these networks and to get governments out of the business of supporting them. But that wasn't something that was going to happen overnight.[18]

In short, it was clear to Wolfowitz that "the old approach to terrorism was not acceptable any longer."[19] Action became less risky than passivity.

FORMULATING A VISION, A STRATEGY, AND TACTICS

Wolfowitz played a key role in helping President George W. Bush formulate the new U.S. antiterrorism strategy and tactics.[20] Wolfowitz, joined by Cheney's Chief of Staff, Scooter Libby, was committed to a policy that would make Iraq a principal target of the first round in the war on terrorism, asserting that the forces supporting Middle East terrorism were all interconnected. If the United States could defeat Saddam Hussein, its most powerful opponent in the Middle East, then all terrorist groups in the region would be weakened. In short, Wolfowitz urged that the United States not limit its initial military response to Afghanistan. Although he did not succeed immediately, he ultimately prevailed.

Since taking office in 2001, Bush had looked for ways to undermine Saddam Hussein. Wolfowitz had pushed efforts to aid opposition groups in Iraq. As will be discussed in chapter 7, Colin L. Powell, now the Secretary of State, sought support for a new set of narrower, but tighter, international sanctions against Saddam's regime.[21] The terrorist attacks of 9/11 gave the United States a new opportunity to go after Saddam.

On the evening of 9/11, Bush addressed the nation, stating that the United States would not distinguish "between the terrorists who committed these acts and those who harbor them."[22] Later that night at a meeting of Bush's senior national security advisors, the president repeated the theme that the United States would punish not only the perpetrators of the horrific attacks but also those who harbored them. Rumsfeld asked Bush and the others to think more broadly about who may have harbored the attackers, including Afghanistan and Iraq. He wondered how much evidence the United States would need to deal with these nations.[23] Thereafter, at a National Security Council meeting on September 12, Rumsfeld again raised the possibility of attacking Iraq along with al Qaeda.[24]

Rumsfeld now questioned whether the United States could use the opportunity offered by 9/11 to immediately overthrow the Iraqi regime. Here, he echoed his deputy, Wolfowitz, who wanted to include Iraq as a primary target in the opening stages of this new war against terrorism. Powell countered that the United States should focus on al Qaeda for now because that was what the

American people expected. Everyone realized that Bush sought a military plan that would destroy the terrorists responsible for the 9/11 attacks. Wolfowitz wanted the president to issue a public warning to nations supporting terrorists. He also sought to prod Bush to include Iraq as the main target in the initial round of the new war on terrorism.[25]

Wolfowitz saw no greater menace in the world than Saddam Hussein, holding that he posed nearly as serious a problem for the United States as Afghanistan. On September 13, Wolfowitz conducted the Pentagon press briefing. Pushing for the broadest possible response to the events of 9/11, he stated, "It's not going to stop if a few criminals are taken care of." Rather, the United States should aim to eliminate the terrorists' support systems. He called for a strategy of "ending states who sponsor terrorism,"[26] which he soon amended to "ending state support for terrorism."[27] The first version caught everyone's attention. Seemingly, Wolfowitz advocated the overthrow of existing regimes. Speculation turned to Iraq.

For over two decades, Wolfowitz had warned about the dangers of a powerful Iraq. Doing little to dispel his support for regime change in Iraq, on September 13, he asserted: "[Hussein] is one of the most active supporters of state terrorism."[28] Wolfowitz also remarked, "It's not just simply a matter of capturing people and holding them accountable, but removing the sanctuaries, removing the support systems, ending states who sponsor terrorism. It will be a campaign, not a single action. And we're going to keep after these people and the people who support them until it stops."[29]

As part of the larger institutional differences between the State and Defense Departments, tensions between Powell and Wolfowitz once again appeared, with Powell publicly distancing himself from the Deputy Defense Secretary. In public, the Secretary of State rebuked Wolfowitz's call for military action against other nations, apart from Afghanistan. He stated, "We are after ending terrorism. And if there are states and regimes, nations, that support terrorism, we hope to persuade them that it is in their interests to stop doing that. But I think ending terrorism is where I would like to leave it, and let Mr. Wolfowitz speak for himself."[30] Privately, Powell told Wolfowitz that his plan would "wreck the coalition" the president was assembling.[31]

Army General Henry H. (Hugh) Shelton, the chairman of the Joint Chiefs of Staff, firmly believed that contemplating military action in Iraq at this point was inappropriate. After Rumsfeld had raised Iraq as a potential target, Shelton tried to get Rumsfeld and Wolfowitz focused on the immediate issues of Afghanistan and al Qaeda, arguing "practicalities and priorities." Wolfowitz, however, resolutely held to his position.[32]

Thereafter, the tensions between Powell and Wolfowitz eased, at least temporarily. The administration focused on Afghanistan as the initial military response to September 11. In the short run, Powell won the day. However, the White House left open the possibility of a future, wider campaign involving an effort to oust Saddam Hussein.

CAMP DAVID: SEPTEMBER 15

On September 15, just days after the attacks, President Bush summoned his top advisors for an intense meeting at Camp David. Present at this marathon session, among others, were Cheney and his Chief of Staff, Libby; CIA Director George J. Tenet, his deputy, John E. McLaughlin, and his counterterrorism chief, Cofer Black; Rumsfeld and Wolfowitz; Powell; Treasury Secretary Paul M. O'Neill; FBI Director Robert Mueller; Attorney General John Ashcroft; General Shelton; White House Chief of Staff Andrew H. Card Jr.; National Security Advisor Condoleezza Rice, and her deputy, Hadley.[33]

Throughout the morning session, Rumsfeld and Wolfowitz pushed to widen the Bush administration's response to al Qaeda. A Defense Department paper prepared for the participants' briefing materials focused on three priority targets for the initial war on terrorism: al Qaeda, the Taliban, and Iraq. Asserting that al Qaeda and Iraq constituted a strategic threat to the United States, the briefing paper cited Iraq's interest in weapons of mass destruction and its long-standing involvement in terrorism.[34] Building on this briefing paper, Rumsfeld and Wolfowitz made the case for an expansive war on terror, targeting not only the terrorists and their organizations but also nations that sponsored them. Specifically, they wanted to target Iraq in the first stage of the war.

The morning began with a briefing by Tenet. He sketched a worldwide campaign against terrorism that focused initially on Osama bin Laden and closing the safe haven provided by the Taliban regime in Afghanistan. He outlined a covert operation strategy. The CIA would send teams into Afghanistan to work with anti-Taliban groups. These CIA teams would conduct joint operations with the Pentagon's Special Forces personnel. He sought presidential approval giving the CIA "exceptional authority" to detain al Qaeda operatives through the use of third parties, with final approval for such operations resting with himself. Tenet's briefing favorably impressed Bush.[35]

After Tenet's briefing, General Shelton presented three options with respect to a preliminary military plan for Afghanistan: a cruise missile attack; a cruise missile attack coupled with an aerial bombing campaign; or a cruise missile and aerial bombardment in concert with ground forces, including Special Forces and possibly even regular Army and Marine units.[36]

In the ensuing discussion, Rumsfeld focused on the need to solve the basic problem of terrorism. He asserted that vilifying Osama bin Laden could rob the United States of its ability to frame this as a larger war against terrorism. Rice expressed concern about the U.S. getting bogged down in Afghanistan. She asked the participants whether they could foresee military success beyond Afghanistan, thereby again making Iraq a potential target.[37]

Wolfowitz took the opening Rice provided, arguing that invading Afghanistan would be fraught with uncertainty. To illustrate his point, he raised the specter of a hundred thousand U.S. troops engaged indefinitely in treacherous mountain fighting. In contrast, Saddam's oppressive regime was brittle and would be easily overthrown. Reflecting a deep suspicion bereft of substantive evidence, he estimated that the possibility that Iraq was somehow implicated in the 9/11 attacks could be as high as 50 percent.[38] Asserting that Iraq was the ultimate "source of the terrorist problem and should therefore be attacked,"[39] he concluded that "the U.S. would have to go after Saddam at some time if the war on terrorism was to be taken seriously."[40] Card thought that Wolfowitz was "just banging a drum," failing to provide any new information or arguments.[41]

During a morning break, Bush joined Cheney, Wolfowitz, and Libby, who were already in a discussion. Wolfowitz directly engaged the president over coffee and "may have sold him on an eventual reckoning with Saddam." Wolfowitz agreed with Bush that "Shelton's plan—a limited series of 'pinprick' bombings—was indeed unimaginative." Wolfowitz noted, however, that "we have very good options for dealing with Iraq. . . . Think about the fact that the second-largest city in Iraq [Basra] is full of Shia who hate Saddam." He urged Bush to consider that Basra lies "within 60 kilometers of the Kuwaiti border and within 60 percent of Iraq's total oil production."[42] He said that "it would be very simple to enable the Iraqi opposition to take over the southern part of the country and protect it with American air power. That would have included a large chunk of Saddam's oil revenues."[43]

Wolfowitz's argument impressed Bush, who responded, "That's an imaginative idea; how come you didn't say so?" Knowing that Shelton opposed attacking Iraq, Wolfowitz replied, "It is not my place to contradict the chairman of the joint chiefs unless the secretary of defense asks me to do so."[44]

The broad outline of Wolfowitz's ideas stuck with Bush. Wolfowitz later put it this way: "To the extent it was a debate about timing and tactics, the president clearly came down on the side of Afghanistan first. To the extent it was a debate about strategy and what the larger goal was, it is at least clear with 20/20 hindsight that the president came down on the side of the larger goal."[45]

Once the general discussion resumed, Rumsfeld asked whether it was the appropriate time to attack Iraq. He remained "deeply worried about the availability of good targets in Afghanistan."[46]

Powell countered that the coalition he had assembled would evaporate if the United States attacked Iraq without evidence of a connection between 9/11 and Saddam. Urging the president to invade Afghanistan now, he concluded, "If we do that, we will have increased out ability to go after Iraq—if we can prove that Iraq had a role [in 9/11]."[47]

Although Bush had strong reservations about immediately attacking Iraq, he allowed the discussion to continue. Bush seemingly felt that military success in Afghanistan would make the rest of the war on terrorism easier. Subsequently he noted that "one of the things I wasn't going to allow to happen is, that we weren't going to let [Powell, Cheney and Wolfowitz's] previous experience in this theater [during the 1991 Gulf War] dictate a rational course for the new war."[48] The new war would not be a resumption of the previous one.

Later that morning, perhaps encouraged by Bush's earlier comments during the break, Wolfowitz interrupted Rumsfeld, expanding on his argument about Iraq. An "awkward silence" followed; ignoring the interruption, Rumsfeld's eyes "narrowed." After Bush "flashed a pointed look in Card's direction," Card took Rumsfeld and Wolfowitz aside during a subsequent break, telling them, "The president will expect one person to speak for the Department of Defense."[49]

Bush thereafter told the group that debate about Iraq was concluded. The afternoon discussions, consisting of the recommendations of Powell, Rumsfeld, Tenet, Card, and Cheney, focused mainly on Afghanistan.

Powell went first, stating "[It's] about al Qaeda and [Osama bin Laden]." He further noted, "All the states that supported terror, you can do at a time of your choosing. . . . They are not going anywhere." Attacking Iraq immediately would undo the emerging coalition, because there was presently no believable connection between Iraq and 9/11. Instead, he continued, "Keep the Iraq options open if you get the linkages," though he doubted it would happen. Though he left it unstated, it was obvious that no military plan had been presented for Iraq, either by Rumsfeld or Wolfowitz.[50]

The others then stated their views. While making no specific recommendation regarding Iraq, Rumsfeld responded that any "argument that the coalition wouldn't tolerate Iraq argues for a different coalition."[51] Tenet supported the position that the initial military focus should be on Afghanistan. Card advanced the idea of a large troop buildup in the Persian Gulf, both to demonstrate a permanent U.S. presence there and to be in a better position to potentially strike Iraq. However, he did not believe that Iraq should be a "principal, initial target."[52] Cheney argued in favor of building a coalition to take advantage of the post-9/11 opportunities. Attacking Iraq would interfere with this process. "If we go after Saddam Hussein, we lose our rightful place as good guy." Despite this reservation, however, Cheney did not rule out overthrowing Saddam at some point in the future.[53] Bush thanked everyone, but did not announce his decision. It came quickly.

THE AFGHAN WAR

Back at the White House on September 16, Bush publicly stated, "This crusade, this war on terrorism is going to take a while, and the American people must be patient."[54] Aides retracted characterizing the war as a "crusade" and apologized. The word had serious negative connotations in the Islamic world, conjuring images of invading European Christian armies in the Middle Ages. The same day Bush told Rice that Afghanistan would be the first target of the war on terror.[55] However, he "still wanted plans for Iraq should the country take some action or the administration eventually determine that it had been involved in the 9/11 attacks."[56]

When the National Security Council reconvened on September 17, Bush chose the most extensive of Shelton's options for Afghanistan. With respect to Saddam Hussein, Bush concluded the lengthy debate of September 15, stating, "I believe Iraq was involved, but I'm not going to strike them now. I don't have the evidence at this point."[57] He wanted military strategists to keep formulating plans for action in Iraq, including a plan to seize Iraq's southern oil fields, in case Baghdad acted against American interests, but indicated that there was no rush to implement these plans.[58] Action against al Qaeda and the Taliban in Afghanistan, however, had to be taken quickly. He also signed top secret orders authorizing new CIA operations against terrorists worldwide, and approving the entrance of CIA paramilitary teams into Afghanistan for the purpose of linking up with Northern Alliance fighters, and ultimately with U.S. Special Forces.[59]

Despite Bush's decision, Wolfowitz continued to press the case for invading Iraq. On September 17, he wrote a memo to Rumsfeld entitled "Preventing More Events," in which he asserted that even a 10 percent chance that Saddam was behind the 9/11 attacks justified making the elimination of that threat a "maximum priority." Based on Saddam's praise for the 9/11 attacks, his extensive record of involvement in terrorism, and the possibility that Iraq had orchestrated the 1993 attack on the World Trade Center, Wolfowitz maintained that the odds were "far more" than 10 percent.[60] The following day, Wolfowitz renewed his argument, writing a second memo to Rumsfeld regarding a possible connection between Iraq and a plot to crash an explosives-laden plane into CIA headquarters.[61]

On September 20, the president ordered General Tommy R. Franks, the commander of CENTCOM, to begin planning the campaign in Afghanistan. Despite the fact that there had been no war plans on the shelf for that country, military operations were underway there by October 7. That evening, Bush delivered an address to the nation, warning both terrorists and the nations that supported terrorism. He stated, "Our war on terrorism begins with al Qaeda, but it does not end there. It will not end until every terrorist group of global reach has been found, stopped, and defeated." He offered an ultimatum to the world: "And we will pursue nations that provide aid or safe haven to terrorism. Every nation, in every region, now has a decision to make. Either you are with us, or you are with the terrorists. From this day forward, any nation that continues to harbor or support terrorism will be regarded by the United States as a hostile regime."[62]

At a National Security Council meeting earlier that day, Rumsfeld had mentioned that there was still a routine request pending to hit some Iraqi targets, including Saddam's weapons and other military capabilities, in order to enforce the two no-fly zones set up after the 1991 Gulf War. Evidencing concern with muddling the thrust of the initial war on terrorism, Bush replied, "If you strike close to Baghdad, which turns on all the warnings in Baghdad, then the clarity of the mission becomes confused." Fearing that the world community as well as Baghdad might believe that such strikes were a response to 9/11, he concluded, "We have to be patient about Iraq."[63]

On September 26, Wolfowitz commented on the White House's strategy, stating, "As the president has said over and over again, it's not about one man or one organization. It's about a network of terrorist organizations. It's about the support and sanctuary and harboring they receive from some states. And while we are going to try to find every snake in the swamp that we can, the essence of the strategy is to try to drain the swamp."[64]

At a September 28 National Security Council meeting, Bush stated, "What we do in Afghanistan is an important part of our effort. It's important to be serious and that'll be a signal to other countries about how serious we are on terror." That message would be particularly poignant to such state sponsors of terrorism as Syria and Iran. Bush further noted, "Many believe Saddam is involved [in 9/11]. That's not an issue for now. If we catch him being involved, we'll act. He probably was behind this in the end."[65]

In October, the poison anthrax was mailed to various addresses in Washington, D.C., New York City, and Florida, killing five people. The National Security Council tackled this issue on October 17. Focusing on al Qaeda as the source, Tenet stated, "I think there's a state sponsor involved. It's too well thought out, the powder's too well refined. It might be Iraq, it might be Russia, it might be a renegade scientist, perhaps from Iraq or Russia."[66] The crisis passed, however, and the Bush administration publicly calmed its rhetoric about Iraqi involvement in the anthrax attacks.[67]

However, these attacks had a definitive impact on Wolfowitz's perception of the danger posed by Iraq. In subsequently commenting on why he favored the need for a more active U.S. military role in supporting regime change in Iraq, Wolfowitz stated, "It was not principally the 9/11 attacks, it was the anthrax scares that came days later. That brought the awareness that it might be too dangerous to take [Saddam Hussein] down slow-motion."[68]

The United States and Britain began the air campaign in Afghanistan in October, and by early November the Taliban had lost control of the northern half of the country. Thereafter the U.S.-backed Northern Alliance entered the capital, Kabul while the Taliban retreated south to Kandahar. Their continued opposition was short-lived and their rule over any part of Afghanistan ended on December 7.[69] Unfortunately, bin Laden managed to elude capture.

The tide of the war in Afghanistan turned in a matter of weeks, showcasing a revolution in combat technology, especially as applied to a primitive battlefield. As one journalist put it, "[T]he war in Afghanistan field-tested some notions of what the new military should be—light on its feet, technologically sophisticated and collaborative."[70] In an interview after the Afghan campaign, Wolfowitz noted:

I think the benefits that come from these advanced capabilities and the ability to fuse them together in new ways I think has been very amply demonstrated in Afghanistan, and in some respects even Afghanistan is almost a model demonstration because it turned out, it's so far away and the resources that we wanted to apply directly because we didn't want to start creating an unnecessarily large American footprint in Afghanistan meant this ability to apply a very small force on the ground and leverage it in a dramatic way not only through precision-guided munitions but through precision communications that would get those munitions accurately to the right target instead of accurately to the wrong target. Accuracy by itself doesn't do you any good if your target identification is wrong. . . .

At some point during the course of the summer [of 2001] when I realized that to a lot of people that meant victory through air power I insisted that we make the point that long range precision strike [sic] can be ground or air or even more significantly the combination of the two. So to me it was particularly gratifying to find guys literally on horseback calling airstrikes from Missouri. It was, the combination of those things, the precision was remarkable.[71]

In another interview, he asserted, "The remarkable ability to put a few people on the ground and thereby create a really devastating capability for long-range close air support. To me that's the revolutionary thing. . . . Taking a 50-year old bomber with 19th Century horse cavalry and turning it into a 21st Century transformation instrument—it does bring out a point that we've been saying often which is that transformation is more than just new technology. It's using the technology to use old things in different ways."[72]

Using the Afghan war as the impetus, Rumsfeld and Wolfowitz pushed for a transformation of the U.S. military, focusing on the future use of agile ground forces coupled with precision, laser or satellite-guided, long-range weaponry and superior information gathering technologies. Wolfowitz summarized this transformation as follows:

U.S. ground forces will be lighter, more lethal, more highly mobile. They will be capable of insertion far from traditional ports and air bases and they will be networked to leverage the synergy that can come from ground forces and long-range precision fires from the air and sea.

Naval and amphibious forces will be able to assure U.S. access even in area denial environments. Air and space forces will be able to locate and track mobile targets over vast areas and strike them rapidly at long ranges without warning.[73]

In short, no longer would the United States be constrained in its ability to project military force when and where it was necessary.

In November 2001, during the last stages of war in Afghanistan, a shift occurred in the rhetoric of the Bush administration. The danger that al Qaeda might obtain weapons of mass destruction surfaced. In an address to the United Nations General Assembly on November 10, Bush warned that the same terrorists who perpetrated the 9/11 attacks were "searching for weapons of mass destruction, the tools to turn their hatred into holocaust. They can be expected to use chemical, biological, and nuclear weapons the moment they are capable of doing so. No hint of conscience would prevent it."[74] Attention turned to potential suppliers from whom terrorists could obtain such weapons.

On November 26, in an exchange with reporters following a Rose Garden appearance, when asked about whether Iraq could be a military target, Bush stated, "Afghanistan is still just the beginning. If anybody harbors a terrorist, they're a terrorist. If they fund a terrorist, they're a terrorist. If they house terrorists, they're terrorists. If they develop weapons of mass destruction that will be used to terrorize nations, they will be held accountable. And as for Mr. Saddam Hussein, he needs to let inspectors back in his country to show us that he is not developing weapons of mass destruction." Asked the consequences if inspectors are not admitted, Bush said, "[H]e'll find out."[75]

Following the success in Afghanistan, U.S. military commanders abroad sent back detailed proposals for action against a variety of countries. Wolfowitz spoke out, making nations such as Somalia, Indonesia, the Philippines, and Yemen targets for the next phase of the anti-terrorist campaign. Defense and intelligence bureaucrats drew up targeting packages for nearly every nation where al Qaeda cells were ever based.[76] Despite these plans, however, the U.S. effort against al Qaeda became primarily one of covert and intelligence activity.

Postwar Afghanistan produced a mix of successes and setbacks. The positives include the country's holding democratic elections and rebuilding a national administration. Unlike postwar Iraq in 2003, the United States did not occupy Afghanistan while awaiting the formation of an interim government. At a conference in Bonn, Germany, brokered by the United Nations, factions of the Afghan opposition to the Taliban agreed on Hamid Karzai, a moderate Pashtun, as their new leader. Karzai took the oath of office in Kabul as Afghanistan's interim administrator on December 22, 2001. Thereafter, Afghanistan adopted a new constitution in January 2004 and Karzai was elected president in October 2004. During the next year, in September 2005, voters selected members of lower house of the nation's first democratically elected parliament in more than three decades, with the new parliament sworn in in December.[77] The negatives include the following: insurgents linked to the Taliban regime keep parts of southeastern Afghanistan ungovernable; portions of the country are under the sway of warlords and tribal leaders; there is widespread corruption and a broken legal system; and the economy is largely based on illicit opium-poppy cultivation.[78]

———————

In the long run, Bush embraced Wolfowitz's strategic vision. The cerebral Wolfowitz had forged a bond with Bush, a self-described "gut player." In time, Bush came to share the view of the man he called "Wolfie," that a democratic, post-Saddam beachhead in Iraq could reshape the entire Arab Middle East.[79] The spread of democratic institutions and the rule of law could transform these nations and protect U.S. strategic and security interests. David Frum, a Bush speechwriter, summarized the consequences of this expansive vision of a broad, far-reaching victory in the Middle East:

Alternatively, should the United States take President Bush's words literally and continue the war on terror until terrorism was entirely uprooted from Middle Eastern and Muslim politics? If the United States overthrew Saddam Hussein next, it could create a reliable American ally in the potential superpower of the Arab world. With American troops so close, the Iranian people would be emboldened to rise against the mullahs. And as Iran and Iraq built moderate, representative, pro-Western regimes, the pressure on the Saudis and the other Arab states to liberalize and modernize would intensify. It was quite a gamble—but also quite a prize.[80]

The Bush administration would soon put this vision into practice.

Chapter 7

The Road to Baghdad, Part Three: Operation Iraqi Freedom

From early 2001 until Operation Iraqi Freedom in March 2003, the Bush White House debated what to do about Saddam Hussein's regime. In a post-9/11 world, the use of force as a proactive tool to effectuate regime change replaced a reliance on containment.

Since the 1986 regime shift in the Philippines, Wolfowitz had sought to spread democracy overseas. After 9/11, he focused on seeding democratic ideals in the Middle East in order to undercut the repressive societies from which terrorist organizations could recruit their forces. As an outspoken advocate for removing Saddam, he held firm to his belief in Iraq's democratic potential. Transforming Iraq and the Middle East generally would require a long-term commitment by the American public. Unfortunately, as chapter 8 will demonstrate, the Bush administration, including Wolfowitz, underestimated the difficulty of regime change in Iraq, a nation marked by sectarian rivalries, ethnic feuds, and ancient grudges.

SOME BACKGROUND ON IRAQ AND ISLAM

Modern Iraq is a artificial construct of diverse tribal and religious groups put together in 1920 as a League of Nations mandate under British control.[1] It consists of three provinces from the defunct Ottoman Empire: Mosul in the north; Baghdad in the center; and Basra in the south. Commerce linked Mosul to Turkey and Syria; the non-Arab Kurds in the north were mostly Sunni Muslims. The Sunni Arabs were concentrated in the west. In and around Baghdad the population was a mix of Shiite and Sunni Arabs. Shiite Arabs dominated the southern cities of Najaf, Karbala, and Basra, with Najaf and Karbala, Shiite shrine cities, oriented toward

Persia. Those in and around Basra looked to commerce with India. Ethnic Turks and Assyrian Christians were found scattered throughout the mandate.

To this day, the Shiite and Sunni sects of Islam are sharply antagonistic although they worship the same God, revere the same Prophet, and read the same Holy Book. This religious friction began with a political dispute more than thirteen hundred years ago. The Sunnis, who comprise the vast majority of the world's Muslims, maintain that the leadership of the faith should be chosen by consensus while Shiites believe that it should be dynastically traced back to the Prophet Mohammed. Today, Shiites follow various ayatollahs, who are religious scholars and jurists. Sunni leadership is more decentralized among local imams.

The Ottoman Turks ruled what is today the modern nation of Iraq, beginning in the sixteenth century. As Sunnis, the Ottomans allowed the then Sunni majority to monopolize power and marginalize the Shiite minority politically. In response, the Shiites strengthened their ties to Persia, their non-Arab, Shiite neighbor. By the early twentieth century, a majority of the Muslims in modern-day Iraq became Shiites as a result of their conversion to that Islamic denomination.[2]

During mandate rule, the British weathered a revolt that began in June 1920, led initially by an Arab tribal chief in the mid-Euphrates. Over the weeks, the rebellion spread first to Baghdad, where part of the population had grown frustrated with the foreign army's heavy-handedness and then through the countryside of central and southern Iraq, creating a nationalistic moment of Sunni-Shiite unity. It took the British army some three months, until October 1920, to crush the revolt and regain control. The uprising brought pressure on the British to withdraw from Iraq and also increased local participation in the burgeoning Iraqi nation.

In 1921, the British turned to indirect rule through a constitutional monarchy. They chose as king a Sunni Hashemite desert chieftain from outside Iraq, who had supported T. E. Lawrence against the Ottomans. Sunnis and other ethnic and religious groups (but not the Shiites), a minority of Iraq's populace, provided the support base for the monarchy. The Shiites generally became a downtrodden underclass.

Under British rule some democratic institutions were put in place. The 1924 constitution, adopted by the Iraqi Constituent Assembly, provided for an elected parliament, a free press, and political parties, which led to expressions of opposition to important government policies and a degree of political competition among the nation's ethnic, religious, and tribal groups. Thus, Iraq, according to one revisionist academic, "had traditions of political pluralism and experience with representative political institutions," allowing "for a multiplicity of political opinions and orientations."[3] The constitution gave the king the right to confirm all laws and call for general elections. Although many Iraqis regarded the constitution as an instrument of British manipulation and continued control, it provided the nation's political and legal structure until 1958. Thus, from 1924 to 1958, Iraq had the rudiments of a democratic tradition and political institutions.

In 1932, Iraq became an independent constitutional monarchy, though the British maintained significant influence. Faced with a possibility of a pro-Axis government in Baghdad, as discussed in chapter 5, British troops put down a revolt in 1941, occupying Iraq until 1948. The pro-Western Hashemite monarchy was overthrown in 1958 by a military coup. After a series of coups, the Baath Party seized power in 1968 with heavy Sunni support. Amid a bloody purge, Saddam Hussein assumed total control in 1979. Under Saddam's dictatorial rule, he exacerbated the Shiite-Sunni rivalry, especially after the 1991 Shiite revolt in the south. Saddam used Sunni tribes to crush the uprising. Thereafter, the Shiites increasingly faced killing, torture, death, and exclusion from Iraqi society.

THE UNITED NATIONS WEAPONS INSPECTION PROGRAM AND SANCTIONS REGIME

In April 1991, in the aftermath of the 1991 Gulf War, the United Nations Security Council passed Resolution 687, which charged Iraq with disclosing and dismantling its weapons of mass destruction (WMD) and any facilities used to manufacture them. The resolution also created an inspections regime to ensure Iraq's compliance with these requirements. The United Nations Special Commission (UNSCOM) would monitor potential violations with respect to chemical and biological weapons and act in conjunction with the International Atomic Energy Administration (IAEA) with respect to nuclear weapons. Once discovered, all such weapons would be destroyed as would be Iraq's remaining long-range surface-to-surface missiles.[4]

The Iraqi government repeatedly delayed, impeded, and disobeyed the U.N. inspectors. The escalating Iraqi resistance culminated in Saddam Hussein forcing UNSCOM to leave Iraq in November 1998. Iraqi intransigence led the United States and Great Britain to launch Operation Desert Fox in December 1998, a four-day air campaign against Iraqi military and suspected WMD sites as well as several of Saddam's palaces. In the wake of this campaign, UNSCOM never returned to Iraq.[5] In an attempt to reconstitute the weapons inspection regime, the United Nations Security Council adopted Resolution 1284 in December 1999. This resolution created a new agency, the United Nations Monitoring, Verification and Inspection Commission (UNMOVIC), to replace UNSCOM.[6] Saddam, however, rejected the resolution, prohibiting UNMOVIC from entering Iraq.[7]

Subsequent to mandating the weapons inspection program, the U.N. Security Council also imposed economic sanctions on Iraq. Resolution 986, passed in April 1995, froze Iraq's overseas financial assets and banned all Iraqi imports and exports except through the Oil-for-Food Program. Pursuant to this program, the U.N. oversaw the limited sale of Iraqi oil and, after funding Gulf War reparations, UNSCOM and the Kurdish autonomous government in northern Iraq released the remaining revenue to Iraq solely for the importation of medical supplies and certain food products.[8]

The nature of the program soon allowed for its corruption. Under Resolution 986, Iraq could choose to whom it would sell its oil—giving Saddam substantial political and economic leverage despite the confines of the sanctions regime—and from whom it would buy its food. Baghdad rewarded nations—in particular France and Russia, both holding a veto power within the Security Council—with oil contracts, including lucrative deals for the development of Iraq's petroleum resources once the sanctions were lifted, in exchange for championing the Iraqi cause internationally and opposing the sanctions regime.[9] As a result, by 2001, both France and Russia actively campaigned to have the sanctions lifted.[10] In addition, Iraq generated income outside the strictures of the program by imposing a surcharge on oil contracts and demanding kickbacks from buyers to even receive such contracts; this money could then be used for purchases other than food and medicine. Moreover, the program failed to stop the continued smuggling of oil out of Iraq.[11]

This weakening of the Oil-for-Food program was so successful that by 2001–2, Iraq was producing an estimated 2.8 million barrels of oil per day, legally exporting over 60 percent of its petroleum production. These 2001–2 exports netted Iraq roughly $12 billion.[12]

THE EVOLVING U.S. POLICY TOWARD IRAQ

While the new administration understood that Iraq presented various policy concerns, before 9/11 it was not yet a top priority. In early 2001, discussion of U.S. policy toward Iraq commenced at both the principals and deputies levels. Iraq surfaced at the first meeting of the National Security Council on January 30, 2001, with principals and deputies in attendance. CIA director Tenet provided a briefing on the latest intelligence on Iraq, offering the possibility that Saddam possessed weapons of mass destruction (WMD). Noting the ineffectiveness of the existing sanctions, Secretary of State Powell advocated restructuring the sanctions so that they would serve as an arms control regime, thereby restricting the import of materials that might be used to manufacture WMD.[13]

On February 5, Rice chaired an NSC Principals meeting, which undertook a comprehensive review of the diplomatic, military, and covert options available with respect to Iraq.[14] Then, on March 1, the principals met again. They delegated to Powell the task of strategizing how the United States might refocus and tighten the U.N. economic sanctions regime, in the face of growing international opposition to the sanctions, and devising a plan to contain Iraq's weapons program.[15]

While the principals dealt with the failing sanctions regime, the deputies discussed the extent to which the United States should support Iraqi opposition groups. Wolfowitz, along with other senior officials from the Department of Defense, favored supporting the controversial Ahmed Chalabi, the leader of the London-based Iraqi National Congress (INC). Founded in 1992, with substantial CIA funding, the INC once fielded a guerrilla army from bases in northern Iraq.

That operation was largely destroyed in 1996, when Saddam sent tanks into the north of Iraq and forced the evacuation of INC operatives and supporters. INC ties to the CIA were effectively severed with both sides exchanging recriminations after failed attempts to promote an uprising against Saddam.[16]

Wolfowitz also floated a novel strategy to aid the anti-Saddam opposition. In the aftermath of the 1991 Gulf War, Saddam drained the marshes in southern Iraq to limit the sanctuary available to Shiite rebels. Wolfowitz suggested bombing the dams to recreate the marshes. When Pentagon attorneys raised objections, Wolfowitz replied his plan was more humane than leaving the Shiites to Saddam's whim.[17]

Meeting four times between the end of May and the end of July to discuss Iraq, the deputies were united by the common goal of increasing pressure on Saddam and creating divisions within the regime. They could not, however, agree on how to implement a strategy to enable the Iraqis themselves to overthrow Saddam. On August 1, the deputies presented the principals with a secret document, "A Liberation Strategy," which envisioned heavy reliance on the Iraqi opposition to pressure Saddam's regime. Thereafter, both the principals and deputies discussed the circumstances by which direct military action by the United States might be used to overthrow Saddam. However, a formal policy recommendation for attacking Iraq was never forwarded to the president.[18]

Wolfowitz remained the "intellectual godfather and fiercest advocate for toppling Saddam," reasoning that it was necessary and would, as it, in fact, turned out, be relatively easy.[19] Realizing that the American public lacked interest in committing U.S. troops to overthrow Saddam, he favored the Enclave Strategy, in which Iraqi opposition groups, supported by U.S. air power, would create a base in southern Iraq. Implementation of this strategy would enable the opposition to seize Iraq's southern oil fields, which generated about two-thirds of the nation's oil production. After the United States recognized the opposition as the legitimate Iraqi government, Saddam's opponents could then foment a rebellion across the country and overthrow the regime.[20]

Powell dismissed the Wolfowitz-supported plan as absurd, but his opposition did not stop Wolfowitz from formulating draft plans. Worried, Powell then spoke directly with the president, telling him, "You don't have to be bullied into this." Bush replied, "I've got it."[21]

Asserting that his support for a U.S. ground war to remove Saddam came only after 9/11, in April 2005 Wolfowitz noted:

I changed my view after 9/11. . . . Contrary to the myth that I have been waiting all along for an excuse to invade Iraq, before then I really didn't want to even think about sending in U.S. ground forces. I had always thought the idea of occupying Baghdad was both unnecessary and a mistake. What was needed was to arm and train the Iraqis to do the job themselves . . . by taking advantage of the fact that a third of the country was already liberated. I advocated supporting them with air power if necessary. . . . It was sometimes called the enclave strategy, disparagingly, although I still don't know what was wrong with it. I have a general strong bias in favor of empowering other people to liberate themselves rather than using American force to do it. I don't like using American troops, and I believe the best alternative to using American troops is to get allies. And the best allies are people who are trying to liberate themselves.[22]

Six days after 9/11, as discussed in chapter 6, Bush signed a secret order authorizing the CIA and the U.S. military to conduct counterterrorism operations globally, with Afghanistan the first priority. While directing Rumsfeld to continue work on contingency plans for a war with Iraq, Bush told Rumsfeld not to make them a primary concern.[23] The October anthrax attacks strengthened the resolve of some key administration officials, notably Cheney, to deal with Iraq because of the possibility that Iraq could distribute chemical or biological weapons to terrorists.

By November, the administration launched an internal review of the U.S. policy options on Iraq. The second- and third-ranking interagency participants from the Defense Department (including Wolfowitz), the State Department, the National Security Council, the CIA, and the Joint Chiefs of Staff wrestled with how to make regime change in Iraq a reality. The participants dismissed the enclave strategy as too slow and unlikely to work. They also ruled out a coup d'état to overthrow Saddam, reasoning that its chances of success were slim. Even if Saddam were overthrown, the strategy would likely result in a senior military official, a Saddam insider, becoming Iraq's leader. This left a U.S.-led military invasion.[24]

With the end of the war in Afghanistan in sight, Bush determined that the time was right to focus on Iraq. On November 21, he told Rumsfeld that developing a modern Iraq war plan had now become a priority.[25] Rumsfeld thereafter, on November 26, asked General Tommy R. Franks, CENTCOM commander, to revisit and update the Pentagon's plans for a possible military campaign to dislodge Saddam from power. Rumsfeld wanted Franks to begin with a "rough concept" of how the war would be waged and how many troops would be needed and then develop the plan through a number of iterations.[26]

On November 29, a dozen policymakers, Middle East experts, and members of policy research organizations gathered in Virginia at Wolfowitz's request. They produced a report for Bush and his war cabinet outlining a strategy for dealing with the Middle East after 9/11. Viewing the United States as likely to face a two-generation battle with radical Islam, the report concluded that "a confrontation with Saddam was inevitable." To transform the region, the report asserted, "Saddam would have to leave the scene before the problem would be addressed."[27]

On January 17, 2002, Wolfowitz attended a briefing on the fourth iteration of the Iraqi war plan. He thought an initial, sustained bombing campaign before the introduction of ground forces could significantly undermine the government. However, Franks was skeptical, noting that previous aerial attacks had failed to bring about the collapse of Saddam's regime.[28]

RECASTING U.S. FOREIGN AND
NATIONAL-SECURITY POLICIES

In January 2002, Bush extended the war on terror to fighting the proliferation of weapons of mass destruction. In his January 29 State of the Union address, Bush proclaimed that the United States would combat the threat posed by an "axis of evil," comprised of Iraq, Iran, and North Korea, rogue states which were "arming to threaten the peace of the world."[29] He thus borrowed from President Reagan, who in 1983 had branded the Soviet Union "an evil empire."[30] However, Iraq, Iran, and North Korea were not collaborating closely with each other as the axis powers had in World War II. Rather, these rogue nations, pursuing disparate strategies, posed a common danger. Connecting weapons and terrorism, Bush noted, "By seeking weapons of mass destruction, these regimes pose a grave and growing danger. They could provide these arms to terrorists, giving them the means to match their hatred. They could attack our allies or attempt to blackmail the United States. In any of these cases, the price of indifference would be catastrophic." With respect to Saddam, the president specifically noted, "Iraq continues to flaunt its hostility toward America and to support terror. The Iraqi regime has plotted to develop anthrax and nerve gas and nuclear weapons for over a decade. This is a regime that has already used poison gas to murder thousands of its own citizens, leaving the bodies of mothers huddled over their dead children. This is a regime that agreed to international inspections, then kicked out the inspectors. This is a regime that has something to hide from the civilized world."[31]

Bush's 2002 State of the Union Address emphasized the administration's concern about terrorists acquiring weapons of mass destruction, linking the war on terrorism to longstanding American efforts to stop the spread of these weapons. Although Wolfowitz did not see the speech in advance, he realized that with the "axis of evil" phrase, Bush had driven a "stake into the ground."[32] Moreover, it reflected the influence that Wolfowitz and Rumsfeld had gained in Bush's thinking regarding the connection between weapons of mass destruction and terrorism. Bush's phrase provided a conceptual framework within which to pursue regime change in Iraq. The speech evidenced a policy change long advocated by Wolfowitz, a shift from compromise or accommodation with rogue nations to a growing reliance on U.S. military power to effectuate change. In light of the sound-bite culture, for Wolfowitz, "Bush had defined the [connection between WMD and terrorism] in graphic, biblical terms without publicly committing to any particular solution."[33] In the speech, the United States also demonstrated its leadership, telling its allies what it wanted to do and asking for their views. To Wolfowitz, it represented a prime time, public consultation with American's allies.[34]

Bush's 2002 State of the Union address also hinted at a strategy of bringing democracy to the Middle East. Bush stated:

America will lead by defending liberty and justice because they are right and true and unchanging for all people everywhere. No nation owns these aspirations and no nation is exempt from them. We have no intention of imposing our culture, but America will always stand firm for the nonnegotiable demands of human dignity, rule of law, limits on the power of the state, respect for women, private property, free speech, equal justice and religious tolerance.

America will take the side of brave men and women who advocate these values around the world, including the Islamic world, because we have a greater objective than eliminating threats and containing resentments. We seek a just and peaceful world beyond the war on terror.[35]

On February 16, Bush signed a new intelligence order that significantly expanded the CIA's covert program to oust Saddam. Although Bush sought some $200 million a year for two years in new covert funds, Congress subsequently cut the funding to $189 million for the first year.[36] In addition to increasing support for Iraqi opposition groups, the order authorized intelligence gathering and paramilitary operations by CIA operatives inside Iraq. In undertaking these steps, CIA director Tenet advised realism. He told Bush that Iraq was not Afghanistan. The Iraq opposition was much weaker. Saddam ran a police state; he was hard to locate. Without accompanying military and other action, Tenet advised Bush, the CIA had only a 10 to 20 percent chance of succeeding. The president concluded that an expanded covert operation would help prepare for a U.S.-led military strike by increasing the flow of intelligence and contacts that might be needed later.[37]

At the same time, the White House escalated its rhetoric against Iraq. On April 6, for example, Bush reiterated that regime change was the official policy of the United States (and had been since 1998), but added that "all options are on the table" to effectuate this goal.[38]

Then, on June 1, at a West Point commencement address, Bush formally declared that he would launch a preemptive attack against any nation believed to pose a serious threat to the United States. In his January 2002 State of the Union address, Bush had hinted at the idea of nipping threats in the bud, asserting, "I will not wait on events while dangers gather. I will not stand by as peril draws closer and closer. The United States of America will not permit the world's most dangerous regimes to threaten us with the world's most destructive weapons."[39]

Now, in his June 1 address, Bush openly called for preemptive action when necessary to protect U.S. national security. In advocating this position, Bush "echo[ed] an old tradition rather than establishing a new one. Adams, Jackson, Polk, McKinley, Roosevelt, Taft, and Wilson would all have understood it perfectly well."[40] Rather than relying on the traditional strategies of deterrence and containment, Bush would now act to prevent future surprise attacks against the United States, which Wolfowitz had feared a year earlier. Bush warned, "If we wait for threats to fully materialize, we will have waited too long. . . . We must take the battle to the enemy, disrupt his plans, and confront the worst threats before they emerge. In the world we have entered, the only path to safety is the path of action, and this Nation will act."[41]

In his June speech, Bush also embraced the vision of military superiority put forth by Wolfowitz's Defense Department staff in 1992: "Competition between great nations is inevitable, but armed conflict in our world is not. . . . America has and intends to keep military strengths beyond challenge, thereby making the destabilizing arms races of other eras pointless, and limiting rivalries to trade and other pursuits of peace."[42] Thus, if the United States maintained an overwhelmingly dominant military, it would preclude attempts by other nations to match it. Moreover, Bush again spoke about the broader goal of spreading democracy as he done in his the 2002 State of the Union Address, asserting:

> We have a great opportunity to extend a just peace by replacing poverty, repression, and resentment around world with hope of a better day. . . .
> The 20th century ended with a single surviving model of human progress, based on nonnegotiable demands of human dignity, the rule of law, limits on the power of the state, respect for women, and private property and free speech and equal justice and religious tolerance. America cannot impose this vision, yet we can support and reward governments that make the right choices for their own people. In our development aid, in our diplomatic efforts, in our international broadcasting, and in our educational assistance, the United States will promote moderation and tolerance and human rights. And we will defend the peace that makes all progress possible.
> When it comes to the common rights and needs of men and women, there is no clash of civilizations. The requirements of freedom apply fully to Africa and Latin America and the entire Islamic world. The peoples of the Islamic nations want and deserve the same freedoms and opportunities as people in every nation. And their governments should listen to their hopes.
> A truly strong nation will permit legal avenues of dissent for all groups that pursue their aspirations without violence. An advancing nation will pursue economic reform, to unleash the great entrepreneurial energy of its people. A thriving nation will respect the rights of women, because no society can prosper while denying opportunity to half its citizens. Mothers and fathers and children across the Islamic world and all the world share the same fears and aspirations: In poverty, they struggle; in tyranny, they suffer; and as we saw in Afghanistan, in liberation, they celebrate.[43]

Over the summer of 2002, bickering arose within the Republican party as well as among members of the Bush administration.[44] For instance, Powell wanted the United States to take its case to the United Nations; while Cheney opposed seeking U.N. approval for military actions in Iraq, fearful that the Security Council would simply talk itself into inaction.[45] In parallel, Wolfowitz derided the U.N. inspection process, maintaining that the inspectors would not be granted access to anything worth inspecting. Furthermore, the process would simply provide Saddam with another opportunity to "play for more time."[46]

Containment of Saddam could not be preserved indefinitely. By the summer of 2002, the international sanctions against Iraq were in disarray, and the U.N. seemed unlikely to continue them, especially given that a number of major nations desired economic engagement with Iraq. For example, French construction firms had already signed lucrative contracts to rebuild Iraq's antiquated petroleum infrastructure once the sanctions were lifted. The White House feared that Iraq, once freed of the sanctions regime, could use the profits from petroleum sales to reconstitute its weapons programs, ensuring that Saddam would again have weapons of mass destruction, if he did not already possess them.[47]

On the evening of August 5, Powell and Rice met with Bush. Powell presented the president with many of the potential difficulties and consequences of a war in Iraq.[48] He asserted that the entire region could be destabilized and the price of oil could increase precipitously. He reminded Bush that if Saddam had weapons of mass destruction, a U.S. invasion would give him every incentive to use them. Moreover, the cost of occupying Iraq after victory could be expensive; the United States would effectively own and thus be responsible for Iraq. Powell invoked what he described as the "Pottery Barn Rule": "You break it, you own it."[49] Finally, he noted that the United States should not act unilaterally; it would need allies at least for basing and logistical purposes. He urged Bush to go to the United Nations to gain an internationalized response to the problem posed by Iraq. If diplomatic efforts to disarm Iraq failed, however, Powell recognized the need to confront Saddam militarily.

On August 14, the national-security principals met in Washington, without Bush. They discussed the president's scheduled September speech before the U.N. General Assembly, agreeing that it made sense for the address to focus on Iraq. Two days later at a National Security Council meeting, the principals, including Cheney, supported giving the United Nations a chance.[50] By late August, Bush had signed a classified statement delineating the objectives for a military operation in Iraq, including not only toppling Saddam, but also implanting democracy there and beginning to redraw the political map of the Middle East.[51]

On September 2, Powell and Rice again met with Bush, who reaffirmed his commitment to seek a new Security Council resolution designed to reconstitute the inspections regime in Iraq, recognizing the possibility that Saddam might comply with the resolution and continue to rule. Then, at a September 6 NSC Principals meeting, Cheney, who had previously agreed with the consensus, now opposed seeking a new U.N. resolution. Evidencing skepticism that Saddam Hussein would ever come clean, Cheney felt that the speech should merely be a tool to demonize Saddam in preparation for possible unilateral action by the U.S. military. Urging a multilateral approach, Powell responded that war could precipitate unanticipated and unintended consequences.[52]

On September 12, Bush addressed the United Nations General Assembly. In a seeming victory for Powell, who wanted to avoid what he foresaw as a long and bloody military action, Bush announced that the United States, despite Saddam's continued violations of previous U.N. resolutions, would work with the Security Council to obtain passage of a new resolution on Iraq. Bush called on Iraq to "disclose, and remove or destroy all of its weapons of mass destruction, long-range missiles, and all related material." He then placed the onus on the United Nations to act: "Iraq has answered a decade of U.N. demands with a decade of defiance.

All the world now faces a test and the United Nations a difficult and defining moment. Are Security Council resolutions to be honored and enforced or cast aside without consequence? Will the United Nations serve the purpose of its founding, or will it be irrelevant?"[53]

The Bush Administration then, on September 17, unveiled its new National Security Strategy (NSS),[54] a comprehensive document spelling out America's relations with the world. Although the strategy adopted many of Wolfowitz's key ideas, the drafting of it was handled by Condoleezza Rice, Bush's national security advisor; her deputy, Stephen J. Hadley; and University of Virginia Professor Philip Zelikow. The NSS, which enunciated what became known as the Bush Doctrine, set forth three key elements. First, it advocated preemptive (in reality, preventive) military action, if necessary, to prevent hostile acts by U.S. adversaries, stating: "Given the goals of rogue states and terrorists, the United States can no longer solely rely on a reactive posture as we have in the past. The inability to deter a potential attacker, the immediacy of today's threats, and the magnitude of potential harm that could be caused by our adversaries' choice of weapons, do not permit that option. We cannot let our enemies strike first." Moreover, "While the United States will constantly strive to enlist the support of the international community, we will not hesitate to act alone, if necessary, to exercise our right of self-defense by acting preemptively against . . . terrorists, to prevent them from doing harm against our people and our country."[55]

Second, the NSS advocated continued American military superiority, noting, "Our forces will be strong enough to dissuade potential adversaries from pursuing a military build-up in hopes of surpassing, or equaling, the power of the United States."[56] Third, in its dealings with other nations, the United States would promote its democratic values overseas, supporting this mission with its unsurpassed military power. Asserting that the "sustainable model for national success . . . [is] freedom, democracy, and free enterprise," the NSS stated, "America must stand firmly for the nonnegotiable demands of human dignity; the rule of law; limits on the absolute power of the state; free speech; freedom of worship; equal justice; respect for women; religious and ethnic tolerance; and respect for private property."[57] The viability of the Bush Doctrine would soon be tested in Iraq.

Thereafter, in October, Congress overwhelmingly passed the Authorization for Use of Military Force against Iraq Resolution of 2002,[58] granting Bush full authority to attack Iraq unilaterally should diplomacy prove ineffective. On October 10, the House of Representatives voted 296 to 133 to authorize Bush to use U.S. armed forces in Iraq as he deemed necessary and appropriate. The next day, the Senate voted 77 to 23 in support the resolution.[59]

On November 1, Hans Blix and Mohamed ElBaradei—the heads of UNMOVIC and the International Atomic Energy Agency (IAEA), respectively—met with Bush, Cheney, Rice, and Wolfowitz. Wolfowitz believed that Blix was ineffectual and would easily be dominated by Saddam, concerns which were shared by Cheney. Bush seemed somewhat mollified, however, by Blix's assurances that Saddam would not dissuade him from inspecting.[60]

The fall of 2002 saw efforts on both the military-strategy and diplomatic fronts. Wolfowitz floated a plan to raise an indigenous opposition Iraqi army. As first conceived, his plan envisioned thousands of Iraqis fighting Saddam's forces along with U.S. troops. At CENTCOM, Franks's deputy, General John Abizaid, supported the concept, which was designed to put an Iraqi face on the combat effort. Franks, however, saw an Iraqi force as only getting in the way. Outside of the Pentagon, only Hadley favored it. The CIA opposed a discrete, Pentagon-trained force and Chalabi's possible influence among the Iraqi troops. The State Department saw Wolfowitz's proposal as a vehicle for the creation of Chalabi's army. Ultimately, even the scaled-back plan produced meager results. Only a small pool of applicants, some seventy-three, completed the training program, despite the expenditure by the United States of millions of dollars. Those who completed the training program were sent in 2003 to a civil-affairs unit supporting U.S. forces in Iraq.[61]

On the diplomatic front, Powell spearheaded an American diplomatic campaign at the United Nations to pass a new Security Council resolution concerning Iraq's WMD. The Security Council unanimously approved Resolution 1441 on November 8, a compromise between the United States and France, giving Iraq a "final opportunity" to comply with its disarmament obligations. The United States gave up its quest for authorization to use force to disarm Iraq if it were found in material breach of any part of the new resolution, which provided that Iraq would be in further material breach of its obligations under U.N. resolutions if it made false statements or omissions in its weapons declaration and failed to "cooperate fully" with the U.N. inspectors. Such a breach would cause the Security Council to reconvene and consider "serious consequences" for Iraq.[62] Disagreement would later ensue concerning whether the United States had to return to the Security Council after a material breach, or whether it could simply use force in response to that breach.[63]

Saddam, while maintaining that he had no WMD, accepted the resolution and agreed to allow the U.N. weapons inspectors into Iraq, seemingly in an attempt to undercut Bush's efforts to internationalize military opposition against him. Given Saddam's history of denial and obfuscation, however, meaningful cooperation with UNMOVIC seemed unlikely. The United States used this diplomatic pause as an opportunity to lay the foundation for action in Iraq, both by ensuring that Turkish and Israeli forces would not become involved, and by gaining basing and overflight rights from nations in the region.[64] While these nations presumed that military action would only be necessary should Resolution 1441 fail, the United States operated under the assumption that war was almost inevitable.

CENTCOM began moving troops and equipment into the Middle East in the fall of 2002. By late November, there were about sixty thousand U.S. military personnel prepositioned in the region, and on December 6, the Pentagon issued the first major deployment order for the American military buildup in Kuwait, Saudi Arabia, and the Gulf States.[65]

On December 7, Iraq provided the United Nations with a detailed report claiming that it had no illicit weapons programs. Wolfowitz, among others, remained less than convinced of Iraq's sincerity. In fact, Wolfowitz had access to CIA intelligence that documented Iraqi attempts to obtain topographic maps of the United States and to develop an unmanned aerial vehicle system that could deliver chemical or biological ordinance.[66] Yet despite this evidence, he could not provide a concrete example of what would prove Saddam's duplicity, noting: "It's like the judge said about pornography. I can't define it, but I will know it when I see it."[67]

Then, on December 21, Tenet and McLaughlin (Tenet deputy) presented Bush, Cheney, Rice, and Card with the CIA's final case concerning the existence of Iraq's WMD programs. Unimpressed with the intelligence, Bush asked Tenet whether the CIA was confident in its assessment. Tenet twice assured the president that it was a "slam dunk."[68]

In January 2003, as the pressures for war built, Wolfowitz became even more convinced that the latest intelligence concerning Iraq's WMD programs was indisputable. On January 23, in a speech to the Council on Foreign Relations, he stated, "It is a case grounded in current intelligence, current intelligence that comes not only from American intelligence, but many of our allies; intelligence that comes not only from sophisticated overhead satellites and our ability to intercept communications, but from brave people who told us the truth at the risk of their lives. We have that; it is very convincing."[69]

At the White House on January 25, Libby briefed Rice, Hadley, and Wolfowitz, among others, on the evidence for an Iraqi WMD program and Saddam's numerous ties to al Qaeda's network. Wolfowitz, a long-time and ardent believer in ties between Iraq and international terrorism, latched onto the connection between Iraq and al Qaeda made by Libby. He thereafter continued searching for a connection between Saddam and the attack on 9/11.[70] Then, in a January 30 op-ed piece, Wolfowitz unequivocally noted: "And there is in controvertible evidence that the Iraqi regime still possesses [weapons of mass destruction]."[71]

THE ROAD TO WAR AND MILITARY OPERATIONS IN IRAQ AGAINST SADDAM'S FORCES

In his State of the Union address on January 28, 2003, Bush laid out the case against Saddam, alleging he had WMD and connections to al Qaeda, noting: "Evidence from intelligence sources, secret communications, and statements by people now in custody reveal that Saddam Hussein aids and protects terrorists, including members of Al Qaida. Secretly and without fingerprints, he could provide one of his hidden weapons to terrorists or help them develop their own."[72]

Powell, who had the most international credibility within the administration, forcefully presented these allegations to the United Nations on February 5, providing evidence of Iraq's secret weapons programs. He also discussed the connection between Iraq and an al Qaeda operative, Abu Musab al-Zarqawi.[73]

Building on the urgency created by Powell's denouncements, the United States then sought Security Council approval for a new resolution, declaring that Iraq had failed to meet its obligations under Resolution 1441. On March 17, however, the United States, the United Kingdom, and Spain conceded that they would be unable to garner passage of such a resolution, and announced that they would withdraw it before a vote. Within an hour of conceding defeat at the U.N., Bush met with Rumsfeld and Wolfowitz for a final review of military preparations for an invasion of Iraq.[74] That evening, Bush gave a forty-eight-hour ultimatum for Saddam and his two sons to leave Iraq. Two days later, Operation Iraqi Freedom began.

On the first full day of the war, Wolfowitz heartedly approved of Franks's decision to advance the commencement of ground operations by twenty-four hours, prior to the start of the air campaign. He thought this adjustment would help to counter the Middle Eastern belief that the United States focused on massive bombing campaigns with the resulting civilian collateral damage, in order to protect its own forces. Why begin the war with an air campaign, if you could achieve success on the ground, with speed and surprise? Wolfowitz reasoned.[75]

Resistance collapsed in Baghdad on April 9, twenty days after the commencement of military operations, marking the end of Saddam's rule. In a fast-moving, light-force campaign, American Marines swept into Baghdad and helped a group of Iraqis topple a 20-foot statue of Saddam.

In contrast to the 1970s, when the United States had almost no military presence in the Persian Gulf and was forced to rely on a partnership with Iran, the United States had mounted a full-scale invasion in 2003. Although Wolfowitz failed to win support to move U.S. troops through Turkey,[76] a previously reliable NATO member, American and British forces, with minimal contingents from other nations, relying on speed and mobility, seized Baghdad and ousted Saddam from power in a three-week campaign. It took another three weeks to complete military operations elsewhere in Iraq.[77] President Bush declared the end of "major combat operations" in Iraq in May 1.[78] Subsequently, on December 13, the U.S. military captured Saddam Hussein, who was later convicted by an Iraqi court and then executed in December 2006.

Overall, Wolfowitz thought that the mobile and lethal campaign in Iraq had been a resounding success. In a May 2003 interview, he noted:

[T]he remarkable speed of the operation, played a role in preventing a number of the worst things that we feared from happening. We'll never know exactly why the oil fields were not destroyed. We did not have an environmental disaster resulting from huge hydrogen sulfide fires in the north. We did not have attacks on Israel. We did not have a fortress Baghdad. We did not have a civil war in northern Iraq or a Turkish intervention in northern Iraq. We didn't have an Iranian intervention to speak of in southern Iraq. We didn't have any Arab governments collapse. . . . The one that had always worried the most was the use of weapons of mass destruction. We still don't know why they weren't used.[79]

Wolfowitz returned briefly to the limelight in December 2003, when he signed a Department of Defense document barring companies from noncoalition nations, including Russia, France, Germany, and Canada, from bidding on prime contracts for the reconstruction of Iraq.[80] Although it represented the administration's decision, Wolfowitz agreed with limiting competition for these contracts to companies from the United States, Iraq, and coalition and force-contributing partners. In an interview, he stated that it was the right policy, not intended to punish any countries but rather to reward those states which had shared in the sacrifice of the military campaign.[81] This went along with Wolfowitz's analysis of the cold war with respect to "the importance of leadership and what it consists of: demonstrating that your friends will be protected and taken care of, that your enemies will be punished, and that those who refuse to support you will regret not having done so."[82]

Unfortunately, the postwar occupation and reconstruction of Iraq would prove to be far more difficult than the invasion itself and would test the limits of the administration's abilities. The speed of the U.S. military victory allowed thousands of Baathists to go into hiding to regroup underground and fight another day. Reflecting signs of a disciplined political approach, perhaps a "guerrilla war was Saddam's plan all along."[83]

The Aftermath of the War and the Quest for Democracy in Iraq and Elsewhere in the Middle East

Regime change in the Middle East became a messy business. Bush and Wolfowitz underestimated the cost and difficulty of rebuilding Iraq and helping it transition to democracy. In reality, the goal of transforming Iraq and, more generally, the Middle East, would require a long commitment, stretching over decades, by the American public.

This chapter begins by analyzing the planning for postwar Iraq. It then considers the evolution of the political process in Iraq, the impact of the insurgency and sectarian strife, and the Iraqi economy. Wolfowitz's reappraisal of the war is examined together with the prospects for democracy in the Middle East and throughout the world.

Despite the widespread disillusionment with the situation in Iraq, cooler heads, recognizing that unexpected troubles arise in the wake of nearly every war, prevailed. President Bush held firm to the belief that the United States needed to create a stable Iraqi government so as to prevent terrorist sanctuary from festering. If the United States failed, Iraq could descend into civil war and the nation would become a new haven for al Qaeda and other terrorist groups, posing a renewed threat not only to the region but also to the security of Western nations. By the United States' not panicking and retreating, but staying until the task was finished, at the time of writing the prospects for a stable, democratic Iraq appear guardedly hopeful, despite numerous strategic and tactical mistakes made by the Bush administration, at least viewed in hindsight.

PLANNING FOR A POSTWAR IRAQ

Even before the conflict started, planning began for postwar Iraq. The State and Defense Departments worked independently for months on postwar planning with little coordination. The Pentagon fought for and basically won the lead role in Iraq's postwar physical, political, and economic reconstruction, which has proved far more difficult than the war.

The postwar planning for Iraq began on April 9, 2002, when Thomas S. Warrick held the first meeting of the State Department's Future of Iraq Project.[1] Warrick, a veteran civil servant in the State Department's Bureau of Near Eastern Affairs, brought together experts at State and the CIA as well as Iraqi exiles in the United States and Europe with professional experience in fields ranging from transitional justice to oil policy. However, as noted by L. Paul (Jerry) Bremer III, the head of 2003–4 Coalition Provisional Authority in Iraq, the project did not provide a comprehensive plan for postwar Iraq. Rather, "[i]ts purpose was to engage Iraqi-Americans thinking about their country's future after Saddam was ousted."[2] One Iraqi exile who participated in the project's democratic-principles working group characterized the endeavor as "mostly busywork for Iraqi exiles whom [the State Department] wanted to guide and control."[3] Ultimately, the project "produced an extremely long and somewhat unfocused set of papers."[4] Although the project failed to offer a practical plan for postwar Iraq, the United States did not begin military operations unprepared for the aftermath.

In May 2002, Rumsfeld ordered General Franks to step up planning for stabilization operations in Iraq, code-named Phase IV, following major combat.[5] The administration also began interagency postwar planning. An interagency Political Military Cell was organized in July, followed by the formation of an Executive Steering Group focused on planning for post-Saddam Iraq, the next month.[6]

At a key meeting of the NSC on August 5, Franks updated the president on the latest iteration of the Iraq war plan, concluding with a discussion of Phase IV stability operations. Franks estimated that U.S. troop levels could be reduced to 50,000 by eighteen months into the occupation.[7] As Franks recalled, Phase IV was "potentially the most important" aspect of the war plan.[8] At the meeting, Rumsfeld noted that the ultimate point was "to get Iraqis in charge of Iraq as soon as possible,"[9] and heads nodded around the table. After Franks offered some brief additional comments, heads nodded again, and National Security Advisor Condoleezza Rice tapped her watch to indicate they were out of time.

In mid-October 2002, Rumsfeld prepared a list of twenty-nine potential pitfalls that might be encountered in invading Iraq. He distributed the bullet-point list throughout the highest levels of the federal government and personally walked President Bush through his various warnings. Some of the difficulties he noted were fairly prescient, including strife between Iraq's Shiites and Sunnis.[10]

By late November 2002, the Deputies Committee began to address the potential issues with respect to the transition of power in Iraq. Rather than simply ensure stability in Iraq as Franks's Phase IV called for, Stephen J. Hadley wanted a more comprehensive postwar plan to effectuate the president's desire to install a democracy in the Middle East.[11] His efforts led to the formation of the Office of Reconstruction and Humanitarian Assistance (ORHA) in January 2003.

ORHA was the brainchild of Douglas J. Feith, Undersecretary of Defense for Policy. It would entail an interagency group within the Defense Department that would transform NSC policy concerning reconstruction into concrete plans and thereafter implement them on the ground in Iraq; the planners would be the implementers. To resolve the interagency dispute over who should control the reconstruction, Powell, now grudgingly on board in the push for military action, agreed that the State Department would be subordinate to the Pentagon in this matter because the Defense Department would have far more personnel in Iraq, as well as the resources and money.[12] Also, it was hoped that, with both the military and civilian commanders in Iraq under Rumsfeld, a unity of command in the reconstruction and a better mobilization of U.S. government resources would result.[13]

On January 20, 2003, Bush signed National Security Presidential Directive 24, setting up ORHA.[14] The new office was charged with seeing to the immediate humanitarian needs of the Iraqi people; repairing Iraqi infrastructure, such as potential sabotage to oil fields; and reshaping the Iraqi military. It would have a temporary mission until new Iraqi leadership emerged.[15]

The Pentagon leadership picked retired Army Lt. Gen. Jay M. Garner to head ORHA and oversee its development. Garner had successfully led the 1991 Operation Provide Comfort that saved the lives of Kurdish refugees in Northern Iraq after the Gulf War. He also assisted the Kurds to establish a governing authority in the area under their control, enabling the coalition forces to withdraw in six months without leaving any peacekeepers behind. However, a lack of local security was not a problem in Kurdistan. While tapping Garner for short-term service in Iraq, the White House had in mind the need for a senior civilian administrator who would eventually manage both the logistical aspects of the reconstruction and the political and diplomatic sides of the process.[16]

After accepting the assignment on February 21, Garner gathered all the prospective participants in postwar administration to go over the planning to win the peace in Iraq after the war was over. However, ORHA lacked the information, the personnel, and the time to plan for the totality of possibilities beyond humanitarian assistance and dealing with potential sabotage to oil fields.[17]

Garner began staffing ORHA. Barbara Bodine, a Foreign Service officer and former U.S. ambassador to Yemen, joined ORHA in early March. After she was given the slot of administrator for Baghdad and central Iraq, she sat down with Wolfowitz with a map of Iraq to determine what would come under the central region. In an expansive mood, Wolfowitz contemplated redrawing Iraq's provincial boundaries. Recalling the secret 1916 Sykes-Picot agreement to divide the Ottoman Empire into British and French zones, Bodine suggested that it would not be a good idea for the United States to redraw Iraq's lines once again, even internally. She told him that the road network had evolved over centuries, adding, "This is how Iraqis see themselves."[18]

Beyond the formation and staffing of ORHA, postwar planning continued even as the commencement of military operations loomed. On March 4, Feith briefed Bush and the NSC on the objectives of the United States and its coalition in Iraq. He noted that the United States would need to ensure the legitimacy of the reconstruction effort by allowing the participation of other nations and international organizations. Hopefully, Iraqi participation in the reconstruction would also lend legitimacy to the endeavor. At this point, disbanding the Iraqi military was not part of U.S. strategy. Feith outlined a policy of retaining and retraining the existing army, but screening the force to remove Saddam loyalists. Furthermore, in a nation racked by unemployment, cutting off the income to hundreds of thousands of men and throwing them onto the streets could be disastrous. He also noted that the extent of de-Baathification of both the military and the government would be a major issue after the war.[19]

Frank Miller, the NSC's senior director for defense, briefed the NSC on March 10 on the plans for post-Saddam Iraq.[20] The top 25,000 members of the Baath Party, constituting 1 percent of all Iraqi government employees, needed to be removed from their posts and other positions of power, Miller urged. As Baathists were expelled, Shiites and Kurds ought to be brought into the public sector. With party membership viewed as a negative, but not a deciding factor, lower-level Baathists could, however, participate in the new order.

To maintain law and order, the United States would rely on Iraqi police, whom Miller claimed had extensive professional training and were not closely tied to Saddam's regime. The reasoning went that by sending in only a limited number of security advisors, who would not have law enforcement powers, the United States would empower Iraqis.

Bush also vetoed Wolfowitz's plan, which he had pushed for months, for building a provisional Iraqi government, even one in exile around Ahmed Chalabi, the head of the Iraqi National Congress. The President did not want the new Iraqi government to be selected in Washington. The dispute over the role of Chalabi had fueled the continuing interagency distrust among the Pentagon and Vice President Cheney, on the one hand, and the State Department and the Central Intelligence Agency, on the other. The State Department opposed Wolfowitz's plan because it would have given too much power to Chalabi. Wanting freedom of action in postwar Iraq, Rumsfeld likely had his own misgivings, seemingly opening his first major difference with Wolfowitz. For Rumsfeld, an Iraqi government dominated by exiles such as Chalabi might have impeded U.S. efforts to root out the Baathists and locate the WMD.

Then, on March 11, Rice provided the NSC Principals with "A Summary of Conclusions," summarizing the strategy for creating an Iraqi interim authority as quickly as possible. This provisional government would consist of an umbrella group, including as broad a spectrum as possible from opposition exiles to Kurds. Once military necessity allowed, a conference would be organized to announce the interim leaders and the guidelines for the transition to a new democratic government. The document also provided guidance on stabilizing Iraq's currency and industry as well as reforming its public-sector bureaucracy.[21]

In a March 12 NSC briefing, Feith outlined U.S. postinvasion policy with respect to Iraq's military and intelligence apparatus. The United States would dismantle the Iraqi Intelligence Service, the Special Republican Guard, and the Special Security Organizations. The regular Iraqi military forces would be downsized and its leadership depoliticized, creating a demilitarized Iraqi society. A small army, with a nucleus of three to five divisions, would be subject to civilian control, be representative of Iraq's heterogenous ethnic and religious composition, and be designed for defensive missions.[22]

ORHA and the Pentagon, in general, focused on a wide variety of potential disasters, including oil fires, a mass exodus of refugees, and epidemics and famines, that never occurred. Unfortunately, ORHA and other planners, including the Joint Chiefs of Staff, and the State, Defense, and Treasury Departments, made four key assumptions that marred postwar planning. First, they used as a template the humanitarian intervention in Iraqi Kurdistan following the 1991 Gulf War, failing to realize that, viewed in hindsight, the most important issues following the 2003 invasion would be ensuring security and rebuilding essential public services.

Second, the planners assumed that a fully functioning Iraqi public sector, including government agencies, army and police forces, and utilities, would remain after the collapse of Saddam's regime and that the United States could quickly transfer responsibility for postwar administration and reconstruction to the Iraqis. Planners worked from the premise that after the defeat of Saddam's forces, public-sector institutions "would hold," as Rice stated in a postwar interview,[23] letting Iraqis rebuild their own nation, without lengthy, costly nation building by the United States. However, the Iraqi public sector crumbled. There was virtually no government to hand power over to, and the United States faced a major postwar challenge, the maintenance of law and order. Moreover, the United States could not rely on the old Iraqi police force because it was "poorly trained, ineffective, and widely distrusted," as Wolfowitz noted in May 2003. He continued, "It turns out that [the police] leadership was hopelessly corrupted by the old regime, and the policemen themselves seem to have been better trained to raid people's homes at night than to patrol the street."[24]

Third, the planners assumed that much of the Iraqi army would survive and play a significant role in keeping postwar order. As Franks subsequently wrote, "[O]ur planning assumption was that we would guide the Iraqi interim government in building a military and a paramilitary security force drawn from the better units of the defeated regular army. These units would serve side-by-side with Coalition forces to restore order and prevent clashes among the religious and ethnic factions."[25]

Fourth, it was assumed that any resistance would quickly end. Pentagon planners, Wolfowitz among them, did not anticipate that the insurgency would continue to operate and then expand after Saddam's capture and the arrest or killing of his top advisors. They underestimated the tenacity of the insurgency and the virulent sectarian animosity.[26] In sum, as a RAND report prepared for the Office of the Secretary of Defense concluded, "Both during the run-up to the war and during the occupation, there was a reluctance among U.S. policymakers to conduct worst-case analysis. This had two effects: (1) a systematic underestimation of the task, costs, and time required to reconstruct and reform the Iraqi security sector [among other sectors], and (2) a failure to undertake contingency planning."[27]

Furthermore, the financial costs to the United States for rebuilding Iraq were not inconsequential. Prior to the commencement of hostilities, Wolfowitz's public estimates, perhaps out of loyalty to the White House, understated the cost of the Iraq war, particularly the postwar phase. His testimony before a House committee on February 27, 2003, illustrated the administration's optimistic view of post-Saddam Iraq. Noting that the containment of Saddam Hussein from 1991 to 2003 had cost "slightly over $30 billion," Wolfowitz added, "I can't imagine anyone here wanting to spend another $30 billion to be there for another 12 years to continue helping recruit terrorists."[28] He refused to be pinned down on the costs of the war and the peace, declining to provide even a ballpark estimate of the potential expenses.

On March 27, with the war underway, Wolfowitz asserted to the Defense Subcommittee of the House Appropriations Committee that Iraq could finance its own reconstruction. Assuming that Iraq's oil wealth would cover a large part of the cost of rebuilding it, his "rough recollection" was that "the oil revenues of that country could bring between 50 and 100 billion dollars over the course of the next two or three years."[29] In April, even before the fall of Saddam's regime, Wolfowitz continued to express this view. In an interview, he stated, "Iraq has enormous resources of its own. It has natural resources wealth and it has incredible human resources wealth. And ultimately it's a country that will, I think, fund its own reconstruction."[30] The postwar insurgency and sectarian strife rendered these hopes unrealistic.

Following the dissolution of the ORHA in mid-June, Rumsfeld put Wolfowitz in charge of managing Phase IV, the Pentagon's day-to-day postwar operations. With the American public bombarded with stories of roadside bombs killing U.S. soldiers, Wolfowitz journeyed to Baghdad in July. Although Rumsfeld refused to admit any postwar planning mistakes at that time, upon returning Wolfowitz publicly acknowledged:

> [S]ome important assumptions turned out to underestimate the problem. Some conditions were worse than we anticipated, particularly in the security area, and there are three.
>
> No army units, at least none of any significant size, came over to our side so that we could use them as Iraqi forces with us today. Second, the police turned out to require a massive overhaul. Third, and worst of all, it was difficult to imagine before the war that the criminal gang of sadists and gangsters who have run Iraq for 35 years would continue fighting.[31]

Rumsfeld appeared before the Pentagon press corps several days later and declined to endorse Wolfowitz's assessment, though he admitted that the reconstruction had "taken longer. . . to get up to speed than anyone would have hoped."[32]

With respect to mistakes made in preparing for and handling the postwar phase, Wolfowitz later stated:

> What I think would have made a difference is: number one, training more Iraqis before war. . . . Other people said: "We don't need trained Iraqis." We ended up with seventy-two as a result in this training program. Second thing would have been to have an Iraqi government recognized from the onset, and we lost that: but the opposing view stemmed from the belief that we could control the country for a much longer period of time. I thought the model of what happened in northern Iraq in 1991 was a model worth trying to emulate. Recognizing northern Iraq was a lot simpler. And the third thing, I think, was that we didn't go after the bad guys in a properly focused way. The usual criticism is that de-Baathification was too harsh, and there's some truth to that. But the other criticism, which isn't made enough, is that we were nowhere near as tough as we should have been on the really hard-core.[33]

Part of the difficulties arose because Rumsfeld held a more circumscribed view of America's role in the world. Not sharing Wolfowitz's enthusiasm for an expansive American effort to bring democracy to the Middle East, he cared less about nation building and wanted to avoid the United States getting bogged down in this effort in Iraq. Rather, he saw the U.S. mission in Iraq in the mold of eliminating threats to American security by removing a hostile regime. Also, since the beginning of the Bush administration, Rumsfeld had sought to modernize the U.S. military, making it lighter, more flexible, and more rapidly deployable abroad, capable of fighting more innovative wars with dramatic improvements in precision weapons and information management.[34]

Given that Rumsfeld saw his transformation of the American military as key to his legacy as defense secretary, he envisioned Iraq as having a far smaller significance than Wolfowitz did. As one journalist wrote, Rumsfeld saw Iraq as:

> just one of many hungry conveyor belts inside his Pentagon. He understood that as soon as the Iraq belt started rolling, it would carry resources away from his preferred investments in the future. . . . "Balance" in this context is another word for "limit"—limit the amount of money, troops, staff and material bound for Iraq. The war he wanted was a short one, involving a relatively small force that would start heading home as soon as Saddam was chased from his palaces. . . . He tried to balance [the] risks of chaos [in Iraq] against the conveyor belts that could otherwise be loaded with resources destined for future transformation.[35]

Rumsfeld's views led to endless debates about the requisite U.S. troop levels and, more specifically, about whether the United States had failed to commit sufficient military personnel to control Iraq's borders and fill the post-Saddam security vacuum.[36] In February 2003, even before the start of military operations, a disagreement surfaced between top U.S. military professionals and Pentagon civilians with respect to the number of American troops needed to stabilize and provide security in postwar Iraq. On February 25, U.S. Army Chief of Staff General Eric Shinseki told the Senate Armed Services Committee that several hundred thousand troops would be needed for this task.[37] Wolfowitz immediately counterattacked, criticizing Shinseki's estimate. At a House Budget Committee hearing two days later, Wolfowitz declared that it was "a particularly bad time to be publishing specific numbers," an obvious rebuke to Shinseki. He described Shinseki's figure as "wildly off the mark," adding, "it is hard to conceive that it would take more forces to provide stability in a post-Saddam Iraq than it would take to conduct the war itself and to secure the surrender of Saddam's security force and his army—hard to imagine." In addition to pointing to the quick success of the 1991 Operation Provide Comfort in northern Iraq, the likely contribution of troops from other nations, and the efforts of the Iraqis themselves, he stated, "There are other differences that suggest that peacekeeping requirements in Iraq might be much lower than our historical experience in the Balkans suggest. There has been none of the record in Iraq of ethnic militias fighting one another that produced so much bloodshed and permanent scars in Bosnia, along with a continuing requirement for large peacekeeping forces to separate those militias."[38]

The number of U.S. military personnel needed to defeat the insurgents and stop the sectarian bloodshed has remained controversial. During the postwar occupation, U.S. military leaders maintained that they had sufficient forces to ensure law and order. Furthermore, additional soldiers might have engendered a "culture of dependency" that would have discouraged Iraqis from assuming responsibilities themselves and might have increased Iraqi hostility toward the United States.[39] Others, such as Bremer, disagreed. He asserted to Rice at one point that "the Coalition's got about half the number of soldiers we need here."[40] The Pentagon ignored Bremer's repeated requests for more troops.

POSTWAR IRAQ: THE FAILURES AND THE SUCCESSES

Slowly and painfully, Iraq's future brightened, particularly in terms of the formal political process, namely, elections and a constitution, but not without significant human costs and many moments of despair in Iraq and Washington brought about by a vicious insurgency and sectarian strife, which created an unsafe, disorderly environment, not conducive to reconstruction. There were many mistakes and setbacks in the long, hard struggle.

In Iraq, the United States faced a number of postwar difficulties: liberating without appearing to dominate; ensuring order without overstaying; securing U.S. interests without trampling on Iraq's; and overseeing democratization without picking winners. Ultimately, the mistakes of the first two months after Saddam's fall continued to haunt the United States years later.[41]

After the liberation of Baghdad on April 9, Garner's small team remained in Kuwait for nearly two weeks. When Garner arrived in Baghdad on April 21, swarms of Iraqis had dismantled nearly every public building in Baghdad, crippling the national government. Lacking clear orders, the U.S. military largely responded with inaction to the widespread looting, burning, and the breakdown of order. Many Iraqis came to believe Americans allowed the looting and the anarchy.[42] U.S. forces did protect the Iraqi Oil Ministry, leading some Iraqis to believe that the United States was in Iraq only for its oil.[43]

Although uncertainty exists as to how much of the looting was random lawlessness and how much of it was organized by elements of Saddam's former regime, Wolfowitz subscribed to the latter view.[44] Regardless, the inability to restore law and order immediately after Saddam's fall from power helped to undermine the confidence of many Iraqis in the Americans and provided a rationale for some to support the insurgents. The Pentagon seemed unprepared to deal with the security vacuum. In its wake came not only gutted buildings, but also lost equipment and destroyed records, which impeded reconstruction efforts. Criminals and insurgents raided Iraq's vast arms storehouses. The vacuum in the first weeks and months after Saddam's fall "created a dynamic in Iraq in which high levels of street crime combined with the growing insurgency increased the population's insecurities, which then also impeded economic recovery activities. With the security environment and the economy both stagnant, dissatisfaction grew, and the resistance thus had more potential recruits to draw upon."[45]

When U.S. forces failed to stop the looting and the anarchy in the weeks after the fall of Baghdad, improvised militias organized by the Shiite religious councils filled the vacuum. Shiite clergy set up roadblocks to deter looters. They mobilized men to protect hospitals and maintain order on the streets. Later, they organized committees to restore public services, including arranging for garbage pickups, setting up free clinics inside mosques, and providing financial help to the destitute.[46]

Facing a collapsing civil order in Iraq, an increase in deadly attacks on American armed forces, and the stalling of the restoration of Iraq's basic services, Washington quickly realized things were not going well. In response, the White House dispatched L. Paul Bremer III as a Special Presidential Envoy, two months before Garner was expected to be replaced as the chief American official in Iraq. Bush designated Bremer the civil administrator of Iraq and head of the Coalition Provisional Authority, responsible for the temporary governance of Iraq and for directing the reconstruction effort, an enormous task. Reporting to the president through the Secretary of Defense, Bremer, a retired U.S. career diplomat with expertise in counterterrorism, had far more political experience than Garner.[47]

Arriving in Iraq on May 12, Bremer implemented major policy changes, including increasing U.S. patrols across Baghdad and aggressively pursuing criminals and imprisoning looters, thereby stemming the chaos in the streets.[48] He also undertook three controversial measures.

First, faced with the collapse of the Iraqi state, rising levels of violence and crime, and bickering among potential leaders, he announced an indefinite postponement

of an earlier plan to form an interim administrative authority by the middle
of May, thereby delaying the establishment of Iraqi self-government.[49] Bremer
opted for a more methodical approach: first, draft a permanent constitution, and
then, hold national elections on the basis of the constitution. Too precipitous elections might empower antidemocratic factions for years to come, he reasoned. In
contrast, Wolfowitz had favored an early transfer of power to an Iraqi Interim
Authority, which would have assumed increasingly greater responsibility for the
administration of Iraq. Wolfowitz envisioned that the authority would draw from
Iraq's religious and ethnic groups and would include both exiles and individuals who had remained in Iraq. It would have provided a means for Iraqis to more
quickly direct the nation's economic and political reconstruction.[50] Wolfowitz's
view did not, however, prevail in the interagency decision-making process.

It remains uncertain whether it would have made a difference if the United
States had followed the Afghan model, discussed in chapter 6, and almost immediately turned sovereignty over to a provisional Iraq government. Giving the
Iraqis more governing responsibility and a more prominent place in the spotlight
might have quickened the return of basic services and security. Any success, however, would have been hindered by the fact that the Iraqi exiles, such as Chalabi,
lacked credibility with a large segment of the population. It is also doubtful
whether an interim Iraqi authority could have stopped the massive looting in
April and May 2003 and then maintained law and order in Baghdad and central
Iraq.

Second, Bremer began the de-Baathification of Iraq's government, signaling
to all Iraqis that the United States really meant to destroy the underpinnings of
Saddam's regime and establish a new, democratic order. On May 16, the CPA
issued a decree which disestablished the Baath Party, removed senior party
members from positions of power in Iraq's government, and banned them from
future public-sector employment, subject to waiver by Bremer on a case-by-case
basis.[51] However, Bremer left the implementation of the policy aimed at the top
1 percent of party members or about 20,000 people to the subsequently formed
De-Baathification Council, a political body within the nascent Iraq government,
which applied it far more broadly than originally intended.[52] Implementation
of the order deprived the nation of experienced administrators, who took with
them knowledge of the nation's electrical grid and its water and sewage systems,
among other public-sector functions, as well as thousands of teachers. By April
2004, the CPA began to began to reinstate teachers and among other government
employees who had joined the Baath Party for professional advancement.[53]

Third, Bremer issued CPA Order No. 2, Dissolution of Entities, dated May 23,
abolishing the Iraqi armed forces.[54] The list of disbanded entities included the
Ministry of Defense, all branches of the armed services, and all intelligence agencies and paramilitary groups. It offered a termination payment to soldiers and other
employees, but senior Baath Party members, with officers at or above the rank
of colonel deemed to be senior party members, were denied this severance package.
Although Bremer formulated the concept of dissolving the army in consultation

with Wolfowitz and Feith, he issued the order only after receiving authorization from Rumsfeld.[55] The rationale for the order was simple. For Bremer and the Pentagon, the United States was left with the shell of a corrupt, cruel, undemocratic army, which was dominated by Sunni officers and which for the most part had ceased to exist. Nearly all Iraqi soldiers, including many Shiite conscripts, had fled their posts in April 2003 and merged with the civilian population. Moreover, every significant Iraqi military installation was unusable due to either coalition attacks, or looting by both departing military personnel and locals. Thus, no bases or equipment existed for any conscripts that might have returned.[56]

However, Bremer's decision sent hundreds of thousands of armed and angry men, deprived of a salary or any work, into the streets. Shortly thereafter, in late June 2003, American authorities, realizing they had created a reservoir of armed recruits for any insurgency, reversed course when Bremer ordered the resumption of payment of monthly salaries to former career members of the Iraq military, except for the most senior Baathist officers, thereby paying a demobilized force without getting anything in return. These payments continued up to and past June 2004.[57]

THE EVOLUTION OF THE POLITICAL PROCESS

With Bremer in place as head of the Coalition Provisional Authority, on May 22, pursuant to Resolution 1483,[58] the U.N. Security Council granted the United States and United Kingdom an international mandate to occupy and reconstruct Iraq. As a result, the United States and the United Kingdom became formal occupying powers. The resolution lifted the sanctions regime and phased out the Oil-for-Food Program, enabling Iraq to sell its oil and get its economy restarted. It required that revenues from the export sales of Iraqi petroleum and petroleum products be deposited into a newly created development fund for the benefit of the people of Iraq. The resolution also called on the Coalition Provisional Authority to work with a new U.N. special representative to facilitate the formation of an interim Iraqi administration, until an "internationally recognized representative government in Iraq" could be established and assume full power.[59]

It took the U.S.-U.K. Governance Team, consisting of about fifty members, working around the clock, about two months to come up with the membership of the Governing Council, an interim, advisory Iraqi administration.[60] Finally, in July, Bremer appointed twenty-five prominent Iraqis from a range of ethnic and religious backgrounds (although exiles were overrepresented) to the Governing Council. The council, split along sectarian and ethnic lines, then began appointing ministers to assist the Coalition Provisional Authority, obtaining a measure of international recognition, setting budgetary policy, and approving a slate of economic reforms. On August 14, the U.N. Security Council passed Resolution 1500, in which it welcomed the Governing Council "as an important step towards the formation by the people of Iraq of an internationally recognized, representative government that will exercise sovereignty of Iraq."[61] However, the Governing Council was subject to Bremer's guiding hand and his veto.

During the summer and early fall of 2003, the Pentagon continued to urge Bremer to transfer governing authority to the Iraqis. Bremer and Wolfowitz met at Wolfowitz's Pentagon office on September 22 to discuss Feith's suggestion that the United States give sovereignty to the Governing Council (GC) by renaming it the Provisional Government, thereby putting Iraqis in a meaningful governance role. Asked about his view concerning the proposed plan, Bremer replied, "Frankly, not much. Your guys don't seem to understand how ineffective the GC is turning out to be. . . . Those people couldn't organize a parade, let alone run the country." Wolfowitz countered that "we've got to move quickly on the political front," asking, "[W]hat if we just expanded the GC to a group of 100 to 200 to make them more representative, and then gave them sovereignty?" Bremer replied, "I guess we could do that, at least in theory. . . . But it'd be enormously time-consuming." Wolfowitz then inquired, "Well, why not just let the GC expand itself, then," to which Bremer responded, "[T]hese guys have shown no capacity to broaden their representation."[62]

As pressures mounted for the United States to turn over sovereignty, the November 15, 2003 agreement between the CPA and the Governing Council set out a detailed timeline for accelerating the political transition.[63] After the adoption of an interim constitution, the plan called for the United States to turn power over to a transitional national assembly chosen in an indirect manner, through a complicated system of caucuses, which would then select a transitional government by June 30, 2004. According to the plan, by mid-March 2005, a directly elected, constituent assembly would then write a permanent constitution and submit it to a referendum, with direct elections for the new government by the end of that year.

It became a contest of wills between Bremer and Grand Ayatollah Ali al-Hussein al-Sistani, Iraq's most powerful Shiite cleric. Bremer was reluctant to replace his ineffective, appointed council of Iraqis with a directly elected, transitional parliament until pro-democracy pressure from Sistani made it clear that he had no choice: only elections could determine Iraq's constitution and its political leaders.[64]

The White House turned to the United Nations to find a way out of the political impasse. Lakhdar Brahimi, an Algerian diplomat serving as a special advisor on Iraq to the United Nations, helped forge a compromise. Grand Ayatollah Sisanti would wait seven or eight months for direct elections; Bremer, forgoing the caucuses, agreed to an elected 2005 transitional national assembly. Brahimi then facilitated consultations among the Bush administration and the various Iraqi factions, which led to the formation of the caretaker government.

On June 8, 2004, the U.N. Security Council, in Resolution 1546,[65] endorsed the timetable for Iraq's political transition. As proposed and implemented, the timeline included holding direct elections no later then the end of January 2005 for a transitional national assembly, the drafting of a permanent constitution, to be approved by the directly elected assembly and then ratified by a public referendum, and a directly elected, permanent government by December 31, 2005.

The interim government took power on June 28, 2004 and saw the country through to the January 2005 elections. A degree of sovereignty passed to this interim regime with Iraq reasserting control over its finances and resources as well as gaining the power to conclude agreements in the areas of diplomatic relations and economic reconstruction. However, the interim government was restricted from taking any actions affecting Iraq's destiny beyond the limited seven-month time frame. Without any competent Iraqi military or police units to defend the new government or maintain order, the United States retained control over security matters.

At Grand Ayatollah Sistani's insistence, the American mission to create a stable, democratic Iraq became more an Iraqi mission. The unfolding political process in 2005 showed the Iraqi desire for freedom and democratic institutions. The January 30 election for an interim national assembly seemed to mark a turning point, at least temporarily, despite a Sunni boycott which gave them disproportionately few seats in the new parliament. A free and fair election, where over eight million people expressed their interest in self-government by voting despite being threatened not to, was held with a minimal level of violence and intimidation. Magnifying the nation's religious and ethnic divisions, the results reflected a divided electorate with nearly all Kurds voting for the combined Kurdish list and most Shiites supporting the United Iraqi Alliance (the so-called Sistani) list, with the Shiites winning the majority of the seats. However, Wolfowitz, quoting an Iraqi-American, proudly announced that on January 30, "the Iraqis liberated Iraq."[66] The interim assembly proceeded to name a second temporary government in late April, led by Ibrahim al-Jaafaari, a Shiite, as prime minister; Jalal Talabani, a Kurd, as president; and Ahmed Chalabi, as deputy prime minister, all of whom had been members of the core group of the Governing Council.

Writing a constitution in a multiethnic and multisectarian society such as Iraq proved a more difficult, but not impossible, undertaking. The interim government designated a constitutional committee to draft a permanent constitution. Shiite-Kurd negotiations with the Sunnis, who considered dominance by the first bloc a threat to their interests, seemed elusive. Ultimately, first the interim national assembly and then on October 15, 2005 the Iraqi voters, apart from Sunni Arabs, approved a permanent constitution, brokered by the Bush administration. The constitution, the most liberal in the Arab world, with a decentralized federal structure, provides for a central government with the powers of a sovereign nation, such as foreign-affairs and defense policy, while enabling regional bodies to make decisions affecting and protecting local interests, including maintaining its own military forces. Significant matters may be revisited, such as the equitable sharing of oil revenues, raising the possibility that the constitution may be amended in the future.[67]

The December 15, 2005 balloting witnessed the election of a full-term, permanent Iraqi government. The strong turnout showed that the insurgency lacked a broad base of support in Iraq. Realizing that they made a fundamental mis-judgment in sitting out the January 2005 election, many Arab Sunnis came to advance their agenda through political action, not violence. The Kurd–religious Shiite alliance won the largest number of seats, with the Shiite (United Iraqi Alliance) coalition comprising the largest bloc in the national assembly, but it fell short of the representation required to form a new government, thus needing the support of other groups to govern.[68]

In the first half of 2006, the bargaining for a four-year government began among Shiite, Kurd, Sunni, and secular groups, who dealt with the real-world consequences of their ideas. The United States used its muscle to ensure a sig-nificant Sunni presence in the cabinet. After dickering over cabinet posts for months, the various factions and their leaders ultimately found their way to form the executive branch of the new government and move ahead. On May 20, they settled on a prime minister, Nuri Kamal al-Maliki, a Shiite former exile, and most of a cabinet, with Talabani, a Kurd, continuing as president.[69] Three key ministries—interior, defense, and national security—were subsequently filled in June. Iraq began nation building by consent. The Shiites, Kurds, and Sunnis began to work out a bargain all could live with.

The new national-unity government sought to bolster security in Baghdad. However, disbanding sectarian militias, most of which are tied to Shiite religious political parties, and rooting out the influence of Shiite militias in Iraqi police forces remain difficult, but critical tasks.[70] With sufficient stability and order, as well as a lessening of corruption, Iraq could start to tap its oil resources and the abilities of its people.

THE INSURGENCY AND SECTARIAN STRIFE

Despite continued progress on the political front, marked by the building of democratic institutions and free elections as Iraqis claimed the right to make them-selves heard, postconflict peacekeeping became real warfare, fought with guer-rilla tactics, having a capacity to kill and instill fear. Tied to the need for security was the need to restore basic infrastructure, such as electricity, discussed in the next section.

The constant, savage violence continued. The war in Iraq never really ended, as the nation became a laboratory for terrorists and sectarian groups. Iraqi and coalition forces, as well as Iraqi civilians, faced an unrelenting insurgency, ini-tially led by remnants of the Baathist regime and then by foreign jihadists, with considerable Sunni Arab support, marked by drive-by shootings, roadside and suicide bombings, and mortar and rocket attacks.[71] Backed by a constellation of forces opposed to the emergence of a democratic Iraq, the guerilla war eroded Iraqi confidence in both U.S. forces and the interim (and permanent) Iraqi gov-ernments and raised sectarian tensions between Shiites and Sunnis. The lack of security created widespread fear among Iraqis and placed important limitations on normal, everyday routines. Although considerable economic activity resumed in major cities, the protracted insurgency and the sectarian violence impeded the nation's economic recovery. For years, public amenities, such as clean water and electricity, continued to function at lower levels than before the war, despite the billions of dollars spent on reconstruction.

The full-fledged insurgency began on August 7, 2003 with the suicide car bombing of the Jordanian Embassy in Baghdad. The attack was designed to send a message to other Arab nations not to embrace post-Saddam Iraq. It was followed by a suicide truck-bomb attack on August 19 that destroyed the United Nations headquarters in Baghdad, killing the U.N. representative in Iraq and at least twenty others. This second attack was designed to discourage the world from playing a significant role in the reconstruction of Iraq. The August 29 assassination of Ayatollah Mohammed Bakr al-Hakim in Najaf deprived the United States of the key mediator between the religious Shiites and the Coalition Provisional Authority. Then, October 27 saw attacks on five Iraqi police stations in Baghdad, beginning the assaults on "collaborators," and on the International Red Cross headquarters there, ending independent humanitarian relief under the occupation, a significant blow to the reconstruction effort. The insurgency grew in size and complexity, with approximately 80 percent of all attacks occurring in Sunni-dominated central Iraq, the so-called Sunni Triangle, with the Kurdish north and the Shiite south remaining relatively calm.

Although the insurgency consisted of several dozen, perhaps as many as one hundred, decentralized groups organized horizontally, not hierarchically,[72] three main, often overlapping, streams fueled the ongoing conflict: Baathists, foreign jihadists, and disgruntled Sunni Arabs. Initially, Saddam Hussein's secret service, Special Operations and Antiterrorism Branch, known within Saddam's government as M-14, was behind the guerrilla roadside bombings, hijackings, assassinations, and other attacks. A few thousand insurgents, with leadership from small numbers of Saddam's intelligence services and military officer corps, true believers in the Baathist ideology, challenged the American occupation with the ultimate aim of restoring themselves to power. With the Baathists relying on recruits from the disaffected Sunni Arab community, a guerilla-style resistance formed, operated, and grew, even after Saddam Hussein's capture and the arrest or killing of his top advisors.[73] Many of the Baathists adopted an Islamic facade to attract more credibility within the country and perhaps support from outside Iraq.

Although bitter Baathist fanatics continued to fight, foreign terrorists came to the fore, sometimes collaborating with the Baathists. From mid-2004 until his slaying in June 2006, Abu Musab al-Zarqawi, a Jordanian militant, and his foreign fighters became the most dangerous terrorists in Iraq, playing an ever-more-prominent role in the violent insurgency.[74] The withdrawal of virtually all U.S. military forces from Saudi Arabia in August 2003, except for small training missions, thereby essentially fulfilling one of bin Laden's primary demands, failed to make a difference in al Qaeda's sponsorship of suicide terror attacks.

Zarqawi established himself as the head of al Qaeda in Mesopotamia, seeking to prevent democracy from gaining a foothold in Iraq. He wanted to establish a Taliban-like state there, based on a reign of repression, and then to topple Jordan's rulers and attack Israel. He saw the negative consequences democracy in Iraq would have on Islamic terrorism. The Islamic fascists realized that with a democratic Iraq their efforts to install Taliban-like regimes in the Middle East would be significantly weakened if not doomed. They realized that a stable, democratic Iraq would be a major victory in the war on terrorism.

By 2005, Zarqawi became a key opposition force and the most immediate threat to U.S. objectives in Iraq. Violence against Iraqi civilians spiked. Although working with the M-14 unit of the old Iraqi intelligence, Zarqaqi's foreign fighters seemingly supplanted Saddam's Iraqi loyalists as the driving force behind the insurgency. Foreigners came to play a disproportionately important role in carrying out the rising number of suicide bombings, which produced extensive casualties.

Able to replenish their ranks as soon as any foreigners were killed or captured, the terrorists grew ever more violent and more sophisticated. Increasingly, foreign jihadists orchestrated and executed the large-scale attacks. By seeking to foster an atmosphere of intimidation and despair, the insurgents, led by Zarqawi, fought to perpetuate disorder, provoke the Shiites into a civil war with the Sunnis, and prevent the establishment of a viable Iraqi government. The war did not become an indigenous rebellion of the Iraqis, who recognized the terrorists sought to take away the democratic gains achieved in 2005.

In addition to becoming a magnet for foreign terrorists, who gained experience in insurgency tactics, Iraq became a breeding ground for terrorists, who then went elsewhere in a phenomenon known as the "bleed out" in the intelligence community. Terrorist cells seeped into neighboring nations such as Jordan and conducted operations there and elsewhere, creating difficult security challenges.[75]

Along with the foreign jihadists, in 2005 and 2006, sectarian tensions rose, as armed militias dispensed justice as they saw fit.[76] The Baathists and al Qaeda terrorists found refuge amid disenchanted and disillusioned Sunni Arabs, many of whom, at least initially, did not view democracy as being to their advantage. With the political ascendancy of the long-trampled Shiite majority, many Sunnis resented their loss of privileged status and sought to reclaim their political and economic power. Linking their domestic struggle with militant, pan-Arab aspirations, thereby becoming increasingly susceptible to Islamic radicalism, angry Sunni Arabs provided support for the insurgents.

Three main Sunni Arab groups fomented the insurgency. The less sectarian Sunni nationalists, who focused on ousting the United States from Iraq, targeted American and Iraqi security forces, seeing them as the symbols (or tools of) a foreign occupation, but not Shiite civilians. Extreme Sunni fundamentalists, inspired by Osama bin Laden, on the other hand, sanctioned attacks against Shiite civilians in an effort to defeat the establishment of a democratic nation-state in Iraq. The vast Sunni middle, who provided a large portion of the insurgency fighters, opposed both the U.S. occupation and a Shiite domination of Iraq.[77]

Apart from active involvement in the insurgency, as a form of passive resistance, the Sunni Arabs granted safe passage to the insurgents and turned a blind eye to numerous acts of terrorism and sabotage. Gradually, more and more Sunnis, wanting jobs and a stake in the new government, evidenced a more conciliatory attitude. It took some two years, until well into 2005, for Sunni sentiment to begin to turn against al Qaeda.[78] However, a critical mass of Sunnis, passively aiding the insurgents or actively engaging in violence, remained unmoved.

Sectarian violence mounted,[79] beginning in 2005, with Sunni-backed terrorists and death squads targeting Shiite civilians in their mosques and their marketplaces, both in Baghdad and the surrounding provinces. Shiites denounced Sunni leaders for supporting the insurgents. In turn, Sunni leaders criticized Iraq's Shiite-dominated security forces for assassinating and torturing Sunnis suspected of ties to the insurgency.[80] The number of private, secretive Shiite militia, affiliated with the nation's largest Shiite political parties, multiplied, increasing the sense of intimidation in Sunni and mixed areas and creating the deadliest threat to security in the central part of Iraq.[81] Mixed neighborhoods became torn along sectarian lines. Thousands died in the low-level sectarian warfare while tens of thousands fled mixed areas into the relative safety of areas dominated by their own religious group or simply left Iraq (the latter alternative was taken especially often by middle-class families and professionals).[82]

The sectarian strife reached new heights after the golden dome of the Askariya shrine in Sammara, one of Iraq's most revered Shiite shrines, was blown apart on February 22, 2006 by a group affiliated with al Qaeda in Mesopotamia,[83] which sought to provoke the Shiites. Shiite-controlled Iraqi police units stood by as an anti-Sunni rampage, led mostly by Shiite militia, ensued. Despite provocations on both sides, Sunni and Shiite clerics and political leaders rose to the occasion, urging restraint. The possibility of an all-out civil war, driven by religious divisions, abated. As Iraqis refused to take the terrorists' bait, the Iraqi army did not crack, the nation pushed back from the brink, and the democratic project kept moving along, albeit with continuing strife among Sunnis and Shiites in central Iraq.

THE POST-SADDAM IRAQI ECONOMY

The post-Saddam Iraqi economy presented a mixed picture, with both failures and successes. U.S. efforts focused on helping Iraq rebuild an infrastructure that could provide petroleum for export and domestic consumption as well as essential services to its population. However, rampant corruption,[84] wasteful contracting,[85] and insurgent attacks, particularly on oil facilities and the electricity grids, severely impeded reconstruction efforts. Significant portions of Iraq's infrastructure remained in a fragile state, resulting in fuel and electricity shortages.

Under Saddam, Iraq's oil infrastructure became run-down.[86] Deterioration occurred as a result of the sanctions regime and trade embargoes, which curtailed

Iraq's access to modern technology and equipment, years of underinvestment, and poor maintenance practices. The post-Saddam damage brought about by looting and the insurgency exacerbated the antiquated production infrastructure and the lack of refineries.

Despite more than $5 billion in U.S. and Iraqi funds available for reconstruction of the petroleum industry, crude oil production in Iraq dropped in 2004 and 2005 from some 2.4 million barrels per day at the beginning of 2004 to about 2.0 million barrels per day during the last quarter of 2005, but then rose to 2.5 million barrels per day by mid-2006. The unrelenting insurgent attacks on pipelines transporting petroleum to refineries and export markets, especially the Iraq-Turkey pipeline,[87] together with corruption, poor pipeline maintenance, and a lack of storage facilities, cost Iraq about 300,000 to 500,000 barrels per day, lessening Iraqi oil exports and resulting in billions of dollars in lost revenues and additional repair expenditures. With crude oil exports at about 1.6 million barrels per day, far less cash remained available for Iraqi-funded reconstruction efforts.[88]

With rising demand and falling supply, domestically produced refined petroleum failed to fill Iraqi needs. Meeting demand through a reliance on petroleum imports caused Iraq to spend some $200–$250 million per month to import refined petroleum in 2004–5 for sale domestically at subsidized prices.[89]

Phasing out the Saddam-era energy subsidies, some of the largest in the world, which had been retained to promote loyalty to the new government, has proven difficult. Because these subsidies swallow a considerable amount of Iraq's revenues, some 30 percent of its gross domestic product in 2004,[90] lessening them would alleviate market distortions and generate additional governmental revenues for investment in infrastructure projects, economic development programs, and social services. The need for economic reform had to be balanced, however, against political realities. A December 2005 five-fold increase in premium gasoline prices, part of a deal Iraqi leaders struck, with U.S. backing, that could wipe out as much as 80 percent of the $120 billion in foreign debts Saddam had accumulated, outraged motorists. The price increase sparked attacks on fuel convoys and gas stations, which led to a temporary upheaval in the Iraqi Ministry of Oil.[91]

After the war, the national electricity grid, intially shut down as a precaution, collapsed. Although 98 percent of Iraqi households are connected to this electricity grid, in 2005 three-quarters of these households reported their electricity supply to be "extremely unreliable."[92]

Public services, especially in Baghdad, notably electricity, but also the water and sewage systems (topics beyond the scope of this book), functioned for a long period at lower levels than before the war, despite the billions spent on their reconstruction. The national electricity grid, which averaged a daily output of 4,000 megawatts in 2005, about 400 megawatts below its prewar level, rose to more than 5,000 by mid-2006.[93] With the electricity grid more off than on, the power supply became a key issue for many Iraqis and the credibility of the government.

In the central region of Iraq, blackouts continued to be the rule, not the exception, into 2006 with Baghdad getting slightly more than eight hours of electricity a day.[94] While the demand for electricity rose as a result of increased salaries and the liberalization of trade, electricity supply remained constrained by three factors: a lack of generating capacity; shortages of fuel at generating plants; and, not unexpectedly, insurgent assaults on the transmission system.[95] Sabotage worsened the electricity problems, which, in turn, exacerbated the security difficulties.

Apart from insurgent attacks on critical petroleum and electricity infrastructure, the lack of a secure environment impeded the effectiveness of reconstruction efforts more broadly. About 25 percent of the U.S. funds allocated to investment in postwar infrastructure were diverted to pay for additional security costs—including training and equipping Iraqi security forces and helping secure the nation's borders—resulting from the insurgency. With the cost of security at each nonmilitary reconstruction project running at from 16 to 22 percent of total costs, up by an estimated 9 percent over original budget projections,[96] security expenses caused authorities to scale back some efforts and abandon other projects.

Despite these difficulties and the postwar hardships endured by ordinary Iraqis, other aspects of the economy present a mixed picture. With the exception of the direct and indirect ownership of natural resources involving primary extraction and initial processing, the economy opened to foreign investment; commercial laws were modernized. Post-Saddam, Iraq witnessed a boom in the number of small and medium-sized private-sector businesses. Per capita income nearly doubled over two years from 2003 to 2005.[97] Joblessness, while high and posing perhaps a bigger threat than even the terrorists, was halved.[98] Along with unemployment, soaring inflation—a 70 percent rise in the cost of living from July 2005 to July 2006—serves as another powerful tool for the insurgents and an obstacle to a stable, functioning democracy.[99]

THE UNITED STATES STAYED THE COURSE

Despite the scope, capabilities, and endurance of the insurgency—a cluster of groups wanting to destabilize Iraq and bring back some version of tyranny, coupled with the sectarian strife—the Iraqi-led political strategy hopefully will enable the forces of democracy to prevail. Given the U.S. experience in Vietnam, the staying power of the American people remained in question. What price, in soldiers' lives, were Americans prepared to pay? What price was Iraqi freedom worth? Would a people content with their own lives have the requisite staying power? Wolfowitz maintained, "The American people are pretty impressive in their ability to keep after something if they think it is doable. I think what they don't want to hear is that all this is for something that can't be done."[100] Political battles in Washington, as much as the physical battles in Iraq, became crucial to the final outcome. America's adversaries the world over watched to see if the United States had the will to remain and win in Iraq.

Although postwar Iraq became a protracted and costly—in human and financial terms—exercise in nation building, most Americans, even Bush critics, realized that a premature withdrawal of the U.S. military from Iraq would likely plunge the nation into chaos and a bloody civil war along sectarian lines in the center of the country, with the possible involvement of Syria in support of the Baathists and Iran favoring the Shiite Arab Iraqis leading to a possible regional war. It would make the terrorist problem there and elsewhere even worse. A retreat under fire would reinforce bin Laden's message: if you hit America hard, it will fold. The Islamic fascists would hail a U.S. departure and the ensuing chaos left behind in Iraq as a major victory. It would be a major foreign-policy and national-security disaster in the vital Persian Gulf oil region and would likely encourage the Islamic fascists to commit more acts of terrorism and violence worldwide.

The continued insurgency in Iraq with its capacity to kill and instill fear became a key part of the larger war on terrorism. With the jihadists' making Iraq a focus on their war against the United States, Iraq became the "central front" in American's global struggle against terrorism.[101] The United States could not accept a terrorist-run nation in the heart of the Middle East. A premature withdrawal from Iraq would be a death sentence for those who struggled to build an Iraqi democracy, from newspaper publishers to politicians to the millions of Iraqis who voted three times in 2005.

Because the war against terror represents a multidecades', if not centuries', effort, the U.S. government must continue to confront al Qaeda globally. Al Qaeda—a loose network of like-minded groups, largely autonomous but sometimes cooperating, who use terrorism to achieve their political goals—understands what Iraq means to its movement and its survival. Allowing the insurgents and sectarian groups to drive the United States out of Iraq would have powerful, worldwide ramifications.

If the United States left Iraq precipitously, moderates in the Middle East would never again believe the United States and its promised support for reform. They would be left alone to face Islamic fascists. An American defeat would likely swell the ranks of jihadists. Islamic terrorism would grow throughout the world, posing a mounting threat to the United States. As President Bush stated in December 2005:

> It is also important for every American to understand the consequences of pulling out of Iraq before our work is done. We would abandon our Iraqi friends and signal to the world that America cannot be trusted to keep its word. We would undermine the morale of our troops by betraying the cause for which they have sacrificed. We would cause the tyrants in the Middle East to laugh at our failed resolve, and tighten their repressive grip. We would hand Iraq over to enemies who have pledged to attack us, and the global terrorist movement would be emboldened and more dangerous than ever before.[102]

With the need to protect against and limit violence in Iraq, the U.S. exit strategy turned on the existence of a viable, legitimate Iraqi government and the growth and the competency of Iraqi security forces. Although it took about one year, until mid-2004, for the United States to become serious about training and equipping the Iraqi security forces,[103] gradually, they became more effective fighters and took up more of the burden beginning in 2005. With a stable government to lead them and stronger ministries of defense and interior to facilitate the supply chain and place them under central control,[104] it is hoped that the Iraq army and police forces will become a real and growing presence. They speak the language; they are culturally aware; they know the terrain and bring a network of informers. Despite horrendous casualties, they confronted the insurgency with courage and resolve. The Iraqi security forces have the potential to defuse the insurgency and the sectarian violence successfully and hopefully permit a significant withdrawal of deployed American troops. The Iraqi police, it is hoped, will fill the security vacuum, especially in Baghdad, and gain popular confidence.

A REAPPRAISAL

Was the war worth it? Wolfowitz pondered the question at the funeral of Army Lt. Col. Chad Buehring, killed on the floor below Wolfowitz in the October 2003 attack at the al Rashid Hotel in Baghdad's Green Zone, and during the dozens of times he visited wounded service personnel at military hospitals. He showed his gratitude for their courage and sacrifice.

Wolfowitz firmly believed that the war was justified and worthwhile.[105] The decision to go to war was an act of personal courage by Bush, he maintained. After 9/11, Wolfowitz became convinced that terrorism was no longer a manageable evil. The intersecting worldwide networks of terrorism and its state sponsors had to be attacked. Specifically, he believed that Saddam's regime long deserved to be overthrown. After 9/11, Wolfowitz concluded that his removal was important enough to risk American lives in a direct military action.

For Wolfowitz, Saddam's Baath Party was a Nazi-like organization of gangsters and sadists. Its removal from power obviated a threat to the United States and presented an opening to a better world. Although healing in Iraq would take time, Wolfowitz believed that much had been accomplished on the positive side for Iraq and the Middle East as a result of the 2003 military action.

Two of the key assumptions and expectations on which the war was based were not vindicated. American forces were unable to find the WMD that the Bush administration claimed that Saddam's forces possessed. The prewar links between Saddam and al Qaeda remain controversial. Wolfowitz subsequently admitted that the supposed cache of Iraqi WMD had never been the most compelling reason for going to war. According to Wolfowitz, for U.S. bureaucratic reasons, "we settled on the one issue that everyone could agree on which was weapons of mass destruction as the core reason."[106]

Months of searching in post-Saddam Iraq produced no chemical or biological weapons. Iraq was not moving toward the development of nuclear weapons. An official U.S. government report intended to offer a near-final judgment about Iraq and its weapons of mass destruction, concluded that Iraq had "essentially destroyed" its illicit weapons stockpiles and abilities shortly after the 1991 Gulf War.[107] Iraq seemingly eliminated its last secret factory, a biological weapons plant, in 1996. Prior to 2003, although Saddam aimed at preserving his capability to reconstitute his WMD when sanctions were lifted, Iraq apparently did not possess chemical and biological weapons, and was not seeking to reconstitute its nuclear program. No evidence was found of any concerted Iraqi effort to restart these programs or make an active effort to regain these abilities. Between 1991 and 2003, Saddam apparently sacrificed Iraq's illicit weapons as part of the larger goal of winning an end to U.N. sanctions. Saddam used this period to exploit avenues, such as the corrupt Oil-for-Food program, to lay the groundwork for a plan to resume production of WMD unfettered if the sanctions were lifted, although the regime had no formal, written plan, post-sanctions, for reviving its WMD. The Iraqi regime seemingly sought to maintain ambiguity about whether it had illicit weapons mainly as a deterrent to Iran, its major Middle East rival, given Iraq's military weakness.[108] However, some time before the start of the 2003 war, Iraq may have moved military matériel, including WMD, to Syria.[109]

At the least, in 2003, Saddam had the means to manufacture WMD and could have developed them some day. He remained interested in and committed to acquiring WMD, which he could have supplied to global terrorist groups such as al Qaeda. Wolfowitz noted, in June 2004, that although United States did not find WMD, Saddam had "the capacity to build those things and to recreate those programs the minute he was out from under sanctions."[110] Wolfowitz subsequently reflected:

> I always thought the nuclear thing was overstated. That was down the road. What really bothered me was biological weapons, and we know they made them. We know they know how to make them. We know there was a lot of deliberate effort to destroy evidence of all kinds of things. "Incontrovertible," I agreed, is a pretty strong word. . . . [L]et me put it this way—they were given a chance to come clean under [U.N. Security Council Resolution] 1441, to declare everything they had and to cooperate fully with inspectors. We caught them lying on the declarations on not insignificant things—mostly on the missiles they were working on and the UAVs [unmanned aerial vehicles] they were working on. And there was lots of evidence of obstructing inspectors and moving things and hiding things. That was supposed to be the test of 1441—not whether we could prove they had stockpiles.[111]

Even absent WMD, Wolfowitz subsequently phrased the rationale for going to war as follows: "You had a very dangerous character who played with terrorists, who had regularly declared hostile intentions toward us and toward our allies in the Persian Gulf, who definitely had a capacity to make these weapons and—absent some kind of fairly fundamental change in his attitude and policy—was extremely dangerous, and much more dangerous in the light of September 11 than before. . . . I think it would have been irresponsible to leave him alone."[112]

The prewar links between Saddam and al Qaeda, among other Islamic terrorist groups, remain a controversial matter. Although the official 9/11 Commission report failed to find evidence of Iraq's connection to the events of September 11, or a "collaborative operational relationship" between Saddam's regime and al Qaeda, it confirmed extensive communications between the two over the years.[113] Wolfowitz believed that Saddam provided "mutual support to al-Qaeda. . . . This is a man who funded terrorists, supported terrorists."[114]

Evidence has begun to emerge regarding the cooperative relationship between Saddam and al Qaeda, thereby legitimizing the 2003 war effort.[115] Terrorist groups, such as Ansar al-Islam, an al Qaeda affiliate, had established bases in northern Iraq prior to 2003. One of the masterminds of the 1993 attack on the World Trade Center, Abdul Rahman Yasin, fled to Baghdad to find a safe sanctuary after the bombing. After the 2001 war against the Taliban, Abu Musab al-Zarqawi escaped from Afghanistan to obtain sanctuary in Iraq. From 1999 through 2002, elite Iraqi military units trained some eight thousand terrorists at different camps in Iraq. Many of the trainees were drawn from North African terrorist groups with close ties to al Qaeda.[116] Because Saddam trained terrorists in Iraq before 2003, many of them likely remained and fought there. Thus, the insurgency may have been an operation led by Saddam's apparatus and those it trained to use violence to achieve their political goals to regain dominance in Iraq or, at least, prevent the formation of a legitimate government. Also, Saddam's government provided financial aid to an al Qaeda offshoot in the Philippines.[117]

The failure to find WMD in Iraq and the inability to conclusively prove relevant connections between Saddam and al Qaeda, at least to date, led the White House to justify the war in Iraq on an idealistic policy of a Middle Eastern political transformation. Iraq formed a key place to test the hypothesis that Arab nations could support democratic institutions.

Freedom is a universal aspiration, Wolfowitz believed, not just a western one. Despite cynical predictions, he had seen democracy spread in East Asia and the world had seen what had happened in post-Communist Eastern Europe. In the next ten or twenty years, Wolfowitz was confident the 2003 war in Iraq would be seen "as an essential stage in the march toward human freedom, democracy, and the defeat of terrorism from which Americans would benefit."[118] Shortly before the end of the 2003 war, on April 6, Wolfowitz voiced the hope that the creation of a democratic Iraq would inspire similar political changes in the Middle East. "I think Iraq can be an inspiration to the Muslim world and the Arab world that Arabs and Muslims can create a democratic country. And that will be positive," he stated. "Many people have done it in the latter part of the 20th century. It's time for the Arabs to do it now."[119]

Even before Iraq's dramatic political steps in 2005 and 2006, in July 2003, Wolfowitz made a four-and-one-half-day visit to Iraq. Acknowledging the huge challenges and that much work remained to be done, he met with the newly elected mayor of Mosul and his council, composed of Arabs, Kurds, Christians, and Turkmens. Rather than zero-sum politics, in which one group's gain resulted in another's loss, Mosul represented the kind of ethnic and religious mix Wolfowitz had long maintained would thrive after Saddam. He told the council, "You don't build a democracy like you build a house. Democracy grows like a garden. If you keep the weeds out and water the plants and you're patient, eventually you get something magnificent."[120] In September 2003, Wolfowitz repeated the gardening analogy as the foundation for democracy. He noted:

> [I]deally what we do is to try to create conditions where people build institutions for themselves. . . . [I]t's more like gardening than it is like architecture. That if you keep the plants watered and keep the weeds out, they can grow into amazing things on their own—not something that you create. . . . I think we can create conditions where people can build a nation for themselves.[121]

THE PROSPECTS FOR DEMOCRACY IN THE MIDDLE EAST AND THROUGHOUT THE WORLD

With Wolfowitz's departure from the Pentagon, President Bush and Secretary of State Condoleezza Rice absorbed Wolfowitz's optimism about the prospects for the spread of democracy in the Middle East and that the growth of freedom in the nations throughout the world could make counties peaceful, prosperous, and pro-American. Bush explicitly declared the spread of democracy and freedom as the central principle and the defining objective of U.S. foreign policy. Making a crusade for democracy a centerpiece of his second term, in his January 2005 Second Inaugural Address, capturing the high moral and ideological ground, he stated:

> So it is the policy of the United States to seek and support the growth of democratic movements and institutions in every nation and culture, with the ultimate goal of ending tyranny in our world. This is not primarily the task of arms, though we will defend ourselves and our friends by force by arms when necessary. Freedom, by its nature, must be chosen and defended by citizens and sustained by the rule of law and the protection of minorities. And when the soul of a nation finally speaks, the institutions that arise may reflect customs and traditions very different from our own. America will not impose our own style of government on the unwilling. Our goal instead is to help others find their own voice, attain their own freedom, and make their own way.
>
> The great objective of ending tyranny is the concentrated work of generations. The difficulty of the task is no excuse for avoiding it. America's influence is not unlimited, but fortunately for the oppressed, America's influence is considerable, and we will use it confidently in freedom's cause. . . .
>
> The leaders of governments with long habits of control need to know: To serve your people, you must learn to trust them. Start on this journey of progress and justice, and America will walk at your side.[122]

On June 20, 2005, in Cairo, Secretary of State Rice delivered a challenge to the closest allies of the United States in the Arab world.[123] She called on Egypt and Saudi Arabia to embrace democracy by holding free elections, allowing freedom of expression for opponents, granting political rights for women, and releasing political prisoners. "For 60 years, my country, the United States, pursued stability at the expense of democracy in the Middle East, and we achieved neither," she declared. "Now we are taking a different course. We are supporting the democratic aspirations of all people." However, these reform goals were different from those sought in Iraq, where change was expected in several years, not over decades. She continued:

> For neighboring countries with turbulent histories, democracy can help to build trust and settle old disputes with dignity. But leaders of vision and character must commit themselves to the difficult work that nurtures the hope of peace. And for all citizens with grievances, democracy can be a path to lasting justice. But the democratic system cannot function if certain groups have one foot in the realm of politics and one foot in the camp of terror.
>
> There are those who say that democracy destroys social institutions and erodes moral standards. In fact, the opposite is true: The success of democracy depends on public character and private virtue. For democracy to thrive, free citizens must work every day to strengthen their families, to care for their neighbors, and to support their communities.
>
> There are those who say that long-term economic and social progress can be achieved without free minds and free markets. In fact, human potential and creativity are only fully released when governments trust their people's decisions and invest in their people's future. And the key investment is in those people's education. Because education—for men and for women—transforms their dreams into reality and enables them to overcome poverty.
>
> There are those who say that democracy is for men alone. In fact, the opposite is true: Half a democracy is not a democracy. As one Muslim woman leader has said, "Society is like a bird. It has two wings. And a bird cannot fly if one wing is broken."

During his second term, Bush sought democratic reforms wherever possible in the Middle East, depending on the circumstances. Slowly, the stirrings of political pluralism, if not democracy, emerged. Beyond Afghanistan and Iraq, the Muslim world's two most important democratic laboratories, the list of nations moving (perhaps, inching) toward democracy is growing and includes the codification of women's rights in Kuwait (including suffrage), the beginnings of political competition in Egypt, local voting in Saudi Arabia, and small steps in the Gulf States.[124]

However, the drive to democratize the Middle East risks the coming to power of Islamic parties, often strong by default, and their upending pro-American alliances. The United States must accept the possibility that democratic elections in the Middle East may bring to power unpalatable, radical Islamic alternatives that are well organized, are generally free from the corruption of entrenched regimes, and have a long history of providing services to local neighborhoods. Democracy and American interests do not always coincide. Consider the examples of Egypt (which accounts for more than one-half of the Arab world's population), where Islamists scored gains in the 2005 parliamentary elections, and the Palestinian Authority, where Hamas achieved a victory in the 2006 elections.

President Hosni Mubarak, under pressure from the Bush administration, allowed Egypt's first multicandidate presidential election in September 2005, a first step toward building a competitive political process in that nation.[125] Although Mubarak won his fifth presidential term in what might be described as a pseudodemocratic election, marked by low voter turnout, the lack of independent monitors, an electoral system slanted in favor of Mubarak's party, and allegations of voter intimidation, democracy activists continue to challenge the president's quarter-century rule.

Too much pressure on Mubarak to offer free and fair elections on the national level, however, might lead to a victory for the Muslim Brotherhood, the most popular Egyptian opposition party, outlawed by the government although it swore off violence decades ago and seemingly has embraced parliamentary democracy. The group, whose candidates run as independents, has registered notable success at the polls despite limits imposed by the Mubarak government on its campaigning and police efforts to block voters from voting.

In February 2006, Mubarak postponed for two years promised local elections scheduled for April 2006 after the Muslim Brotherhood won a record one-fifth of the seats in the December 2005 parliamentary elections. In his reelection campaign, Mubarak had promised to amend the constitution to give more power to the parliament; help political parties to grow; and replace a 1981 emergency law allowing the government to detain prisoners, in reality, indefinitely, without charges, prohibiting gatherings of more than five people and limiting speech and association. However, in April 2006, Mubarak pushed through parliament a two-year extension of the emergency law. Mubarak's government also denied requests to create new political parties and reprimanded a judge who publicly alleged fraud at the polls in the 2005 parliamentary elections.

Hamas (the Islamic Resistance Movement), won seventy-six out of 132 seats in the January 2006 Palestinian legislative council elections.[126] Palestinian leaders of the Muslim Brotherhood's Gaza and West Bank outposts launched Hamas, a militant Islamic party sworn to the destruction of Israel, in the late 1980s. Running on a platform of good government and having earned the respect of voters in municipal councils as a result of keeping its promises, improving government services, and avoiding corruption, Hamas won an out-and-out victory in the parliamentary elections. Having won a parliamentary majority, Hamas formed a cabinet and took effective control of the Palestinian Authority. Power confronted Hamas with difficult choices and uncertain prospects, including whether to renounce its Islamic outlook and violence as well as recognize Israel's legitimacy and the 1993 Oslo peace accords that led to the creation of the Palestinian Authority.

The 2006 Palestinian election results suggested the risks inherent in Bush's campaign to bring democracy to the Middle East, balancing support for elected governments with a refusal to deal with groups linked to terrorism. Bush praised the Palestinians' exercise in democracy but warned about their choice, and cut off aid, except for humanitarian assistance, to the Palestinian Authority.

This new phase of political reform and the transition to democracy faces serious challenges. Arab regimes, enjoying full power with no accountability, are not eager to have a vibrant civil society, and they resist political liberalization, citing a desire to protect their nation's security and sovereignty. Rulers appeal to fears of instability and to the need to implement economic reforms in a bid to win domestic and international support and justify harsh measures against any political opposition. The official, state-controlled press provides maximum opposition to radical and violent groups.

Overcoming inertia in the Middle East requires a push from both within and without.[127] From within, democratization requires political leaders with the vision and political skill to challenge those in power who resist liberalization. From without, democratization will require Western nations, especially the United States, to continue their gentle prodding. However, even within the Bush administration, because of circumstances, the president's words are not always translated into policies—for example, in Egypt—that back up his faith in freedom and democracy.

In reflecting on Wolfowitz's and George W. Bush's promotion of democracy, it is important to ask what we mean by "democracy."[128] We may place too much emphasis on elections. Spurious elections may obscure infirm and corrupt governing institutions. Balloting and even free and fair elections do not necessarily bring the protection of civil liberties, such as freedom of speech and the press, or a legal system based on an impartial judiciary and the protection of private property. In short, democracy rests on a broader range of institutions than merely free elections.[129] A movement toward democracy needs to promote good governance and the establishment of institutions that form the preconditions for an effective democracy, including the rule of law and a free press to ferret out corruption and bureaucratic incompetence. Its foundation includes the development of an independent civil society, devoted to the cultivation of reason and enlightened understanding; effective, widespread participation; and a public that demands better performance from the public sector.

Some maintain that liberal democracies and their institutions and practices require indigenous antecedent qualities, specifically, a democratic cultural base for freedom to take root, especially where a democratic tradition never existed or it was long suppressed.[130] But ideas, such as tolerance for others' views, a belief in the equality of all, education as a fundamental right, and valuing the questioning of authority, can change human minds along with incentives, such as economic, technical, and security assistance. Antidemocratic ideologies and institutions faded and democracy took root in Japan after World War II, in Latin America and East Asia in the 1980s, and in South Africa in the 1990s. Many believed these nations' and regions' religious and cultural traditions made self-government and freedom impossible. Because people want to rule them-selves, democracy and freedom are universal values although nations differ in their implementation.[131]

Dysfunctional, autocratic rule in the Middle East has helped fostered virulent forms of Islamic extremism. Too speedy a removal of the autocrats may create conditions for radical Islamic groups to come to power and install their ideology. It will take time, most likely decades, for Middle Eastern countries to develop democratic institutions and practices that comport with their culture, traditions, and history. However, if authoritarian governments in the Middle East fail to open themselves to reform, Islamic radicals may not only grow in numbers but also blow up these regimes. Increased political openness in the Middle East is thus essential to American, and, more generally, Western security.

Some maintain that democracies are more prone to militarism and war.[132] How-ever, the conventional wisdom, which I believe is correct, asserts that democra-cies favor peace and that they are generally unthreatening and are less externally aggressive than dictatorships.[133] More democratic institutions and the accompa-nying limitations on the power of rulers, a greater openness in governance, and a meaningful commitment to human rights will mean more peaceful, but not nec-essarily perfect, relations between and among other nations. Democracies may not get along with nondemocracies. Because alienated individuals, especially the able-bodied young men and women frustrated by a lack of opportunity, stag-nant economies, and rampant corruption, often turn, in the struggle for recogni-tion and the assertion of their dignity and worth, to radical Islamic ideology and violence, increased democracy in the Middle East will likely reduce the terror-ist threat and make America and Western nations generally safer. As President Bush stated in his Second Inaugural Address: "The survival of liberty in our land increasingly depends on the success of liberty in other lands. The best hope for peace in our world is the expansion of freedom in all the world."[134]

Despite all the benefits democracies offer, in a more circumspect moment, Wol-fowitz noted the difficulties inherent in establishing a viable, liberal democracy. Writing in 2000, before joining the Bush 43 administration, he stated that:

> one should be wary of a policy that devotes equal effort to promoting democracy everywhere, regardless of the particular circumstances. Aside from the question of the importance of a country for U.S. interests, we cannot ignore the uncomfortable fact that economic and social conditions may better prepare some countries for democracy than others. . . .
>
> Promoting democracy requires attention to specific circumstances and to the limitations of U.S. leverage. Both because of what the United States is, and because of what is possible, we cannot engage either in promoting democracy or in nation-building as a exercise of will. We must proceed by interaction and indirection, not imposition.[135]

For the next leg of his illustrious career, Wolfowitz became president of the World Bank. Based on the premise that a successful transition to democracy generally requires meaningful economic development,[136] Wolfowitz sought to couple increased infusions of financial capital and the promotion of human capital through multilateral loans and grants as well as debt relief with an emphasis on more open, less corrupt third world governments.

Chapter 9

Wolfowitz at The World Bank

On June 1, 2005, Wolfowitz moved from one challenge to the next, taking over as president of the World Bank Group. A respected development group issued a report on his assent to his new position, entitled "The Hardest Job in the World."[1]

As Wolfowitz saw it, the bank's mission of economic development and reducing worldwide poverty levels by funding projects that would enable developing countries to grow and take part in the global marketplace matched the philosophy that motivated America's 2003 war in Iraq. His statement, "We are all better off when other people are better off,"[2] shows that he sees limited prospects for peace and stability in the world where much of its population exists below the poverty line and many are starving. Harkening back to 9/11, he maintained that underdeveloped countries provide breeding grounds for discontent and that poverty serves as fuel for hate-filled terrorists.

With this in mind, Wolfowitz moved from his U.S. government position to one of international leadership, much as Robert S. McNamara had done in 1968. McNamara, the U.S. Secretary of Defense from 1961 to 1967, also shifted from the Pentagon to the World Bank. Both McNamara and Wolfowitz were Pentagon leaders linked with controversial and heavily criticized wars, and both took a similar exit route to new careers when the outcome of the wars remained unresolved. McNamara, however, had left the Pentagon shaken by doubts about the Vietnam War; while Wolfowitz left at a moment of confidence, after the January 2005 Iraqi elections. In Wolfowitz's case, the move was made not because he disagreed with the administration, but to enable him, in part, to leave behind the nightmare of the insurgency and the slow progress of reconstruction in Iraq. As president of the World Bank, he could work anew on governance issues that he cared a great deal about, focusing on stemming corruption in third world nations.

THE WORLD BANK GROUP: AN OVERVIEW

The World Bank Group was founded in 1944 with the original purpose of financing reconstruction in post–World War II Europe. It is owned by 184 member states, including both economically developed and developing countries. The United States, with 16 percent ownership, is the bank's largest shareholder. This dominance enables the American president to nominate the bank's president, as President Bush did with Wolfowitz.

The bank is the world's largest development organization, with some ten thousand employees. It has as many units—five—as the Pentagon has sides. The bank moves more than $23 billion each year out its doors in the form of loans and grants.[3]

The bank's most prominent unit is the International Development Association (IDA), which makes outright grants—some $1.8 billion in fiscal year 2006—and affordable (so-called "soft") loans, interest free (or low 1.5–2 percent interest loans) with the principal due in thirty or forty years, another $7.6 billion in fiscal year 2005, to some eighty-one of the globe's poorest nations. The IDA gathers contributions of cash from wealthy nations and redistributes these funds, roughly $9.5 billion in fiscal year 2006,[4] to poorer nations. However, the process of gaining regular, three-year commitments from developed countries leaves the bank vulnerable to pressure from its donor nations.

The bank's second unit is the International Bank for Reconstruction and Development (IBRD), which lent about $14.1 billion in fiscal year 2006.[5] With its AAA-credit rating, the IBRD can borrow cheaply on the international capital market and lend, at slightly higher interest rates, to middle-income developing nations, such as China. The industrialized nations' subscribed capital, both paid-in and callable, guarantees the IBRD's AAA-bond rating. Because the bank's borrowings are always held below the level of its subscribed capital and its accumulated reserves, the bank's creditworthiness is unshakable.

The IBRD's best middle-income clients, such as China, India, and Brazil, have increasingly abandoned it in favor of private international capital markets. These nations cite the so-called "hassle" factor of working with the IBRD, including the slow pace of the IBRD's decision-making process and the need to deal with bank-mandated social and environmental safeguard policies, as their impetus for preferring private financing.

The bank's third arm, the International Finance Corporation, makes loans to and equity investments in private-sector enterprises without any government guarantees.[6] Its fourth unit, the Multilateral Investment Guarantee Agency, offers political risk insurance against noncommercial risks, such as expropriation and currency nonconvertibility, so as to encourage foreign direct investment in developing nations.[7] The fifth side, the International Centre for Settlement of Investment Disputes, hears investment disputes between foreign lenders and sovereign borrowers.[8]

WOLFOWITZ PONDERED A NEW POSITION AND
THEN GAINED APPROVAL

Wolfowitz seriously started thinking about leaving the Pentagon in early 2005, spurred, at least in part, by a three-day tour of the December 2004 tsunami's devastating effect on Southeast Asia. As he put it, "Economic development supports political development, and it really came home to me with the Asian tsunami."[9]

The scenes of destruction he saw in Sri Lanka and Indonesia played into his interest in alleviating poverty in third world nations. He called the tsunami trip "a big deal" that "may have crystallized" his views about a new career move to the area of economic development. "Nothing is more gratifying than being able to help people in need—as I experienced once again when I witnessed the tsunami relief operations in Indonesia and Sri Lanka," he indicated in a written statement explaining his interest in the presidency of the World Bank. He continued, "It is also a critical part of making the world a better place for all of us."[10] He wanted to be viewed as a bringer of help rather than conflict.

On a less idealistic note, President Bush declined to name Wolfowitz as his National Security Advisor in 2005, stalling out his advancement in the federal government. Snubbed in this regard by the Bush administration, Wolfowitz as president of the World Bank would be able to run his own show. Moreover, a move to the World Bank would remove Wolfowitz from Defense Secretary Rumsfeld's shadow, affording him more prominence and power than he might have had if he had stayed at the Pentagon or at another position in the Bush administration.

President George W. Bush approved of Wolfowitz's career move, nominating him as the tenth head of the World Bank on March 16, 2005. In a news conference on that date, Bush stated:

> I appreciate the world leaders taking my phone calls as I explain to them why I think Paul will be a strong president of the World Bank. I've said he was a man of good experience. He helped manage a large organization. The World Bank is a large organization. The Pentagon is a large organization; he's been involved in the management of that organization. He's a skilled diplomat, worked at the State Department in high positions. He was ambassador to Indonesia, where he did a very good job representing our country. And Paul is committed to development. He's a compassionate, decent man who will do a fine job in the World Bank.[11]

As President Bush saw it, Wolfowitz was a good choice for the position because of his bureaucratic skills. Wolfowitz was an experienced public-sector manager and a persuasive communicator, knowing how to function in and get results from a vast bureaucracy, such as the bank's. Moreover, dealing with the Philippines and Indonesia had given him firsthand experience with what poverty is like in a developing nation as well as with the corruption that often accompanies third world projects.

Despite President Bush's glowing endorsement, an outcry from bank member governments, the bank's staff, and nongovernmental organizations met Wolfowitz's nomination. Summing up a body of sentiment, the German Development Minister, Heidemarie Wieczorek-Zeul noted that "the enthusiasm [about Wolfowitz's nomination] in 'old Europe' is not exactly overwhelming."[12]

Following Wolfowitz's nomination, the bank's Staff Association set up a web-based comment line to which bank staffers could send confidential e-mails detailing their opinion of Bush's choice. Within forty-eight hours, the comment line logged some 1,300 e-mails, about 87 percent of which expressed opposition to Wolfowitz's appointment.[13] Staffers cited Wolfowitz's close links to the White House and his advocacy of the Iraq war as the reasons for their hostility and criticized his selection as an overtly political move on President Bush's behalf. Moreover, they feared that Wolfowitz's connection with a controversial administration and the overt unilateralism manifested in its foreign and national-security policies would damage the bank's credibility and its effectiveness. The staff's resistance also carried with it an undercurrent of cliquishness; the bank is a vast organization powered by an intricate bureaucracy, which evidenced suspicion of Wolfowitz, an outsider who had little experience with global poverty alleviation.

Nongovernmental organizations worldwide also objected to the nomination. Over three hundred of these organizations from sixty-two countries signed a letter protesting Wolfowitz's ascent to the position.[14]

Although Germany, France, Japan, and Great Britain signed off on his nomination almost immediately and no country offered an alternative nominee, some other governments resented his nomination because of Wolfowitz's role as a key intellectual architect of the 2003 Iraq War, to which many of the bank's member states were adamantly opposed. The anti-Wolfowitz faction also feared that he would use the bank to promote America's foreign and economic policies, serving as the United States' puppet and making the bank nothing more than another arm for imposing the Bush administration's policies on developing nations.

Wolfowitz immediately conducted a whirlwind diplomatic "charm effort," designed to give his critics, both external and within the bank, a chance to vent their concerns and himself a chance to respond to them.[15] To win over the bank staff, Wolfowitz sought to convince its employees that he would both respect and operate within the bank's bureaucracy and cut his ties with the White House. He reached out to leaders in the bank's staff, seeking to convince them that he planned to lead them by consensus. His campaign also included assuring the bank's executive directors that he understood the organization's mission and that he would not use the presidency to promote the Bush administration's foreign-policy goals. He told the directors what they wanted to hear: that he respected the bank's multilateral nature and its goal of reducing world poverty, and that his loyalty would be to the bank and no other authority.

Running the gauntlet of what amounted to the European Union's confirmation hearing on March 30 in Brussels, Wolfowitz responded to various governments' opposition by disavowing his unilateralist image. He stressed to European finance and development ministers that he would be prepared to clash with the Bush administration, if necessary, to uphold the bank's mission. He again vowed to serve the international community and to created a multilateral team to run the bank although he stopped short of promising to appoint a European as his senior deputy.[16]

On March 31, a little more than two weeks after his nomination, Wolfowitz won unanimous approval from the bank's 24-member board of executive directors to serve a five-year term as the bank's president. Upon his confirmation, Wolfowitz described the bank's goal of "helping the poorest of the world to lift themselves out of poverty" as a "noble mission." He continued, "I believe deeply in that mission. Nothing is more gratifying than being able to help people in need and developing opportunities for all the people of the world to achieve their full potential."[17]

In his first meeting with the Bank's staff on June 1, Wolfowitz again tried to reassure the group that he understood the bank's mission and its multilateral nature. Responding to a question, he stated, "Politically neutral development can serve everybody's interests in a region, and it can actually expand the area on which people can come to agree on what are sometimes difficult political differences." He added that the bank often brings a "unique objectivity" to development and that he would "do everything in [his] power to preserve that objectivity."[18]

Although some bank staffers and development activists remained hostile, most staffers, development experts, and officials from nongovernmental organizations seemed reassured by their encounters with Wolfowitz. As his presidency continued and fears of a sharp change in the bank's direction proved unfounded, skeptics began to accept that he would not use the institution to push Bush's foreign-policy agenda.

Many initial critics came around to the view that Wolfowitz's links to the Bush White House could translate into powerful support for antipoverty initiatives. As Wolfowitz noted, "I've encountered more, 'Gee, you could help us obtain access to the White House and Congress'" than criticism.[19]

However, relations between Wolfowitz and the bank Staff Association remained tense. By early 2006, two high-ranking Bank officials—Managing Director Shengman Zhang, the Bank's most powerful staffer under former president James D. Wolfensohn, and General Counsel Roberto Danino—announced their departures from the bank, reportedly because they no longer were given active roles in decision making. Meanwhile, Wolfowitz, following the practice of past presidents and in conformity with the IBRD's Articles of Agreement,[20] exercised his discretion and appointed an American group of advisors with ties to the Bush administration to top bank positions. Robin Cleveland, an associate director of the U.S. Office of Management and Budget, became Wolfowitz's chief advisor; Kevin S. Kellems, formerly a special advisor to Wolfowitz when he served as Deputy Secretary of Defense, became the bank's top communication strategist; and Suzanne Rich Folsom, a Republican party loyalist, became acting and then permanent head of the Department of Institutional Integrity, a unit that investigates corruption on Bank projects and staff misconduct.[21] Kellems is also senior advisor to Wolfowitz; Folson is counselor to the president. Wolfowitz consults with the trio on most major decisions.

These appointments, together with the departures of Zhang and Danino, set off discontent at the Staff Association, which interpreted the personnel changes as Wolfowitz's attempting to distance himself from bank veterans and flood the bank with high-ranking Americans sympathetic to his viewpoint. Some of the staff, who had feared that Wolfowitz would use the bank as a vehicle to push an American agenda, saw their doubts realized in Wolfowitz's appointments. Others disapproved of Wolfowitz's trio because they felt that the American advisors would cut off the rest of the staff from access to the president. Wolfowitz, for his part, scoffed at these employees' fears. He stated in an interview, "I really like hearing different points of view. . . . I like to encourage people to disagree with me."[22] He tried many tactics to win over the staff, including approaching employees in the cafeteria to ask them candid questions, holding town meetings with the staff to give them a chance to air their concerns, and giving out his personal e-mail address to staff members to encourage them to advise him of any concerns they might have. He also selected a New Zealander and a Salvadoran to be managing directors and a Spanish national to serve as general counsel, in an effort to temper criticism.[23] However, despite Wolfowitz's attempts to ingratiate himself, the staff's reception of him continued to be somewhat chilly.[24]

THE WORLD BANK IN A TIME OF TRANSITION

During James D. Wolfensohn's tenure as president in the 1990s, the World Bank began to intervene in recipient nations' governance matters. Although not encouraging overt regime changes, it started to promote good governance, a civil society, and empowerment as part of the conditions attached to its grants and loans. Gradually, the bank became committed to changing the political institutions in the countries where it operates. Although the bank is in the business of lending and giving grants for economic and social development, it has come to try to build nations and reform regimes.

The Articles of Agreement of both the IBRD and the IDA require bank officials to remain apolitical. Both charters mandate that the bank officials "shall not interfere in the political affairs of any member; nor shall they be influenced in their decisions by the political character of the member or members concerned. Only economic considerations shall be relevant to their decisions, and these considerations shall be weighed impartially in order to achieve the [unit's] purposes."[25] Until 1996, the bank did not overtly take political considerations into account in making grants or loans, nor did it make a concerted effort to address corruption in developing nations.

However, such a policy became increasingly counterproductive as the bank's focus turned to Africa, Asia, and Latin America. In regions subject to frequent regime changes and with its economic goals amounting to "construction" rather than "reconstruction" as was the case in post-World War II Europe, an assessment of political culture relies more on a government's ability to benefit from a loan or grant than on making value judgments about the ideology behind that government. Beginning in 1980, as the bank gave out an increasing portion of its funds in the form of structural adjustment loans, money not designated for a specific project but rather designed to finance recipient nations' economies, it also became necessary for the bank to address corruption in borrowing countries. It would be absurd for the bank to distribute substantial funds to corrupt governments even if the loans were subject to various economic conditions.

Under the ten-year reign of Wolfensohn, a wealthy former Wall Street financier, the bank began to deal overtly with the problem of corruption in recipient nations. At the bank's 1996 annual meeting, Wolfensohn stated, "And let's not mince words, we need to deal with the cancer of corruption." He continued:

> In country after country, it is the people who are demanding action on this issue. They know that corruption diverts resources from the poor to the rich, increases the cost of running businesses, distorts public expenditures, and deters foreign investors. They also know that it erodes the constituency for aid programs and humanitarian relief. And we all know that it is a major barrier to sound and equitable development.
>
> Corruption is a problem that all countries have to confront. Solutions, however, can only be home-grown. National leaders need to take a stand. Civil society plays a key role as well. Working with our partners, the Bank Group will help any of our member countries to implement national programs that discourage corrupt practices. And we will support international efforts to fight corruption and to establish voluntary standards of behavior for corporations and investors in the industrialized world.
>
> The Bank Group cannot intervene in the political affairs of our member countries. But we can give advice, encouragement and support to governments that wish to fight corruption and it is these governments that will, over time, attract the larger volume of investment. Let me emphasize that the Bank Group will not tolerate corruption in the programs that we support; and we are taking steps to ensure that our own activities continue to meet the highest standards of probity.[26]

Under Wolfensohn, the bank sought to identify corruption and confront it as a key obstacle to economic growth and development in the third world. Over the next ten years, the bank's anticorruption measures, which included strengthening its procurement and auditing requirements, blossomed into a portfolio of six hundred anticorruption programs in more than a hundred countries.[27] Among multinational development organizations, it maintains the only public blacklist of corrupt individuals and entities.

At the bank's urging, many countries developed national anticorruption commissions. However, such measures achieved little; rather than proactively

discouraging corruption, these commissions were often set up following the dis-
covery of a scandal to point a retrospective finger at a scapegoat. Moreover, the
bank did not consistently cut off corrupt recipient nations.

The bank openly addressed the topic of good government in its 1997 *World
Development Report*.[28] The report reexamined the importance of political institutions in the development process and set out an agenda for action to improve the
performance of governments.

Indicators of good government, such as accountability and transparency, the
rule of law, an independent judiciary, protection of property rights, a free press,
and bureaucratic competence, helped bank staffers derive measures of political misrule. From this data, it became possible to draw broad comparisons and
changes over time.

In 2000, the bank took stock of its post-1997 work on governance, gauging
how the bank could most effectively help client nations implement an agenda
of reforming public-sector institutions and strengthening good governance.[29]
While the reform of political institutions does not inexorably lead to good economic outcomes, it increases the likelihood of positive results. A strong causal
link has come to be seen between the bank's indices of sound governance and a
nation's economic growth and prosperity.

Between 2000 and 2006, the bank's support to improve governance rose, and
its assistance to promote economic reforms fell. In its 2006 fiscal year, the IDA,
for example, committed 28 percent of its total support, some $2.8 billion, to
public administration, including law and justice.[30] The bank's direct efforts were
mostly confined to poorer nations dependent on the IDA for grants and soft
loans. Middle-income countries with well-established political institutions generally did not want to cede any ground to outsiders such as the bank, rejecting
loans conditioned on political change.

The bank now openly uses political means to alleviate poverty. IDA money
flows to poorer countries based on two key criteria: how poor the country is and
how well it is run. Each year the bank's staff assesses the quality of each eligible
IDA borrower's performance. The IDA's performance criteria, more specifically,
its Country Performance Rating (CPR), is calculated as a weighted average of the
Country Policy and Institutional Assessment (CPIA) and the Annual Report on
Portfolio Performance (ARPP), with the former accorded a weight of 80 percent
and the latter 20 percent. The CPIA represents the average of a nation's score on
twenty indicators grouped into four clusters: economic management. structural
policies, policies for social inclusion and equity, and public sector management
and institutions. To produce the final CPR, the weighted average of the CPIA and
the ARPP is multiplied by a governance factor composed of seven governance
indicators.[31] Countries with better governance scores receive significantly more
IDA grants and soft loans while those lacking the capacity to manage their development and implement projects receive far less money.

However, the IDA does not completely shun corrupt, disastrously run nations.
Each of the poorer nations gets a "small" allocation of funds regardless of the

performance of its political institutions. Some also qualify for money from the bank's trust fund for failed nations, called "low-income countries under stress." Richer nations, even if badly run by corrupt leaders, can still borrow from the IBRD, the bank's commercial loan arm.

THE WORLD BANK UNDER WOLFOWITZ

Reflecting the need to marshal the bank's resources to achieve a limited number of objectives and not to further alienate disgruntled staffers by unnecessarily disrupting the bank's status quo, Wolfowitz sought to give the bank a clearer focus without offering a grand vision or one comprehensive blueprint for change. He emphasized five areas: extreme poverty alleviation, lessening corruption both in recipient nations and at the bank, partnering with developing countries, continuing to lend to middle-income countries, and increasing the funding for infrastructure projects.

Extreme Poverty Alleviation

Wolfowitz understood the dire need to focus the bank's efforts on facilitating economic and social development in the world's poorest nations, especially those in Africa; they particularly needed debt relief, increased aid, and lower trade barriers. He indicated, "A clear message from modern history is that this is a small world . . . and that leaving people behind is a formula for failure—for all of us."[32] For him, the bottom line of development is that poor nations' troubles could grow to affect the lives of people in the developed world. Moreover, from a national-security perspective, helping third world countries grow and develop could prevent more governmental failures that otherwise could lead to more terrorist bases.

Wolfowitz initially pledged to make poverty reduction his first priority, particularly in Africa; subsequently it became coupled with the goal of fighting corruption. Just before assuming the presidency, he noted, "I would find nothing more satisfying than, at the end of my tenure at this institution, to feel that we played a part in what hopefully could be a period that Africa went from being a continent of despair, to a continent of hope."[33] His zeal about Africa, a departure from his longtime obsession with the Middle East, underscored his transition from U.S. Deputy Secretary of Defense, an American civil servant, to World Bank president, an international civil servant.

Africa was the first continent Wolfowitz visited after he assumed leadership of the bank. Then, in September 2005, the bank launched the Africa Action Plan, one of Wolfowitz's first steps to fulfilling his commitment to make economic and social development in Africa top priority.[34] The bank designed the plan, which was initiated under Wolfensohn, to help African nations accelerate their economic growth, improve the lives of the poor and women, and achieve tangible results over three years (2006–8). The plan sets forth twenty-five concrete initiatives, focusing on four broad areas: first, building capable nations and improving governance; second, strengthening the drivers of growth including an enhanced private sector and expanding exports, investing in health and education infrastructure, and improving agricultural productivity; third, participating in and sharing economic growth; fourth, increasing the impact of partnerships among recipient governments, donor nations, and development agencies. It offers a variety of donor commitments, such as increased financial support for free primary education in fifteen countries and increased infrastructure funding. The plan translates priorities and directions into country-specific projects and sets out country-led strategies to implement these priorities. All the commitments made by donors and African nations to lift the continent out of poverty are consolidated into one action plan, which would be monitored on an annual basis.

Debt Relief

Wolfensohn recognized the need for multilateral debt relief as part of a global poverty alleviation strategy and gradually brought rich nations around to his position.[35] Wolfowitz actualized debt relief, visualizing it as a foundation, but not a panacea, for development. When leading industrial nations agreed to cancel billions of dollars of debt owed by some of the world's poorest nations, Wolfowitz's handicraft was clearly visible.

Wolfensohn's had achieved much, by the end of his tenure as president, by convincing the rich nations to accept the prospect of funding debt relief; however, negotiations had stalled for several weeks in the spring of 2005. The United States and the United Kingdom could not reconcile their differing views as to how to cancel the debts of eighteen, mostly African, nations. Wolfowitz's arrival at the bank seemed to encourage the United States to compromise and accept the U.K. strategy. In advocating the arrangement proposed by the British, he may have persuaded the Bush administration to put up extra cash to fund the write-off. Furthermore, the U.S. acceptance of the U.K. proposal seemed to embarrass the other G-7 members into following the U.S.-U.K. lead.

On June 11, 2005, at a meeting of the G-8, the world's leading economic powers, the finance ministers of the G-7 (the United States, the United Kingdom, Canada, Germany, France, Italy, and Japan) agreed to cancel $40 billion of World Bank, International Monetary Fund (IMF), and African Development Bank (ADB) debt owed by eighteen nations, including fourteen in Africa, thereby easing the drain of scarce funds from these impoverished debtor countries.[36] The heads of the G-8 nations in July 2005 ratified the debt-relief agreement.[37]

Keeping up with interest payments of their indebtedness had forced most of these eighteen nations to take a number of detrimental steps. For instance, as many countries partially funded their interest payments by charging tuition to attend public elementary schools, attendance rates, especially among girls, plummeted. Basic health care was often denied those who were unable to pay the entry fees levied at local clinics and hospitals. Moreover, countries often took out additional loans in order to cover the required interest payments, sending them further in a downward debt spiral. Freeing these countries from the crushing repayment burden allowed them to start with a clean slate.

The eighteen debtor countries owed the three international lenders some $55.6 billion. G-7 members agreed to compensate the bank and ADB for the principal and interest payments on the cancelled debt, thereby freeing funds with which the two institutions could make new loans. The G-7 cost to compensate the two lenders is estimated at $16.7 billion based on the principal and interest payments the lenders would have expected to receive from the debtor nations between 2005 and 2014. Replenishing the bank's and the ADB's reserves would cost the United States some $1.3 to $1.75 billion over ten years. The IMF would use some of its existing resources, but not its gold reserves, to cancel $6 billion it was owed by these poor nations.

In September, finance ministers from the 184 member nations of the bank endorsed the G-8 debt-relief agreement. Although most acknowledged that debt repayment imposed a crushing burden on those countries least able to deal with the added economic strain, several smaller European nations expressed the concern that the debt-relief proposal would leave the bank short of funds for its development mission.[38] In response to these concerns, the G-8 finance ministers sent a letter to Wolfowitz, pledging a public commitment not only to pay the principal and interest costs of the relieved debt to the bank over the next forty years, but also not to reduce their regular contributions to the IDA to make up for their debt forgiveness obligations.[39] Under the agreement, money paid to the IDA for debt relief would be counted separately from its general funding. Rich countries would compare their future contributions to the IDA with their funding levels after adjusting for inflation during the 2006–8 period. This benchmark for constant IDA funding in real terms before debt relief would indicate whether the wealthy nations were providing the extra funds to cover debt relief.

In the spring of 2006, the bank's executive directors and then the IDA's Board of Governors approved the debt-relief plan's financing and implementation details. On July 1, 2006, the Multilateral Debt Relief Initiative cancelled the IDA debt of seventeen of the world's poorest countries.[40]

Increased Aid

Wolfowitz emerged as a crucial ally for British Prime Minister Tony Blair, who saw an important role for increased aid to developing nations. Blair placed aid for Africa on the agenda at the G-8 July 2005 summit. Before the meeting, Wolfowitz stated, "I certainly hope to use my position at the bank to encourage increased resource commitments from the donors and certainly from the U.S."[41]

Blair sought a Marshall Plan for Africa. As proposed by Blair, wealthy nations would double their foreign aid, including an extra $25 billion per year for Africa, by 2010. At the July 2005 G-8 meeting, he obtained an agreement to gradually double aid by the G-8 nations for Africa in five years, reaching $50 billion in 2010,[42] which may, however, face a future compliance shortfall by these countries.[43]

Even with debt relief and increased aid, Wolfowitz remained skeptical that the only successful development path centers on developed nations giving poor nations enough money. Money, he stated, "is a necessary but far from sufficient condition."[44]

Lower Trade Barriers

Seeing the need for a more level trade playing field as a poverty-alleviation strategy, Wolfowitz sought to promote freer trade, particularly of agricultural products, among rich and poor nations. In the early years of the twenty-first century, wealthy nations spent some $280 billion a year subsidizing their farmers, with taxpayers paying $112 billion a year in direct subsidies and consumers paying $168 billion a year because of tariffs on agricultural imports, more than quadruple the total amount they spent on overseas aid.[45] By lowering the prices for agricultural goods in global markets, subsidies make it harder for farmers in poor nations to compete. High tariffs keep agricultural products from developing nations out of the wealthy markets. "Most important . . . is the responsibility of developed countries to open markets themselves and to reduce activities that distort markets," Wolfowitz stated, noting, "The sums of money that are spent on subsidies that take opportunities away from African farmers are staggering."[46]

In the fall of 2005, Wolfowitz, seeking to play a role in the public debate on trade, boosted the so-called Doha Development Round of world-trade talks, which are called the Doha Round because they started in Doha, Qatar at a 2001 World Trade Organization meeting there. Designed to help lift poor, developing nations out of poverty, the talks are called a development round.

The central part of the Doha Development Round focused on the need for rich nations to reduce protectionist practices for their own farmers, thereby helping developing nations gain more from world trade. Because third world nations are heavily agrarian, they often lack access to markets in rich countries. Recognizing that nations need to trade and sell goods to reduce poverty, Wolfowitz asserted, "It is trade, not aid, that holds the key to creating jobs and raising incomes. It is trade that will allow poor countries to generate growth; forgiving debt alone will not do that. It is trade that has helped 400m Chinese people escape poverty in the past 20 years and the same can happen elsewhere."[47]

Progress was agonizingly slow because decisions on multilateral trade issues must be made by consensus of all World Trade Organization (WTO) member countries. An enormous gap separated the United States from the European Union,[48] with the European Union balking at joining the United States and other major trading nations and blocs in offering more significant cuts in farm tariffs.[49]

In December 2005, representatives from the countries that make up the WTO met in Hong Kong and were unable to negotiate successfully on any major issue. With the continued spread of globalization, an increasing number of developing countries have entered the global marketplace, each bringing a divergent set of priorities and goals to the table. Finding a way to incorporate both the developed and developing nations' priorities into such a large multilateral agreement proved nearly impossible.[50]

Despite Wolfowitz's efforts in July 2006 to pressure the United States, leaders of European nations, Japan, Russia, China, and Brazil, among other countries, to make further compromises, the Doha Round collapsed.[51] At the time of writing, the Doha Round appears destined to be the first multilateral trade negotiations to fail since the 1930s. The failure of the global trade talks serves as a sign that post–World War II era of lessening trade barriers is coming to an end, with major powers striking more bilateral and regional trade partnerships.

Lessening Corruption

Wolfowitz reiterated that the emphasis on lessening corruption launched by Wolfensohn would be maintained. Realizing that grants or loans do not help people in corrupt, poorly governed nations, Wolfensohn had forcefully spoken out against corruption. Wolfowitz stated, "I like the legacy that Mr. Wolfensohn has left me and his emphasis on fighting corruption. If he had not done it I would have done [it]."[52] Realizing that good development policies require competent public-sector institutions to implement and deliver them, Wolfowitz frankly and continuously discussed the subject of corruption in his meetings with government leaders. Seeing corruption as a barrier to building democratic institutions in developing nations, he went as far as to suggest, "Corruption is the biggest threat to democracy since communism."[53] Battling graft became a top priority.

Wolfowitz knew the developing world and its problems, particularly corruption and cronyism, from his service as American ambassador to Indonesia. Corruption shows itself in many ways. Perhaps the most egregious is nepotism and patronage derived from political connections.

During his ambassadorial tenure, Wolfowitz fought and documented government corruption, an important learning experience for the bank presidency. He ended a U.S. food aid program because the wife of Suharto, the Indonesian dictator, profited from the program through her partial ownership of a flour mill that milled American wheat.[54]

Corruption not only rots public-sector institutions but also stunts economic growth and private investment by distorting economic markets, spiraling the costs of doing business, and encouraging people to apply their talents and energies to nonproductive tasks. Seeing that corruption harmed the level playing field on which development and prosperity depends, Ambassador Wolfowitz criticized government corruption in a 1989 farewell speech to the American Chamber of Commerce in Jakarta. "The cost of the high-cost [corrupt] economy remains too high," he stated. "For the private sector to flourish, special privilege must give way to equal risk for all."[55]

Looking back on his ambassadorial experience, Wolfowitz indicated he even learned some lessons from the bank's missteps in Indonesia, when the bank financed huge infrastructure projects during Suharto's presidency. The bank, Wolfowitz noted, "did some wonderful work" in Indonesia but "it didn't do enough to empower those advocating" better development strategies against the Suharto regime. Focusing on the corruption problem, he asserted, "The bank itself assessed that money had gone off to places it shouldn't have."[56]

In his first address to the annual meetings of the bank and the IMF in September 2005, Wolfowitz identified better leadership and more accountability in developing nations as key priorities. He stressed the need to address corruption and also strengthen checks and balances on governments, such as the rule of law and impartial judicial institutions, as well as enhancing civil-society organizations, which play an important role in building a bridge between citizens and their governments.[57] Realizing that economic development could not be separated from political development, particularly when it comes to issues such as corruption, he noted in July 2005, "[T]o the extent that corruption is an obstacle to development. . . . [o]ne of the best tools for combating corruption, in fact, is public exposure, and that obviously requires a press that is free to criticize."[58]

Under Wolfowitz, the bank sought to implement a hard-line policy against public-sector officials in recipient nations skimming off funds from any of its projects, and did not hesitate to make public examples of corrupt governments. Focusing on sub-Saharan Africa, Wolfowitz noted that corruption "is an incredibly crippling factor on countries' efforts to develop,"[59] diverting resources from the bank's clients, the world's desperately poor. Beginning in 2006, Wolfowitz acted, freezing (and even canceling) funds to African and Asian nations. Troubled by allegations of corruption on bank projects in Kenya, he froze $265 million in new loans to that nation. As part of a $2.9 billion debt-relief package, after an acrimonious meeting with his board, a compromise imposed anticorruption measures on the Republic of Congo, before debt relief would become irrevocable. Following evidence of graft in one healthcare project involving drug procurement, Wolfowitz also put on hold $800 million in new loans for healthcare projects in India. When it became clear that some bids were rigged, a $35 million loan to Bangladesh for road building was cancelled. Most dramatically, perhaps, in January 2006, the bank suspended grants and loan disbursements to Chad after the African nation went back on its 1999 commitment to the bank to use oil revenues for funding agreed-on development targets. Based on Chad's agreement that 72 percent of the country's oil revenues would be spent on priority sectors, including health, education, and rural development, with 10 percent of the revenues placed in a fund for future generations to ensure some benefits once the oil reserves were exhausted, the bank had funded part of the Chad-Cameroon oil pipeline project.[60]

In addition to addressing corruption in the bank's client nations, Wolfowitz also turned a spotlight on the bank's internal affairs and the dealings of its staffers and consultants. During his presidency, Wolfensohn had created a system designed to monitor not only bank-financed projects but also its personnel, which consists of the Department of Institutional Integrity (DII) and a separate sanctions committee. However, the DII under Wolfensohn was largely ineffective; when Wolfowitz took the helm, the department, with twenty-two investigators, had a backlog of nearly four hundred cases and it was severely underfunded.

Wolfowitz soon added $5 million to the DII's coffers and augmented its staff. When DII director Maarten de Jong retired in the fall of 2005, Wolfowitz appointed Suzanne Rich Folsom, as the acting and then the permanent head of the DII. In response to criticism, Wolfowitz maintained that he hired Folsom because he thought her competent, not because of her political affiliations, noting that the department under de Jong had been run with "very puzzling negligence" during the Wolfensohn era, and that staffers were angry because they felt more comfortable operating with a crippled DII overseeing them. Although Wolfowitz stressed that he believed that the vast majority of the bank's staff was honest, it seemed to him that the discontent with Folsom "comes from people who had gotten comfortable with an [Institutional Integrity] unit that has 387 open cases. I have a real problem with that."[61]

In April 2006, Wolfowitz announced a broad, long-term strategy to help third world nations combat corruption and halt fraud in bank-supported projects.[62] Rather than simply suspending loans where corruption was suspected, his plans to make fighting corruption pervasive throughout the Bank's operations ranged from the heightened monitoring of projects to an enhanced focus on reforming public-sector institutions, including the procurement process in order to make governments more accountable. To lessen corruption in bank-funded projects, the bank initiated the deployment of anticorruption teams to work with government auditors, among others, fighting corruption in recipient nations. The bank also changed the way it designs projects to emphasize incentives to combat corruption from the start. To help countries build institutions of accountability and the ability to combat corruption on their own, the bank increased the funds it allocates for judicial and civil-service reform and for media and freedom-of-information projects in developing countries. The bank also expanded its partnership with a range of groups, including the private-sector, multilateral development banks and civil-society organizations that have a stake in enhancing governance and lessening corruption. Wolfowitz emphasized that managers and staffers at the bank would be rewarded "as much for saying no to a bad loan as for getting a good one out the door."[63]

Then, in September 2006, the Development Committee, the highest policy-making body of the World Bank and the IMF, endorsed Wolfowitz's plan to crack down on corruption in the bank's lending, but with reservations. Wolfowitz's anticorruption policy had stirred unease among some European and developing nations, who were fearful that it might be overly punitive and result in fewer funds for poor countries. While supporting the anticorruption campaign, the Development Committee "stressed the importance of Board [of Executive Directors of the bank] oversight of the strategy as it is further developed and then implemented" and "emphasized that predictability, transparency, and consistent and equal treatment across member countries are the Bank's guiding principles."[64] This reflected European demands for objective criteria and developing countries' insistence on equal treatment. While Wolfowitz was pleased with the approval given him to proceed with a signature issue, the wording seemingly reflected some discomfort with his crackdown on corruption.

Partnering with Developing Countries

Wolfowitz reiterated that developing countries would be "treated as partners [rather] than clients," another theme of his predecessor. Gradually, the bank came to realize that foisting unwanted loans or grants upon unwilling countries would not facilitate development; third world countries had to take a greater degree of control over their progress. "The best approach is to put people in developing countries in the driver's seat," he indicated, adding that empowering local institutions and people often requires patience and humility.[65] In addition to the better coordinating development projects and aid programs, Wolfowitz wanted recipient governments to take a bigger role in deciding how the money would be spent, and then to judge such initiatives according to the specific needs of each country. Following a country ownership strategy, he realized that recipient nations needed good public-sector institutions and the political will to implement sound policy prescriptions. This approach requires the bank to ask a nation what its development targets and economic goals are and to listen to a trusted government in order to understand what is politically feasible. After hearing various approaches through a strategy of broad consultation, the bank would then analyze how it could help implement projects, offering expert advice as well as funds.

The country ownership strategy originated in the late 1990s. In 1998, the bank's research department concluded that the key to more successful projects centered on putting locals in developing countries in control, by first asking them what their own priorities were.[66] Reasoning that policies and programs must be owned by countries, not imposed on them by the bank, Wolfensohn had sought to make the bank more responsive to the concerns of its recipient nations. Allowing countries with a proven track record to set and manage their own comprehensive, participatory development strategies and priorities and then cooperate with other bilateral and multilateral agencies, including U.N. agencies, regional developmental banks, and international and local NGOs, would, in theory, help in implementing projects and facilitating governmental reforms.

Despite the bank's best intentions, a gap continues to exist between the rhetoric and the reality. Although the bank's staff increasingly brings a greater degree of respect for and willingness to partner with local efforts, the bank often expects to remain in control of setting priorities and selecting projects to meet these priorities. Many of the poorest nations continue to lack the institutions and the will to assume the requisite degree of responsibility for the implementation of a country ownership strategy. The bank could only reach those nations with interested, competent, noncorrupt governments, ones committed to the assessment of priorities and to project selection and implementation.

Another problem stems from the fact that even competent governments often do not have the resources to make the broad, in-depth policy studies the bank requires. In 1999, the bank began requiring countries to submit Poverty Reduction Strategy Papers (PRSP) designed to streamline the grant and lending process. As a national plan, PRSPs contain a detailed description of a country's development strategies, as well as an in-depth account of donor funding for each strategy. Furthermore, the conclusions contained in a country's PRSP must be supported by a broad, participatory agreement among its civil society, its private sector, and its national government.[67] Many poorer nations do not have the time, budget, or expertise to construct a PRSP. Among those PRSPs that are prepared, these documents often reflect what each country believes the bank wants, not a nation's own priorities.

Given the realities in the third world, the bank ought to continue to play an active role in helping formulate poor countries' priorities and strategies. Although the bank ought not to mechanically impose its agenda on poor nations that have no choice but to accept it, the bank has the resources to develop effective strategies and projects, whereas most poorer countries do not. It would be foolhardy and wasteful to give or lend large sums to governments having no idea how to spend the funds or lacking the discipline to spend the funds well.

Continuing to Lend to Middle-Income Nations

Wolfowitz hoped to make World Bank loans more attractive to fast-growing developing nations. Under Wolfensohn, the appeal of loans by the bank to middle-income nations, such as China and India, with access to international capital markets, declined. Bank-imposed environmental and social safeguards, designed to limit the adverse impact of infrastructure projects and restore the bank's reputation, particularly among nongovernmental organizations, raised the cost of borrowing and imposed delays on borrowers. Thus, loans became less appealing to countries able to raise funds from other sources.

As a result of the long time lag between a government's initiating a loan request and its approval, and the accompanying administrative burdens, such as compliance with environmental and social safeguards, the bank's lending to middle-income countries over ten years, from fiscal 1995 though fiscal 2004, for example, fell from $15–$18 billion to $10 billion a year.[68] During this period, the bank became more of an IDA institution, lending or giving to poor nations.

Technical assistance is included with the bank's funding. Technical assistance became necessary after the well-documented human-rights and environmental problems caused by project loans in the 1980s, and is included to safeguard the environment, protect workers, and empower indigenous peoples. Critics of bank loans to middle-income nations estimate the cost of the bank's technical advice at 3 to 4 percent of the borrowed funds per year.[69] When the cost of compliance with the bank's standards exceeds the interest rate subsidy, the subsidy disappears and middle-income borrowing nations vanish.

Wolfowitz's efforts to reverse this trend rested on two factors: idealism and practicality. From an idealistic perspective, two-thirds of the world's poor live in middle-income countries, with China and India accounting for some 45 percent of the total.[70] In October, 2005, Wolfowitz defended the continuation of IBRD loans to China, seeing that nation still needed assistance in the form of loans on commercial terms, as it strove to lift tens of millions of people out of poverty. He noted, "For all of the huge success, there is a lot of poverty in [China]." He continued, "While the government has huge resources to tackle that and we [the bank] only bring an addition at the margin in some respects, it is a very important margin."[71]

He also took pride that the World Bank could be a vehicle for learning, even for China, indicating that senior Chinese officials told him, "It's what we learn from the relationship [with the bank]," the soft factor. Noting the importance of building strong public-sector institutions in middle-income countries, he pointed to an answer from a midlevel official in the Chinese Ministry of Finance, who stated, "When we launched our economic reform program, we learned that we needed to introduce modern accounting standards."[72] As part of a bank program to build a cadre of accountants, who, in turn, would be knowledgeable about modern accounting standards, this official spent one year in the United States training with private accounting firms.

On the graduation of the Czech Republic from needing bank assistance in February 2006, Wolfowitz reiterated the importance of middle-income nations to the bank's mission of fighting poverty. He stated:

> [T]hey are valuable not only for the lessons of experience.
>   When countries like [the Czech Republic] open your borders to goods and migrant workers from poorer neighbors, middle-income countries bring stability and prosperity to their region. . . .
>   Middle-income countries also help integrate markets and contribute to the upgrading of shared roads and infrastructure.[73]

A bottom-line financial strategy also entered into Wolfowitz's approach. The bank uses revenues from the interest on loans to middle-income countries to keep it in business and finance its operations elsewhere, including heavily subsidizing interest rates on loans to the world's poorest nations, sustaining its professional expertise, and financing its administrative activities.[74] The continued decline in middle-income country borrowing would lessen the bank's financial independence and make it more reliant on grants from developed donor nations, which, in turn, would make it more vulnerable to pressure from these countries in its overall strategies and its decision-making process.[75]

In sum, the bank's financial model depends on its continuing to lend funds to middle-income nations. Middle-income borrowers are good for the bank because these loans are likely to be repaid. However, the bank's efforts to retain middle-income borrowers drain funds otherwise available for the poorest nations.

Increased Funding for Infrastructure Projects

Returning the bank to its historic roots, Wolfowitz placed more emphasis on infrastructure projects, such as roads, bridges, and power plants, than did his predecessor, who seemed not to care about concrete. During Wolfensohn's reign, project lending declined by 40 percent.[76]

Infrastructure projects often presented environmental problems and human-rights violations, such as the demolition of villages and involuntary relocation of entire groups of indigenous peoples. Bowing to pressure from nongovernmental organizations and their strident incarnation, advocacy pressure groups, under Wolfensohn, the bank moved away from infrastructure projects in favor of less controversial areas, such as health, education, and other social-capital projects, including empowering the poor.[77] The bank also lessened its funding of infrastructure projects because of problems with corruption in project procurement and implementation. However, the bank may have come to accord excessive influence to NGOs at the expense of its real clients, the populace of poor nations.

Toward the end of Wolfensohn's tenure, it became apparent that noninfrastructure project lending and grants had not brought about the expected results. A 2005 report by the bank's Operations Evaluation Department, an internal watchdog unit, concluded that the bank's health and education programs, despite increased funding, had "fallen short of bringing about qualitative and sustainable improvements in human development outcomes such as better learning achievement and improved health status."[78] Moreover, the expansion of health and education systems often encounter management and human-resource limitations in developing countries.

"Infrastructure," Wolfowitz said, "has fallen too far out of fashion. Development is not just pouring concrete, but it does require concrete and water and electricity."[79] In his September 2005 presidential address to the annual meetings of the bank and the IMF, he noted, "One of the most persistent messages I have heard during the past few months from people in developing countries, poor and rich, citizens and leaders alike, was the need to restore our role in infrastructure investment." He continued, "Infrastructure is a lifeline to many other things: to healthcare, to education, to jobs, to trade."[80]

Lacking electricity, roads, and ports to move goods to market, farmers, entrepreneurs, and larger businesses are hamstrung and cannot realize their potential. Furthermore, a solid infrastructure foundation is requisite to introducing foreign capital effectively into a developing economy. Encouraging foreign investment represents part of the bank's development package; however, a private company is unlikely to turn a sufficient profit in a country with inadequate roads or electricity. Thus, the bank needs to deliver infrastructure projects if it intends to fight poverty and promote economic growth. These big infrastructure projects also mesh with the bank's multidisciplinary nature across a range of topics, including engineering, analysis of environmental and social impacts, and financing, as well as its country-specific knowledge and expertise.

Refocusing on infrastructure and, more broadly, on economic growth, and cutting back on social programs may, however, be difficult. Caving into pressure from NGOs and Western activists, the bank under Wolfensohn adopted cumbersome environmental and social safeguards for infrastructure projects.

ASKING THE BIGGER QUESTIONS

Wolfowitz's move to the bank came at a time when experts again asked fundamental questions about what effectively pulls nations out of poverty. As Wolfowitz noted at a meeting with reporters just before assuming the bank's presidency, "There's been a healthy change in the development approach. It's no longer one size fits all."[81] Beyond a country's macroeconomic health based upon sound monetary policy and low tax rates, the keys to poverty-reducing, sustainable economic growth and development vary from nation to nation. A focused, piecemeal problem-solving approach, relying on on-the-ground feedback from locals to figure out what works, may provide the best chance of success.[82] Wolfowitz stated, "I think one of the lessons of the development experience of the last 40 years is there is no single unified theory of development that can explain or predict everything, and that countries and institutions that adapt, that reinforce success and correct failure will do best. So I want to sustain the efforts to measure results and strengthen that effort as much as possible."[83]

In short, a need exists to tailor the bank's loans and grants to each recipient nation's needs and to focus more on results rather than on good intentions or getting money out the door. Reviewing which bank programs are effective and analyzing why they work will enable the bank to retain and expand successful programs. Conversely, programs that are ineffective ought to be curtailed, if not eliminated. The bank's own analysts or outside experts can perform the necessary evaluations.

In addition to this analytical work, bank funds ought to be distributed with greater selectivity at the country level and with an enhanced focus on the private sector, particularly strengthening microfinance institutions in developing nations. The bank's current policy logically leans toward giving more funds to well-governed countries and less to corrupt, thuggish, or incompetent governments. The bank ought to reward countries with track records for using funds well. Specifically, it ought to direct IDA loans and grants to nations with good governance institutions, marked by an absence of corruption, the existence of transparent and accountable public finances, and a striving to raise living standards. Following the country ownership strategy, the bank ought to take this trend further and not only provide more funds to well-governed nations, particularly those with a significant internal demand for strong institutions, whether by a small elite or, hopefully, a broader civil society, but also reward them by allowing them more autonomy and less bank oversight regarding how the money is spent. This approach would not only free up bank resources, but also help lessen the more successful countries' resentment at being "nannied" unnecessarily by the bank and the delays that go hand-in-hand in moving project proposals through a large bureaucracy.

Conversely, less well-governed nations, those that are either corrupt or ineffective because of bad policies or weak implementation, require a different approach. The bank has traditionally sought to control such governments' actions by attaching conditions that require various stringent reforms. However, promises made by governments too weak, inept, or corrupt to keep them are meaningless; corrupt nations will discount them, as did Chad, and weak governments become even weaker as their dependency on the bank grows. Because attaching conditions generally does not work, funds need to be given more selectively. The bank ought to simply stop lending or making grants to corrupt nations and other nations that achieve little because of self-defeating policies and incompetent governments. Historically, loans and grants given to such countries are rarely effective, and the bank's resources would be better used to provide technical assistance to these nations.

As with loans and grants generally, incentives ought to play a larger role with respect to infrastructure projects. More funds ought to be available in the future to nations that successfully complete projects in a timely, noncorrupt manner. In short, a need exists to provide incentives for countries to perform and succeed.

The role of private investment and enterprise creation in the development process needs clarification and expansion. Funds ought to promote a climate conducive to a dynamic, productive private sector, particularly for indigenous private investors.

In this context, Wolfowitz sought to get the IFC more engaged in small-, rather than big-business, funding. Under Wolfensohn, the bank began to shift more resources to private-sector projects in the developing world designed to fight poverty. Wolfowitz saw the need for an increased emphasis on small-business creation.[84] He noted:

A vibrant private sector is the most important engine of growth and job creation.
    One of the biggest obstacles to the growth of small and medium businesses is lack of credit. The Bank Group has provided sound policy advice to support micro-lending, but we need to explore innovative ways to expand access to financial services, including both local and regional needs and approaches.[85]

In addition to increased infrastructure funding, the bank ought to focus its resources on micro-capitalism, a low-end development strategy, particularly as a means to improve women's access to credit and education. Micro-credit lending originated in South Asia in the 1970s with the advent of the Grameen Bank in Bangladesh. Micro-lending agencies, which have spread all over the world, give small loans, as low as $25, to poor persons, who have not been traditionally served by commercial banks. Borrowers use the funds to establish businesses, such as making handicrafts or buying livestock or seed and fertilizers for family farms, thereby creating opportunities for themselves and jobs for others.[86]

The World Bank Group's Micro-Finance Initiative currently exceeds $1 billion. Of this total, the IFC has a micro-finance portfolio of $256 million, reaching over 1.3 million clients in 38 countries, with a projected portfolio of $500 million by fiscal year 2006.[87] While remaining cognizant of the limits regarding absorptive capacity and the management of micro-credit lending organizations, the bank ought to expand its initiatives to provide financial services and offer a range of products to the broadest possible numbers of people, focusing initially on those with the greatest need.

Micro-credit borrowers need businesses to run. Large companies realize they need inexpensive ways to distribute their products to the bottom of the economic pyramid. In 2002, Hindustan Lever Ltd., Unilever PLC's Indian subsidiary, approached the Andhra Pradesh state government and requested access to clients of the state-run micro-credit program. The government agreed to establish a pilot project that quickly grew and expanded to twelve Indian states. The project, known as the Project Shakti, provides a livelihood for hundreds of thousands of Indian women who sell Unilever products in their villages. The company helps train them and provides local marketing support. A micro-loan of $200 to buy sachets of soap, toothpaste, and shampoo helps the budding female entrepreneurs start their own businesses.[88]

Micro-credit and its accompanying services, such as savings plans, crop and life insurance, and money transfers, today bracketed under the category of micro-finance, have proven especially useful for women. In some nations, such as Bangladesh, women represent some 90 percent of micro-credit borrowers. Micro-lending has contributed to the social inclusion of women as well as improving their living standards. By freeing children from the need to work, the profits from these businesses help send poor women's children, especially daughters, to school in large numbers. Thus, micro-credit helps promote the education of girls, an important poverty alleviation strategy.

Wolfowitz has stressed the importance of making more women partners in the process of development and poverty alleviation. He strongly backed gender equality in primary and secondary education, noting, "I've seen in my travels the unmistakable role women play—not only in improving the lives of their children and families but also in revitalizing their communities and contributing to their countries' economic progress. All they need is opportunity. It is time we do everything we can to help them get it."[89]

In the first months of his presidency, Wolfowitz witnessed firsthand the importance of women's self-help groups in India. The statewide creation of some five hundred thousand women's self-help groups in the Indian state of Andhra

Pradesh helped women not only improve their livelihoods, educate their children, and buy assets, but also campaign against oppressive social practices and become a force for development in their villages. As Wolfowitz stated in a visit to India:

> But something else even more remarkable seems to have happened, which is that these women have learned by helping one another how to give voice to their concerns that go far beyond material concerns and that they have been able to defend their rights as women, to defend their rights as underprivileged classes in society in a way that probably couldn't have been imagined when this program started 10 years ago.[90]

Recognizing the impact of the self-help group in this one Indian state, the bank approved $260 million to fund a new program for self-help groups that gives rural Indian women one rupee (two U.S. cents) a day to save toward starting a small business, provided they can set aside the same amount themselves.[91]

When Wolfowitz left the Pentagon to become president of the World Bank Group, he changed his stick for a carrot as his tool for making the world a better place. Although his nomination was fraught with controversy, many of his initial opponents came to understand that he had abandoned his ties to Washington when he made the move, and that his commitment to development was sincere. Wolfowitz's framework reflected a return to the basics of development, focusing on poverty alleviation, increased infrastructure funding, and maintaining the bank's resources by continuing to lend to middle-income nations. His passion for democracy became apparent in the fervor with which he promoted his main initiative: reducing corruption in recipient nations.

Postscript

After reaching a March 2007 accord with the board's executive board on a revised anti-corruption strategy, Wolfowitz's difficulties boiled over the next month. He came under fire for the special professional arrangements he made for his romantic interest, Shaha Ali Riza, who worked at the bank when he assumed the presidency.

In the summer of 2005, after reviewing the matter, the board's ethics committee concluded that Ms. Riza should be transferred to a position outside of Wolfowitz's supervision to avoid any conflict of interest and that she be compensated for the damage to her career. It instructed him to work out the details. An outside law firm approved the terms of Ms. Riza's pay and promotion arrangement, which Wolfowitz dictated to the bank's human resources department, in exchange for her temporarily leaving her position at the bank during his tenure. She was then detailed to a post at the U.S. State Department.

Although Wolfowitz apologized for his role in arranging for the package, the bank's Development Committee, its highest policy making body, expressed "great concern" about the matter and its impact on the institution's mandate, its credibility, and staff morale. While the bank's executive board reviewed the situation, leaving it to Wolfowitz to resign, he dug in, stating that the bank "has important work to do, and I will continue to do it."

If he remains as president, Wolfowitz faces two huge tasks. First, he must rebuild his sometimes rocky, now nearly broken, relationship with the bank's Staff Association, particularly its leaders. Second, over the next three years, he must raise more than $30 billion from donor nations for the bank's International Development Association.

Wolfowitz's ongoing difficulties at the bank stem from three broader sources. First, some European nations, led by France and Germany, want the bank presidency to go to one of their own. Second, Wolfowitz's opponents, including certain European nations and Staff Association leaders, among others, dislike his anti-corruption campaign. They want to shame rich nations into providing ever-increasing amounts of aid to developing countries but cynically turn a "blind eye" to corruption which diminishes poverty alleviation efforts. Third, his opponents, who dislike an assertive American foreign policy, want to force the United States to become more accepting of the international status quo.

Notes

CHAPTER 1.   INTRODUCTION

1. See, e.g., Jane Perlez, "Iraq Shadow Government Cools Its Heels in Kuwait," *New York Times*, April 3, 2003, sec. B.

2. Paul D. Wolfowitz, Committee on Armed Services Form, Biographical and Financial Information Requested of Nominees, Part A—Biographical Information, February 15, 2001, in Senate Armed Services Committee, *Nominations before the Senate Armed Services Committee*, 107th Cong., 1st sess., Senate Hearing 107–749, February 27, 2001, 288–89.

3. Eric Schmitt, "The Busy Life of Being a Lightning Rod for Bush," *New York Times*, April 22, 2002, sec. A. See also Deputy Secretary of Defense Paul Wolfowitz, "Interview with New York Times," April 18, 2002, *U.S. Department of Defense*, http://www.defenselink.mil/Transcripts/archive.aspx (accessed September 7, 2005).

4. Mark Bowden, "Wolfowitz: The Exit Interviews," *Atlantic Monthly*, July–August 2005, 120.

5. Thomas E. Ricks, "As Critics Zero In, Paul Wolfowitz Is Unflinching on Iraq Policy," *Washington Post*, December 23, 2003, sec. C. James Fallows, *Blind into Baghdad: America's War in Iraq* (New York: Vintage, 2006), 3–4, offers a critique of the Nazi analogy, seeing World War I as a more apt parallel.

6. Norman Podhoretz, "World War IV: How It Started, What It Means, and Why We Have to Win," *Commentary*, September 2004, 17–54. See also Joseph Rago, "Unrepentant Neocon," *Wall Street Journal*, August 12–13, 2006, sec. A.

7. Paul Wolfowitz, "Glasnost in Order on Regional Clashes," *Wall Street Journal*, November 7, 1989.

8. See, e.g., Stephen Kinzer, *Overthrow: America's Century of Regime Change From Hawaii to Iraq* (New York: Times Books/Henry Holt and Co., 2006); Lloyd C. Gardner and Marilyn B. Young, eds., *The New American Empire: A 21st Century Teach-In on U.S. Foreign Policy* (New York: New Press, 2005). The classic work detailing American foreign policy as rooted in economic growth, expansion, and the scramble for new markets and

raw materials is William Appleman Williams, *The Tragedy of American Diplomacy* (Cleveland: World Publishing Co., 1959). Paul M. Buhle and Edward Rice-Maximin, *William Appleman Williams: The Tragedy of Empire* (New York: Routledge, 1995), surveys the life of a historian who rejected the conventional wisdom.

CHAPTER 2.   THE PERSONAL AND INTELLECTUAL ROOTS OF PAUL WOLFOWITZ'S WORLDVIEW

1. I have drawn on David Dudley, "Paul's Choice," *Cornell Alumni Magazine*, July–August 2004, 48–57; James Mann, *Rise of the Vulcans: The History of Bush's War Cabinet* (New York: Viking, 2004), 22–36.

2. "Bibliographical Note on Jacob Wolfowitz," in *Selected Papers of Jacob Wolfowitz*, ed. Jack Kiefer (New York: Springer-Verlag, 1980), vii–viii; *Dictionary of Scientific Biography*, vol. 18, supplement 2, ed. Frederic L. Holmes (New York: Charles Scribner's, 1970), 996–97.

3. Wolfowitz, "Interview with New York Times."

4. Deputy Secretary of Defense Paul Wolfowitz, "Interview with Los Angeles Times," April 29, 2002, *U.S. Department of Defense*, http://www.defenselink.mil/Transcripts/archive.aspx (accessed September 7, 2005).

5. John Hersey, *Hiroshima* (New York: Alfred A. Knopf, 1946).

6. For background on the Telluride House, see Beatrice MacLeod, "The House That Nunn Built," *Cornell Alumni News*, September 1982, 24–25 and Brad Edmondson, "The House of Triple-I," *Cornell Magazine*, March–April 1997, 42–48.

7. Allan Bloom, *The Closing of the American Mind: How Higher Education Has Failed Democracy and Impoverished the Souls of Today's Students* (New York: Simon and Schuster, 1987). See also Walter Nicgorski, "Allan Bloom: Strauss, Socrates, and Liberal Education," in *Leo Strauss, the Straussians and the American Regime*, ed. Kenneth L. Deutsch and John A. Murley (Lanham, MD: Rowman and Littlefield, 1999), 205–19; Jim Sleeper, "Allan Bloom and the Conservative Mind," *New York Times Book Review*, September 4, 2005, 27.

8. Deputy Secretary of Defense Paul Wolfowitz, "Interview with Sam [Tanenhaus], Vanity Fair," May 10, 2003, *U.S. Department of Defense*, http://www.defenselink.mil/Transcripts/archive.aspx (accessed June 13, 2005).

9. Quoted in Dudley, "Paul's Choice," 54.

10. Wolfowitz, "Tanenhaus Interview."

11. Bill Keller, "The Sunshine Warrior," *New York Times Magazine*, September 22, 2002, 54.

12. Paul Wolfowitz, "Statesmanship in the New Century," in *Present Dangers: Crisis and Opportunity in American Foreign and Defense Policy*, ed. Robert Kagan and William Kristol (San Francisco: Encounter Books, 2000), 315.

13. Mann, *Vulcans*, 53.

14. Keller, "Sunshine Warrior," 54. See also Todd S. Purdum, *A Time of Our Choosing: America's War in Iraq* (New York: Times Books, 2003), 14.

15. Richard M. Pfeffer, ed. *No More Vietnams? The War and the Future of American Foreign Policy* (New York: Harper and Row, 1968), 138. See also Albert Wohlstetter, "On Vietnam and Bureaucracy," appendix on Mini-Brute Force in Vietnam, July 17, 1968 (revised), *RAND Corporation*, http://www.rand.org/publications/classics/wohlstetter/D17276.1/D17276.1.html (accessed October 27, 2005).

16. Mann, *Vulcans*, 53.

17. Wolfowitz, "Tanenhaus Interview."

18. Mann, *Vulcans*, 26.

19. Ibid., 29.

20. Wolfowitz, "Tanenhaus Interview."

21. Fred Kaplan, *The Wizards of Armageddon* (New York: Simon and Schuster, 1983), 89–110, 117–24. See also Khurram Husain, "Neocons: The Men behind the Curtains," *Bulletin of the Atomic Scientists* 50, no. 6 (November/December 2003): 63–67.

22. Paul D. Wolfowitz, "Nuclear Proliferation in the Middle East: The Politics and Economics of Proposals for Nuclear Desalting" (Ph.D. diss., University of Chicago, 1972). See also Paul D. Wolfowitz, "Nuclear Desalting in the Middle East," in *Communication in International Politics*, ed. Richard L. Merritt (Urbana: University of Illinois Press, 1972), 339–60.

23. Wolfowitz, "Nuclear Proliferation," 35.

24. Deputy Secretary of Defense Paul Wolfowitz, "Interview with Baltimore Sun," April 12, 2002, *U.S. Department of Defense*, http://www.defenselink.mil/Transcripts/archive.aspx (accessed September 7, 2005). See also Deputy Secretary of Defense Paul Wolfowitz, "Interview with Baltimore Sun," April 26, 2002, *U.S. Department of Defense*, http://www.defenselink.mil/Transcripts/archive.aspx (accessed September 7, 2005).

25. Paul H. Nitze, with Ann M. Smith and Steven L. Rearden, *From Hiroshima to Glasnost: At the Center of Decision* (New York: Grove Weidenfeld, 1989), 294–95. For background on the formation of the Committee to Maintain a Prudent Defense Policy see Kaplan, *Wizards*, 136–41, 343–55, 388; Strobe Talbott, *The Master of the Game: Paul Nitze and the Nuclear Peace* (New York: Alfred A. Knopf, 1988); Jay Winik, *On the Brink: The Dramatic, Behind-the-Scenes Saga of the Reagan Era and the Men and Women Who Won the Cold War* (New York: Simon and Schuster, 1996), 52–53; William Beecher, "Acheson Group Seeks 'Balanced' Defense Debate," *New York Times*, May 27, 1969.

26. Robert G. Kaufman, *Henry M. Jackson: A Life in Politics* (Seattle: University of Washington Press, 2000), 211. See also Deputy Secretary of Defense Paul Wolfowitz, "Remarks on the Receipt of Henry M. (Scoop) Jackson Distinguished Service Award," November 18, 2002, *U.S. Department of Defense*, http://www.defenselink.mil/Transcripts/archive.aspx (accessed December 4, 2005); James Bamford, *A Pretext For War: 9/11, Iraq and the Abuse of America's Intelligence Agencies* (New York: Doubleday, 2004), 275.

27. Nitze, *From Hiroshima*, 295.

28. *Congressional Record* 115, no. 17 (August 6, 1969): S22497–98. See also Warren Weaver Jr., "Nixon Missile Plan Wins in Senate by a 51–50 Vote," *New York Times*, August 7, 1969.

29. "Treaty between the United States of America and the Union of Soviet Socialist Republics on the Limitation of Anti-Ballistic Missile Systems," signed by President Richard Nixon and Leonid I. Brezhnev, General Secretary of the Central Committee of the Central Committee of the CPSU, on May 26, 1972, ratified by the U.S. Senate on August 3, 1972, and entered into force on October 3, 1972, *United States Treaties and Other International Agreements* 23 (1972): 3437–47.

30. Wolfowitz, "Tanenhaus Interview." See also Paul Wolfowitz, "A Bomber for Uncertain Times," *Wall Street Journal*, June 12, 1995, sec. A. Andrew J. Bacevich, *The New American Militarism: How Americans Are Seduced by War* (New York: Oxford University Press, 2005), 158–63, summarizes Wohlstetter's efforts to reconceptualize warfare.

31. Winik, *On the Brink*, 120–21.

32. Steven V. Roberts, "Haig Is Confirmed by Senate, 93 to 6," *New York Times*, January 22, 1981, sec. B.

33. Mann, *Vulcans*, 109.

34. Deputy Secretary of Defense, Paul Wolfowitz, "Interview with Business Week," December 18, 2001, *U.S. Department of Defense*, http://www.defenselink.mil/Transcripts/archive.aspx (accessed September 7, 2005).

35. Mann, *Vulcans*, 231 and "Adviser Comments on Bob Dole's International Policy," *CNN*, September 4, 1996, Transcript #1279-12.

36. *National Defense Authorization Act for Fiscal Year 1997*, Public Law 104-201, Title XIII, Subtitle B, September 23, 1996.

37. Executive Summary of the *Report of the Commission to Assess the Ballistic Missile Threat to the United States*, July 15, 1998, *Federation of American Scientists*, http://www.fas.org/irp/threat/bm-threat.htm (accessed November 30, 2005). See also Mann, *Vulcans*, 241–42; Eric Schmidt, "Panel Says U.S. Faces Risk of a Surprise Missile Attack," *New York Times*, July 16, 1998, sec. A; Michael Killian, "Panel Disputes CIA Assessment, Fears Attack by Rogue States," *Chicago Tribune*, July 16, 1998; Richard L. Garwin, "What We Did," *Bulletin of the Atomic Scientists* 54, no. 6 (November/December 1998): 40–45.

38. Mann, *Vulcans*, 249.

39. Ibid., 251. See also John Lancaster and Terry M. Neal, "Heavyweight 'Vulcans' Help Bush Forge a Foreign Policy," *Washington Post*, November 19, 1999, sec. A; Eric Schmidt, "A Cadre of Familiar Foreign Policy Experts Is Putting Its Imprint on Bush," *New York Times*, December 23, 1999, sec. A.

40. Mann, *Vulcans*, 253.

41. Rowan Scarborough, *Rumsfeld's War: The Untold Story of America's Anti-Terrorist Commander* (Washington, DC: Regnery, 2004), 39.

42. Wolfowitz, "Baltimore Sun April 26 Interview."

CHAPTER 3.   WOLFOWITZ, THE PRACTICAL IDEALIST

1. Richard Pipes, "Team B: Reality behind the Myth," *Commentary*, October 1986, 25–40; Nitze, *From Hiroshima*, 530–35; David Binder, "New C.I.A. Estimate Finds Soviet Seeks Superiority in Arms," *New York Times*, December 26, 1975. Anne Hessing Cahn, *Killing Detente: The Right Attacks the CIA* (University Park: Pennsylvania State University Press, 1998), 138–40, 148–52, 155–57, critically chronicles the birth of Team B, its membership, and its workings.

2. Ivo H. Daalder and James M. Lindsay, *America Unbound: The Bush Revolution in Foreign Policy* (Washington, DC: Brookings Institution Press, 2003), 26.

3. Report of Team "B," "Intelligence Community Experiment in Competitive Analysis: Alternative View," December 1, 1976, *Central Intelligence Agency*, http://www.foia.cia.gov/ (accessed September 19, 2005). See also Don Oberdorfer, "Report Saw Soviet Buildup for War," *Washington Post*, October 12, 1992, sec. A; Cahn, *Killing Detente*, 165; Keller, "Sunshine Warrior," 55.

4. Cahn, *Killing Detente*, 165; Keller, "Sunshine Warrior," 55.

5. Jack Davis, "The Challenge of Managing Uncertainty: Paul Wolfowitz on Intelligence Policy-Relations," *Studies in Intelligence* 39, no. 5 (1996), www.odci.gov/csi/studies/96unclass/davis.htm (accessed June 21, 2005).

6. Wolfowitz, "Tanenhaus Interview." See also Gary J. Schmitt and Abram N. Shulsky, "Leo Strauss and the World of Intelligence (by Which We Do Not Mean *Nous*)" in Deutsch and Marley, *Leo Strauss*, 410–11.

7. I have drawn on Senate Select Committee on Intelligence, *Report On the U.S. Intelligence Community's Prewar Intelligence Assessments on Iraq*, 108th Cong., 1st sess., July 7, 2004, 307–12; "Briefing on Policy and Intelligence Matters," June 4, 2003, *U.S. Department of Defense*, http://www.defenselink.mil/Transcripts/archive.aspx (accessed December 1, 2005); Secretary of Defense Donald Rumsfeld, "Press Briefing," October 24, 2002, *Federation of American Scientists*, http://www.fas.org/irp/news/2002/10/dod102502.html (accessed December 4, 2005). See also James Risen, *State of War: The Secret History of the CIA and the Bush Administration* (New York: Free Press, 2006), 73; Daniel Benjamin and Steven Simon, *The Next Attack: The Failure of the War on Terror and a Strategy for Getting It Right* (New York: Times Books/Henry Holt, 2005), 167–70; James Bamford, *A Pretext For War: 9/11, Iraq, and the Abuse of America's Intelligence Agencies* (New York: Doubleday, 2004), 287–91, 317–18; James Risen, "How Pair's Finding on Terror Led to Clash on Shaping Intelligence," *New York Times*, April 28, 2004, sec. A; Dana Priest, "Feith's Analysts Given a Clean Bill," *Washington Post*, March 14, 2004, sec. A; Dana Priest, "Pentagon Shadow Loses Some Mystique," *Washington Post*, March 13, 2004, sec. A; Greg Miller, "Spy Unit Skirted CIA on Iraq," *Los Angeles Times*, March 10, 2004, sec. A; Eric Schmitt, "Aide Denies Shaping Data to Justify War," *New York Times*, June 5, 2003, sec. A; Senate Armed Services Committee, *Report of an Inquiry into Alternative Analysis of the Issue of an Iraq-al Qaeda Relationship by Senator Carl Levin* (D-MI), Ranking Member, October 21, 2004; Robert Dreyfuss, "The Pentagon Muzzles the CIA," *American Prospect*, December 16, 2002, 26–29.

8. Senate Select Committee on Intelligence, *Report*, 307.

9. Ibid. See also Peter J. Boyer, "The Believer," *New Yorker*, November 1, 2004, 52.

10. Senate Select Committee on Intelligence, *Report*, 308.

11. Ibid., 309.

12. Ibid.

13. Quoted in Eric Schmitt and Thom Shanker, "A C.I.A. Rival," *New York Times*, October 24, 2002, sec. A.

14. Priest, "Feith's Analysts." See also Bamford, *Pretext for War*, 318.

15. Mann, *Vulcans*, 78–80.

16. Ibid., 80; Michael R. Gordon and Bernard E. Trainor, *The Generals' War: The Inside Story of the Conflict in the Gulf* (Boston: Little, Brown, 1995), 6–9, 480 n2.

17. Mann, *Vulcans*, 81(emphasis omitted); Gordon and Trainor, *Generals' War*, 480 n. 2.

18. Mann, *Vulcans*, 82.

19. Ibid., 87.

20. Steve Coll, "Paul Wolfowitz, Devising U.S. Policy in a Turbulent Time," *Washington Post*, February 7, 1986, sec. D.

21. Mann, *Vulcans*, 87–88.

22. Ibid., 88–89.

23. James Earl Carter, "The State of the Union," January 23, 1980, *Weekly Compilation of Presidential Documents* 16, no. 4 (January 28, 1980): 197. President Carter's policies were set forth in Secret Presidential Directive, PD NSC-63, "Persian Gulf Security Framework," January 15, 1981, *Digital National Security Archive*, http://nsarchive.chadwyck.com/marketing/index.jsp (accessed October 5, 2005) and Walter Slocombe, Deputy Under Secretary of Defense (Policy Planning), Secret Memorandum, "Persian Gulf Secu-

rity Framework," January 16, 1981, *Digital National Security Archive*, http://nsarchive. chadwyck.com/marketing/index.jsp (accessed October 5, 2005).

24. Bacevich, *New American Militarism*, 192.

25. Mann, *Vulcans*, 172–73.

26. Wolfowitz, "Tanenhaus Interview."

27. Coll, "Wolfowitz."

28. Mann, *Vulcans*, 128.

29. Mike Tharp, "South Korean Leader Ends 456 Days of Martial Law," *New York Times*, January 25, 1981; Bernard Gwertzman, "U.S. Applauds Seoul for Sparing Opposition Leader," *New York Times*, January 24, 1981; William Chapman, "South Korea Follows Clemency for Kim with Lifting of Martial Law," *Washington Post*, January 24, 1981, sec. A.

30. Bernard Gwertzman, "U.S. Is Expected to Use Chun Visit to End Tension with South Korea," *New York Times*, February 1, 1981.

31. Bernard Gwertzman, "U.S. Put Off Report on Human Rights to Avoid Embarrassing Chun," *New York Times*, February 3, 1981, sec. A.

32. Lou Cannon, *President Reagan: The Role of a Lifetime* (New York: PublicAffairs, 2000), 272.

33. Ronald W. Reagan, "Address to Members of Parliament," June 8, 1982, *Weekly Compilation of Presidential Documents* 18, no. 23 (June 14, 1982): 768, 770. See also R. W. Apple Jr., "President Urges Global Crusade for Democracy," *New York Times*, June 9, 1982, sec. A; Lou Cannon, "President Calls for 'Crusade,'" *Washington Post*, June 9, 1982, sec. A.

34. See David Lowe, "Idea to Reality: NED at 20," *National Endowment for Democracy*, http://www.ned.org/about/nedhistory.html (accessed September 19, 2005); National Endowment for Democracy, "Statement of Principles and Objectives," http://www.ned. org/about/principlesobjectives.html (accessed September 19, 2005).

35. For background on Elliot Abrams, see Winik, *On the Brink*, 425–37.

36. George P. Shultz, *Turmoil and Triumph: My Years as Secretary of State* (New York: Charles Scribner's Sons, 1993), 970.

37. Paul Wolfowitz, "Asian Democracy and American Interests" (B.C. Lee Lectures, Heritage Foundation, March 2, 2000), 5. See also Paul Wolfowitz, "Interview with Atlantic Monthly," January 2, 2002, *U.S. Department of Defense*, http://www.defenselink.mil/ Transcripts/archive.aspx (accessed September 7, 2005).

38. For this and the following paragraphs, I have drawn on Walter LaFeber, *The New Empire: An Interpretation of American Expansion* (Ithaca, NY: Cornell University Press, 1963), 410–11, 413, 416–17; Stanley Karnow, *In Our Image: America's Empire in the Philippines* (New York: Ballantine, 1989), 78–79, 99–140, 150–54, 168–80; Frank Ninkovich, *The United States and Imperialism* (Malden, MA: Blackwell Publishers, 2001), 57–62, 75–86; Michael Adas, "Improving on the Civilizing Mission? Assumptions of United States Exceptionalism in the Colonization of the Philippines," in Gardner and Young, *New American Empire*.

39. Treaty of Peace (Treaty of Paris), signed December 10, 1898, entered into force, April 11, 1899, *U.S. Statutes-at-Large* 30 (1899): 1754.

40. For background on the Filipino-American war see Brian McAllister Linn, *The Philippine War: 1899–1902* (Lawrence: University of Kansas Press, 2000); Stuart Miller, *"Benevolent Assimilation": The American Conquest of the Philippines, 1899–1903* (New Haven, CT: Yale University Press, 1982).

41. Public Law 57-235, July 1, 1902.

42. Public Law 64-240, August 29, 1916.

43. Public Law 73-127, March 24, 1934.

44. Ninkovich, *United States and Imperialism*, 80.

45. Karnow, *In Our Image*, 356–88, chronicles the Marcos era and its legacy of mismanagement and venality.

46. Philip Taubman, "Schultz, in Manila, Affirms Support of U.S. for Marcos," *New York Times*, June 26, 1983.

47. Paul D. Wolfowitz, "Statement," in *Situation in the Philippines and Implications for U.S. Policy*, Hearing Before the Subcommittee on East Asian and Pacific Affairs of the Foreign Relations Committee, United States Senate, 99th Cong., 2nd sess., S. Hrg. 98–1063, September 18, 1984, 3, 4. See also Paul D. Wolfowitz, "Recent Developments in the Philippines," *Department of State Bulletin* 84, no. 2092 (November 1984): 54–56.

48. Eduardo Lachica, "U.S. Worries about Erosion of [Marcos's] Power, Growth of Communist Rebels in Philippines," *Wall Street Journal*, October 3, 1983.

49. Steve Lohr, "Democracy Gains Steam in the Philippines," *New York Times*, January 27, 1985, sec. 4. See also Raymond Bonner, *Waltzing with a Dictator: The Marcoses and The Making of American Policy* (New York: Times Books, 1987), 367–68; Eduardo Lachica, "U.S. Plugs for Philippines' Acting Defense Chief, Hoping to Restore Army's Morale, Effectiveness," *Wall Street Journal*, January 24, 1985. For background on crony capitalism in the Philippines, see Bonner, *Waltzing*, 327–28; David D. Kang, *Crony Capitalism: Corruption and Development in South Korea and the Philippines* (New York: Cambridge University Press, 2002), 23–34, 74–84, 136–45.

50. Secret Cable, Assistant Secretary Wolfowitz Meeting with Foreign Minister Tolentino, April 1, 1985, *Digital National Security Archive*, http://nsarchive.chadwyck.com/marketing/index.jsp (accessed September 21, 2005); Secret Cable, Assistant Secretary Wolfowitz's Meetings with Opposition Figures, April 1, 1985, *Digital National Security Archive*, http://nsarchive.chadwyck.com/marketing/index.jsp (accessed September 21, 2005); Secret Memorandum, Paul D. Wolfowitz to George P. Shulz, Your Meeting with Ambassador Bosworth, February 6, 1985, *Digital National Security Archive*, http://nsarchive.chadwyck.com/marketing/index.jsp (accessed September 21, 2005). The phrase "quiet diplomacy" appears in National Security Decision Directive Number 163, United States Policy toward the Philippines, February 20, 1985, *Federation of American Scientists*, http://www.fas.org/irp/offdocs/nsdd-163.htm (accessed September 29, 2005).

51. Shultz, *Turmoil*, 612–13.

52. National Security Decision Directive, February 1985, quoted in Leslie H. Gelb, "Marcos Reported to Lose Support in Administration," *New York Times*, January 26, 1986, sec. 1. See also Karnow, *In Our Image*, 408; Bonner, *Waltzing*, 367.

53. Paul D. Wolfowitz, "The Pacific: Region of Promise and Challenge" (February 22, 1985, U.S. State Department Current Policy Document no. 660). See also *New York Times*, "U.S. Official Prods Manila," February 23, 1985.

54. Paul D. Wolfowitz, "Statement," in *Foreign Assistance Legislation for Fiscal Years 1986–87 (Part 5)*, Hearings and Markup before the Subcommittee on Asian and Pacific Affairs Committee on Foreign Affairs, House of Representatives, 99th Cong., 1st sess., March 12, 1985, 550, 551. He outlined the White House's position on the need for reforms in Paul D. Wolfowitz, "Asia: U.S. Encourages Constructive Change in the Philippines," *Wall Street Journal*, April 15, 1985. See also Lena H. Sun, "Philippine Crisis Grows, Top U.S. Officials Warn," *Washington Post*, March 13, 1985, sec. A.

55. Paul D. Wolfowitz, "Statement," in *Foreign Assistance Legislation*, 12.

56. Bonner, *Waltzing*, 373.

57. Ibid., 378–80.

58. Shultz, *Turmoil*, 615. See also Bonner, *Waltzing*, 386–87; Lou Cannon and Bob Woodward, "Reagan to Warn Marcos on Peril of Overthrow," *Washington Post*, October 15, 1985, sec. A; Bernard Weinraub, "U.S. Sends Laxalt to Talk to Marcos," *New York Times*, October 15, 1985, sec. A; Bill Keller, "Laxalt Reports Pledges by Marcos on Political and Military Changes," *New York Times*, October 23, 1985, sec. A.

59. David Ottaway, "A Diplomatic Dilemma," *Washington Post*, October 27, 1985, sec. A.

60. Paul D. Wolfowitz, "Statement," in *Administration Review of U.S. Policy Toward the Philippines*, Hearing Before the Committee on Foreign Relations, United States Senate, 99th Cong., 1st sess., S. Hrg. 99-435, October 30, 1985, 5, 13. See also Paul D. Wolfowitz, "Developments in the Philippines," *Department of State Bulletin* 86, no. 2106 (January 1986): 49–52.

61. Paul D. Wolfowitz, "Statement," in *Recent Events in the Philippines, Fall 1985*, Hearings and Markup before the Committee on Foreign Affairs and Its Subcommittee on Asian and Pacific Affairs, House of Representatives, 99th, Cong., 1st sess., November 12, 1985, 6, 25, 66, 67. The appendix to Wolfowitz's statement detailed specific political, economic, and military reforms (29–33). See also David B. Ottaway, "U.S. Puts Marcos on Notice," *Washington Post*, November 13, 1985, sec. A.

62. Paul D. Wolfowitz, "Testimony," in *The Philippine Presidential Election*, Hearing before the Committee on Foreign Relations, United States Senate, 99th Cong., 2nd sess., S. Hrg 99-535, January 23, 1986, 45, 53. See also Joel Brinkley, "U.S. Voices Fears Fraud Could Mar Philippine Voting," *New York Times*, January 24, 1986, sec. A.

63. Gelb, "Marcos Reported to Lose Support."

64. Bonner, *Waltzing*, 438.

65. Ronald W. Reagan, "Statement by the President on the Philippine Election," January 30, 1986, *Weekly Compilation of Presidential Documents* 22, no. 5 (February 3, 1986): 110–11. See also Bernard Weinraub, "U.S. Vows Rise in Aid if Manila Changes Policy," *New York Times*, January 31, 1986, sec. A.

66. Shultz, *Turmoil*, 618–19. President Reagan provides a summary of the events in the Philippines in Ronald Reagan, *An American Life* (New York: Simon and Schuster, 1990), 362–67.

67. Ronald W. Reagan, "Statement by the President on the Philippine Elections," February 15, 1986, *Weekly Compilation of Presidential Documents* 22, no. 8 (February 24, 1986): 228–29. Secret Memorandum from Paul D. Wolfowitz to George P. Schultz, Briefing the President, February 10, 1986, *Digital National Security Archive* http://nsarchive.chadwyck.com/marketing/index.jsp (accessed September 21, 2005), set forth a postelection briefing strategy for Reagan. See also Leslie H. Gelb, "President Faults Marcos for Fraud but Announces No U.S. Response," *New York Times*, February 16, 1986, sec. 1.

68. Bonner, *Waltzing*, 437.

69. "Statement on the Situation in the Philippines," February 22, 1986, *Weekly Compilation of Presidential Documents* 22, no. 9 (March 3, 1986): 260. See also Bernard Gwertzman, "White House Signals Its Support for 2 Military Men in Philippines," *New York Times*, February 23, 1986.

70. Statement, "Situation in the Philippines," February 23, 1986, *Weekly Compilation of Presidential Documents* 22, no. 9 (March 3, 1986): 261. See Secret Cable 055988, Message to Marcos from George P. Shultz to Stephen W. Bosworth, February 23, 1986, *Digital National Security Archive*, http://nsarchive.chadwyck.com/marketing/index.jsp (accessed September 21, 2005); National Security Decision Directive 215, Philippines, February 23, 1986, in Christopher Simpson, *National Security Directives of the Reagan and Bush Administrations: The Declassified History of U.S. Political and Military Policy, 1981–1991*

(Boulder, CO: Westview Press, 1995), 636–37, 665. See also Bernard Gwertzman, "U.S. Warns against Use of Force," *New York Times*, February 24, 1986, sec. A; David Hoffman and George C. Wilson, "U.S. Threatens Arms Aid Halt, Offers to Fly President Out," *Washington Post*, February 24, 1986, sec. A.

71. Statement, "Situation in the Philippines," February 24, 1986, *Weekly Compilation of Presidential Documents* 22, no. 9 (March 3, 1986): 263. See also Don Oberdorfer and Joanne Omang, "In Reversal, Reagan Urges Philippine President to Resign," *Washington Post*, February 25, 1986, sec. A; David Hoffman, "Attack Plan Led Reagan to Switch," *Washington Post*, February 25, 1986, sec. A; Bernard Weinraub, "U.S. Says Staying On Is 'Futile' and Offers to Be 'of Assistance,'" *New York Times*, February 25, 1986, sec. A; Gerald M. Boyd, "U.S. Had Warnings of Manila Revolt," *New York Times*, February 25, 1986, sec. A; Don Oberdorfer and David Hoffman, "Marcos' U.S. Support Ended Sunday Night," *Washington Post*, February 27, 1986, sec. A.

72. Leslie H. Gelb, "As Options Narrow, U.S. Moves against an 'Old Friend,'" *New York Times*, February 25 1986, sec. A. The White House's reaction to Marcos's last days in power are summarized in Karnow, *In Our Image*, 418–21. Mark Fineman, "The 3-Day Revolution," *Los Angeles Times*, February 27, 1986, part 1, provides an excellent summary of the "people power" revolution. Helpful summaries of the unfolding crisis are offered by Amy Blitz, *The Contested State: American Foreign Policy and Regime Change in the Philippines* (Lanham, MD: Rowman and Littlefield, 2000), 157–91; Jennifer Conroy Franco, *Elections and Democratization in the Philippines* (New York: Routledge, 2001), 165–81; Don Oberdorfer, "Crisis Germinated for Years," *Washington Post*, February 24, 1986, sec. A. For background on U.S.-Filipino relations and the democratic revolution in the Philippines, see Sandra Burton, *Impossible Dream: The Marcoses, the Aquinos, and the Unfinished Revolution* (New York: Warner, 1989).

73. Shultz, *Turmoil*, 638–39.

74. Ibid., 642.

75. Mann, *Vulcans*, 134.

76. Wolfowitz, "Asian Democracy and American Interests," 6.

77. Mann, *Vulcans*, 136. See also Coll, "Wolfowitz."

78. Wolfowitz, "U.S. Encourages Constructive Change."

79. Paul Wolfowitz, "Remembering the Future," *National Interest* 59 (Spring 2000): 39. See also Paul Wolfowitz, "Statesmanship in the New Century," in *Present Dangers: Crisis and Opportunity in American and Defense Policy*, ed. Robert Kagan and William Kristol (San Francisco: Encounter, 2000), 320.

80. John Burgess and Lena H. Sun, "South Korean Party Bows to Opposition," *Washington Post*, June 29, 1987, sec. A; Lena H. Sun and John Burgess, "S. Korean President Accepts Reforms," *Washington Post*, July 1, 1987, sec. A; Clyde Haberman, "A Full Turnabout," *New York Times*, July 1, 1987, sec. A; Neil A. Lewis, "U.S. Spoke Softly For Seoul Change," *New York Times*, July 1, 1987, sec. A; Don Oberdorfer, "Carefully Timed U.S. Advice Played Role in S. Korean Events," *Washington Post*, July 5, 1987, sec. A.

81. Robert Pear, "U.S. May Give Up One of Its Bases in the Philippines, Official Says," *New York Times*, May 14, 1990, sec. A.

82. Keith B. Richburg, "U.S. to Start Phasing Out Military Bases in Philippines," *Washington Post*, September 14, 1990, sec. A; William Branigin, "U.S. to End Presence in Philippines," *Washington Post*, September 18, 1990, sec. A.

83. William Branigin, "U.S. Agrees to Quit Base in Philippines, Keep Use of Subic," *Washington Post*, July 18, 1991, sec. A; William Branigin, "U.S. Says Mt. Pinatubo Has

Ended Clark Field's Attraction as a Base," *Washington Post*, July 16, 1991, sec. A; Philip Shenon, "U.S. Will Abandon Volcano-Ravaged Air Base, Manila is Told," *New York Times*, July 16, 1991, sec. A.

84. Philip Shenon, "Philippine Senate Votes to Reject U.S. Base Renewal," *New York Times*, September 16, 1991, sec. A; William Branigin, "Base Treaty Rejected by Philippines," *Washington Post*, September 17, 1991, sec. A.

85. David E. Sanger, "Philippines Orders U.S. to Leave Strategic Navy Base at Subic Bay," *New York Times*, December 28, 1991; William Branigin, "Given One Year's Notice, U.S. Begins to Pull Out of Subic Base," *Washington Post*, December 28, 1991, sec. A; *New York Times*, "Manila Gives Formal Notice to U.S. on Base Withdrawal," December 31, 1991, sec. A.

86. Seth Mydans, "Filipinos Find It Easy to Deride, but Not Depose, Their President," *New York Times*, March 6, 2006, sec. A; Seth Mydans, "For Philippine Military, Politics Remains a Crucial Mission," *New York Times*, March 5, 2006, sec. 1; Seth Mydans, "Political Turmoil Again Thwarts Progress in Philippines," *New York Times*, February 26, 2006, sec. 1; Carlos H. Conde, "Emergency Rule in Philippines after Failed Coup Is Cited," *New York Times*, February 25, 2006, sec. A; Alan Sipress, "In 20 Years since Marcos, Little Stability for Philippines," *Washington Post*, February 24, 2006, sec. A.

87. Elizabeth Becker, "For McNamara and Wolfowitz, a War and Then the World Bank," *New York Times*, March 22, 2005, sec. C. See also Paul Wolfowitz, "The Tragedy of Suharto," *Wall Street Journal*, May 27, 1998, sec. A.

88. Alan Sipress and Ellen Nakashima, "Jakarta Tenure Offers Glimpse of Wolfowitz," *Washington Post*, March 28, 2005, sec. A. See also Paul Wolfowitz, "Testimony," in *United States Policy toward Indonesia*, Hearing before the Subcommittee on Asia and the Pacific of the Committee on International Relations, House of Representatives, 105th Cong., 1st sess., May 7, 1997, 59.

89. Mann, *Vulcans*, 280.

90. George W. Bush, "Remarks on the Middle East," June 24, 2002, *Weekly Compilations of Presidential Documents* 38, no. 30 (July 1, 2002): 1089. See also Patrick E. Tyler, "Debate on Arafat Stalls U.S. Policy, Aides to Bush Say," *New York Times*, May 26, 2002, sec. 1; Elisabeth Bumiller and David E. Sanger, "Bush Demands Arafat's Ouster before U.S. Backs a New State," *New York Times*, June 25, 2002, sec. A; Karen DeYoung, "President Outlines Vision for Mideast," *Washington Post*, June 25, 2002, sec. A; Robin Wright and Tracy Wilkinson, "A Vision for Peace—after 28 Drafts," *Los Angeles Times*, June 27, 2002, sec. A; Glenn Kessler, "Cutting Arafat Loose, but Not by Name," *Washington Post*, June 30, 2002, sec. A; Patrick E. Tyler, "With Time Running Out, Bush Shifted Mideast Policy," *New York Times*, June 30, 2002, sec. 1.

91. George W. Bush, "Remarks to the American Enterprise Institute Annual Dinner," February 26, 2003, *Weekly Compilation of Presidential Documents* 39, no. 9 (March 3, 2003): 248. See also Dana Milbank and Peter Slevin, "President Details Vision for Iraq," *Washington Post*, February 27, 2003, sec. A.

CHAPTER 4.   WOLFOWITZ VIEWS THE UNITED STATES AS THE WORLD'S SOLE SUPERPOWER

1. Paul D. Wolfowitz, "Statement," in *United States Security Interests in the Post-Cold-War World*, Committee on National Security, House of Representatives, 104th Cong., 2nd sess., H.N.S.C. No. 104-17, June 6, 1996, 25, 31–32.

2. Francis Fukuyama, *The End of History and the Last Man* (New York: Free Press, 1992), argues that Western-style, free-market-oriented democracy represents the last ideological stage in history.

3. For background on Khalilzad, see Elizabeth Bumiller, "Afghan Adviser: The Country's in His Blood," *New York Times*, October 28, 2001, sec. 1B; Jon Lee Anderson, "American Viceroy," *New Yorker*, December 19, 2005, 54–65; Julian Borger, "The Guardian profile: Zalmay Khalilzad," *Guardian* (London), March 10, 2006.

4. Christopher Madison, "Haig's Planning Chief Finds Rewards, Risks in Helping Keep State Straight," *National Journal* 15 (April 10, 1982): 623.

5. George W. Bush, "Remarks at National Defense University," May 1, 2001, *Weekly Compilation of Presidential Documents* 37, no. 18 (May 7, 2001): 687, 688. See also David E. Sanger and Steven Lee Myers, "Bush Seeks Missile Shield along with Nuclear Cuts," *New York Times*, May 2, 2001, sec. A; Mike Allen, "Bush Calls for Missile Shield," *Washington Post*, May 2, 2001, sec. A; David E. Sanger, "Bush Calls Allies in Advance of Missile Speech," *New York Times*, May 1, 2001, sec. A.

6. Deputy Secretary of Defense Paul Wolfowitz, "Press Availability with Deputy Secretary Wolfowitz in Berlin," May 10, 2001, *Department of Defense*, http://www.defenselink.mil/Transcripts/archive.aspx (accessed September 7, 2005). See also Roger Cohen, "Germany's Question: Could U.S. Missile System Be Cooperative?" *New York Times*, May 11, 2001, sec. A; Peter Baker, "Bush Seeks Backing for Missile Plan," *Washington Post*, May 12, 2001, sec. A; Patrick E. Tyler, "Talks Don't Calm Foes of Antimissile Plan," *New York Times*, May 12, 2001, sec. A.

7. Deputy Secretary of Defense Paul Wolfowitz, "Statement," in *Department of Defense Authorization for Appropriations for Fiscal Year 2002, Part 1*, Hearing before the Committee on Armed Services, United States Senate, 107th Cong., 1st sess., S. Hrg. No. 107-355, Pt. 1, July 12, 2001, 439, 440, 445, 446; Deputy Secretary of Defense Paul Wolfowitz, "Statement," in *Missile Defense Programs and Policy*, Hearing before the Committee on Armed Services, House of Representatives, 107th Cong., 1st sess., H.A.S.C. No. 107-26, July 19, 2001, 58, 60. See also Vernon Loeb and Thomas E. Ricks, "Bush Speeds Missile Defense Plans," *Washington Post*, July 12, 2001, sec. A; Vernon Loeb, "Senate Democrats Blast Bush's Missile Defense Plan," *Washington Post*, July 13, 2001, sec. A; James Dao, "Pentagon Sets Ambitious Tests of Missile Plan," *New York Times*, July 13, 2001, sec. A.

8. George W. Bush, "Remarks at the Citadel in Charleston, South Carolina," December 11, 2001, *Weekly Compilation of Presidential Documents* 37, no. 50 (December 17, 2001): 1779. See also David E. Sanger and Elisabeth Bumiller, "U.S. to Pull Out of ABM Treaty, Clearing Path for Antimissile Tests," *New York Times*, December 12, 2001, sec. A; David E. Sanger and Patrick E. Tyler, "Officials Recount Road to Deadlock over Missile Talks," *New York Times*, December 13, 2001, sec. A; Steven Mufson and Dana Milbank, "U.S. Sets Missile Treaty Pullout," *Washington Post*, December 14, 2001, sec. A.

9. Michael Wines, "Facing Pact's End, Putin Decides to Grimace and Bear It," *New York Times*, December 14, 2001, sec. A.

10. Caspar W. Weinberger, *Fighting for Peace: Seven Critical Years in the Pentagon* (New York: Warner Books, 1990), 47.

11. *Taiwan Relations Act*, Public Law 96-8, April 10, 1979.

12. Ibid., codified at *U.S. Code* 22 § 3301(b).

13. Alexander M. Haig Jr., *Caveat: Realism, Reagan, and Foreign Policy* (New York: Macmillan, 1984), 194. See also Don Oberdorder, "Haig Recommends Limits on Arms

Sales to Taiwan," *Washington Post*, July 2, 1982, sec. A; Bernard Gwertzman, "U.S. Seeks a Breakthrough with Peking over Taiwan," *New York Times*, July 3, 1982.

14. James Mann, *About Face: A History of America's Curious Relationship with China, from Nixon to Clinton* (New York: Alfred A. Knopf, 1999), 128.

15. Ibid., 129.

16. Francis X. Cline and Warren Weaver Jr., "Briefing," *New York Times*, March 30, 1982, sec. B.

17. Haig, *Caveat*, 314. See also Lou Cannon, "Departure," *Washington Post*, June 26, 1982, sec. A; "Haig's Quick Shifts Had Reagan Aides Looking at Ceiling," *Washington Post*, June 26, 1982, sec. A; Lou Cannon, "Inner Circle Was Ready to Let Haig Go," *Washington Post*, June 27, 1982, sec. A.

18. Mann, *Vulcans*, 116.

19. Ibid. See also Paul Wolfowitz, "The Interests and Policies of the United States," in *National Security Interests in the Pacific Basin*, ed. Claude A. Buss (Stanford, CA: Hoover Institution Press, 1985), 29.

20. Shultz, *Turmoil and Triumph*, 382.

21. Richard Nations, "A Tilt towards Tokyo," *Far Eastern Economic Review* 120, no. 16 (April 21, 1983): 36–37.

22. Mann, *About Face*, 153–54.

23. Heritage Foundation and the Project for the New American Century, "Statement on the Defense of Taiwan," August 20, 1999, *Project for the New American Century*, http://www.newamericancentury.org/Taiwan defensestatement.htm (accessed September 29, 2005).

24. Steven Mufson, "President Pledges Defense of Taiwan," *Washington Post*, April 26, 2001, sec. A.

25. George W. Bush, "Speech at the Ronald Reagan Library: Topic: Foreign Policy," November 19, 1999, Federal News Service, http://www.lexis-nexis.com/.

26. ABC News, "President Bush Discusses His First 100 Days in Office," *Good Morning America*, April 25, 2001. See also Steven Mufson, "Clash with China Strengthens Hard-Liners," *Washington Post*, April 23, 2001, sec. A; Mufson, "President Pledges."

27. George W. Bush, "Remarks in Kyoto, Japan," November 16, 2005, *Weekly Compilation of Presidential Documents* 41, no. 46 (November 21, 2005): 1728, 1729. See also Dan Blumenthal and Tom Donnelly, "Bush to Asia: Freedom Is More Than Markets," *Washington Post*, November 27, 2005, sec. B.

28. Paul Wolfowitz, "Asian Democracy and American Interests" (B.C. Lee Lecture, Heritage Foundation, March 2, 2000), 7, 8. See also Paul Wolfowitz, "Remembering the Future," *National Interest* 59 (Spring 2000): 42; Wolfowitz, "Statesmanship in the New Century," 325.

29. See, e.g., Keith Bradsher, "As Trade Deficit Grows, So Do Tensions with China," *New York Times*, March 10, 2006, sec. C.

30. Wolfowitz, "Tanenhaus Interview."

31. The quotations in this and the next two paragraphs are from "Excerpts from Pentagon's Plan: 'Prevent the Re-Emergence of a New Rival,'" *New York Times*, March 8, 1992, sec. 1. See also Patrick E. Tyler, "U.S. Strategy Plan Calls for Insuring No Rivals Develop," *New York Times*, March 8, 1992, sec. 1; Patrick E. Tyler, "Lone Superpower Plan: Ammunition for Critics," *New York Times*, March 10, 1992, sec. A; Barton Gellman, "Keeping the U.S. First," *Washington Post*, March 11, 1992, sec. A; Charles Krauthammer, "What's Wrong with the 'Pentagon Paper'?" *Washington Post*, March 13, 1992, sec. A; Barton Gellman, "Pentagon Abandons Goal of Thwarting U.S. Rivals," *Washington Post*,

May 24, 1992, sec. A; Patrick E. Tyler, "Pentagon Drops Goal of Blocking New Super-powers," *New York Times*, May 24, 1992, sec. 1; James Mann, "The True Rationale? It's a Decade Old," *Washington Post*, March 7, 2004, sec. B. Khalilzad subsequently discussed the need to maintain U.S. global leadership and preclude the rise of another global rival in Zalmay M. Khalilzad, *From Containment to Global Leadership? America and the World after the Cold War* (Santa Monica, CA: RAND Corporation, 1995).

32. Patrick E. Tyler, "Senior U.S. Officials Assail Lone-Superpower Policy," *New York Times*, March 11, 1992, sec. A.

33. Mann, *Vulcans*, 211.

34. Secretary of Defense Dick Cheney, "Defense Strategy for the 1990s: The Regional Defense Strategy," January 1993, 4, *Information Clearing House*, http://www.informationclearinghouse.info/pdf/naarpr_Defense.pdf.

35. Ibid., 7.

36. Ibid., 9. See also p. 4.

37. Ibid., 4.

38. Wolfowitz, "Remembering the Future," 36–37. The Buchanan quotation is from Patrick J. Buchanan, *A Republic, Not an Empire: Reclaiming America's Destiny* (Washington, DC: Regnery, 1999), 9.

CHAPTER 5. THE ROAD TO BAGHDAD, PART ONE: OPERATION DESERT STORM

1. For background on the Iraq-Kuwait disputes, see Phebe Marr, *The Modern History of Iraq*, 2nd ed. (Boulder, CO: Westview Press, 2004), 218–21.

2. George Bush and Brent Scowcroft, *A World Transformed* (New York: Alfred A. Knopf, 1998), 308–9; James A. Baker III, with Thomas M. Defrank, *The Politics of Diplomacy: Revolution, War and Peace 1989–1992* (New York: G.P. Putnam's Sons, 1995), 271. See also Youssef M. Ibrahim, "Iraq Threatens Emirates and Kuwait on Oil Glut," *New York Times*, July 18, 1990, sec. D.

3. Bob Woodward, *The Commanders* (New York: Simon and Schuster, 1991), 210.

4. Ibid.

5. Baker, *Politics*, 271; Gordon and Trainor, *Generals' War*, 19; H. Norman Schwarzkopf, with Peter Petre, *It Doesn't Take a Hero* (New York: Bantam, 1992), 291–93.

6. Pete Williams, "Department of Defense Briefing," July 24, 1990, Federal News Service, www.lexis-nexis.com. See also Michael R. Gordon, "U.S. Deploys Air and Sea Forces after Iraq Threatens Two Neighbors," *New York Times*, July 25, 1990, sec. A; "U.S.-Arab Maneuvers Denied," *New York Times*, July 26, 1990, sec. A.

7. Woodward, *Commanders*, 215. Gordon and Trainor, *Generals' War*, 23–24, describe the objections to the proposed message by Arthur G. Hughes, Deputy Assistant Secretary of Defense for Near East Affairs. Jock P. Covey, a high-ranking official in the State Department's Bureau of Near Eastern and South Asian Affairs, showed a draft to Hughes at a "chance meeting." Hughes objected to the "almost obsequious tone of the draft" (24).

8. Woodward, *Commanders*, 215; Gordon and Trainor, *Generals' War*, 23–24; Bush and Scowcroft, *World Transformed*, 312–14.

9. Woodward, *Commanders*, 215–16.

10. Ibid., 216.

11. Ibid.

12. Ibid.

13. Woodward, *Commanders*, 223–24; Bush and Scowcroft, *World Transformed*, 304.

14. *National Security Act, U.S. Statutes at Large* 61 (1947): 496, codified at *U.S. Code* 50 § 402.

15. For background on the National Security Council see David J. Rothkopf, *Running the World: The Inside Story of the National Security Council and the Architects of American Power* (New York: Public Affairs, 2005).

16. Woodward, *Commanders*, 229–30; Bush and Scowcroft, *World Transformed*, 315–18.

17. Gordon and Trainor, *Generals' War*, 33.

18. Ibid., 34.

19. For this meeting I have drawn on Bush and Scowcroft, *World Transformed*, 322–25; Woodward, *Commanders*, 236–37; Colin L. Powell, with Joseph L. Persico, *My American Journey* (New York: Random House, 1995), 463–646.

20. Woodward, *Commanders*, 236–37.

21. Ibid., 237.

22. National Security Directive, "Covert Operations Against Iraq," in Simpson, *National Security Directives of the Reagan and Bush Administrations*, 929–30. See also David Hoffman and Dan Balz, "Bush Plans Effort Aimed at Toppling Saddam," *Washington Post*, August 6, 1990, sec. A; Woodward, *Commanders*, 237.

23. Woodward, *Commanders*, 241–44; Powell, *American Journey*, 465; Bush and Scowcroft, *World Transformed*, 325–26.

24. Woodward, *Commanders*, 245.

25. Ibid.

26. Ibid.

27. For background on CENTCOM and its origins see Dore Gold, *America, the Gulf and Israel: CENTCOM (Central Command) and Emerging U.S. Regional Security Policies in the Mideast*, JCSS Study no. 11 (Boulder, CO: Westview Press, 1988), 29–56.

28. Gordon and Trainor, *Generals' War*, 47; Powell, *American Journey*, 466; Schwarzkopf, *It Doesn't Take*, 300–302; Woodward, *Commanders*, 249.

29. Bush and Scowcroft, *World Transformed*, 327–30. See also Ann Devroy and Dan Balz, "For Bush, Moment of Decision Came Saturday at Camp David," *Washington Post*, August 9, 1990, sec. A.

30. George H. W. Bush, "Remarks and an Exchange with Reporters on the Iraqi Invasion of Kuwait," August 5, 1990, *Weekly Compilation of Presidential Documents* 26, no. 32 (August 13, 1990): 1209. See also Bush and Scowcroft, *World Transformed*, 332–33; Powell, *American Journey*, 466–67; Thomas L. Friedman, "Bush, Hinting Force, Declares Iraqi Assault 'Will Not Stand'," *New York Times*, August 6, 1990, sec. A.

31. George H. W. Bush, "Address to the Nation Announcing the Deployment of United States Armed Forces to Saudi Arabia," August 8, 1990, *Weekly Compilation of Presidential Documents* 26, no. 32 (August 13, 1990): 1216–17. See also Bush and Scowcroft, *World Transformed*, 340–41; Dan Balz and Molly Moore, "Bush Asks Nation to Back 'Defensive' Mission as U.S. Forces Begin Arriving in Saudi Arabia," *Washington Post*, August 9, 1990, sec. A. The decision-making process is summarized in Maureen Dowd, "The Longest Week: How President Decided to Draw the Line," *New York Times*, August 9, 1990, sec. A.

32. For the meeting in Saudi Arabia, I have drawn on Paul Wolfowitz, "Rebuilding the Anti-Saddam Coalition," *Wall Street Journal*, November 18, 1997, sec. A; Woodward, *Commanders*, 266–73; Bush and Scowcroft, *World Transformed*, 335; Powell, *American Journey*,

467–68; Schwarzkopf, *It Doesn't Take*, 302; Gordon and Trainor, *Generals' War*, 51–52. See also Michael R. Gordon, "First American Deployment to Gulf Is 'Tip of Wedge,'" *New York Times*, August 9, 1990, sec. A; "Excerpts from News Conference by Cheney and Powell at the Pentagon," *New York Times*, August 9, 1990, sec. A.

33. Gordon and Trainor, *Generals' War*, 71.

34. Ibid.

35. Ibid.

36. Gordon and Trainor, *Generals' War*, 71–72.

37. Woodward, *Commanders*, 299; Powell, *American Journey*, 478–80, 535–36; Rick Atkinson, *Crusade: The Untold Story of the Persian Gulf War* (Boston: Houghton Mifflin, 1993), 122.

38. Woodward, *Commanders*, 303–4; Gordon and Trainor, *Generals' War*, 128–29.

39. Woodward, *Commanders*, 304–6; Gordon and Trainor, *Generals' War*, 131–34; Powell, *American Journey*, 484–85.

40. Bush and Scowcroft, *World Transformed*, 381; Gordon and Trainor, *Generals' War*, 135–39; Powell, *American Journey*, 485.

41. Gordon and Trainor, *Generals' War*, 141. See also Atkinson, *Crusade*, 111.

42. Powell, *American Journey*, 486–87; Woodward, *Commanders*, 309.

43. Gordon and Trainor, *Generals' War*, 143–44; Mann, *Vulcans*, 187.

44. Gordon and Trainor, *Generals' War*, 144.

45. Ibid., 144–45.

46. Ibid., 145.

47. Schwarzkopf, *It Doesn't Take*, 368–69; Gordon and Trainor, *Generals' War*, 151.

48. Schwarzkopf, *It Doesn't Take*, 368.

49. Mann, *Vulcans*, 188.

50. Gordon and Trainor, *Generals' War*, 147, 151; Schwarzkopf, *It Doesn't Take*, 362.

51. Woodward, *Commanders*, 319–20; Gordon and Trainor, *Generals' War*, 153–55; Powell, *American Journey*, 487–89; Schwarzkopf, *It Doesn't Take*, 370.

52. Woodward, *Commanders*, 320.

53. Ibid.

54. Ibid.

55. George H. W. Bush, "The President's News Conference on the Persian Gulf Crisis," November 8, 1990, *Weekly Compilation of Presidential Documents* 26, no. 45 (November 12, 1990): 1789–91. See also Michael R. Gordon, "Bush Sends New Units to Gulf to Provide 'Offensive Option,'" *New York Times*, November 9, 1990, sec. A; Patrick E. Tyler, "New Deployment Signals U.S. Switch to Offensive," *Washington Post*, November 9, 1990, sec. A; Andrew Rosenthal, "Buildup in Gulf Seen as a Signal on Use of Force," *New York Times*, November 10, 1990, sec. 1. For a list of the ten U.N. Security Council resolutions adopted in response to the Persian Gulf crisis see James Schwartz, "The Previous Resolutions," *Washington Post*, November 30, 1990, sec. A.

56. United Nations Security Council, Resolution S/678 (1990), adopted by the United Nations Security Council, November 29, 1990. See also Bush and Scowcroft, *World Transformed*, 414–16; Powell, *American Journey*, 489–90; John M. Goshko, "U.N. Vote Authorizes Use of Foreign against Iraq," *Washington Post*, November 30, 1990, sec. A; David Hoffman, "Gulf Turning Points," *Washington Post*, December 2, 1990, sec. A.

57. Bush and Scowcroft, *World Transformed*, 415.

58. Gordon and Trainor, *Generals' War*, 193, 307.

59. Woodward, *Commanders*, 347.

60. Ibid., 348–49.

61. Gordon and Trainor, *Generals' War*, 194–96, 231–33.

62. Woodward, *Commanders*, 363.

63. Ibid., 354.

64. "Text of Letter from Bush to Hussein," *New York Times*, January 13, 1991, sec. 1.

65. Bush and Scowcroft, *World Transformed*, 441–43; Woodward, *Commanders*, 361; Gordon and Trainor, *Generals' War*, 197–98. Secretary of State Baker recounts the meeting with Aziz in Baker, *Politics*, 355–63. See also David Hoffman, "Bush Letter Left on Conference Table 6 1/2 Hours," *Washington Post*, January 11, 1991, sec. A.

66. *Congressional Record* 137 (January 12, 1991): S1018–19, H1139–40. See also Bush and Scowcroft, *World Transformed*, 438–39, 441, 443–46; Adam Clymer, "Congress Acts to Authorize War in Gulf," *New York Times*, January 13, 1991, sec. 1; Tom Kenworthy and Helen Dewar, "Divided Congress Grants President Authority to Wage War against Iraq," *Washington Post*, January 13, 1991, sec. A; Adam Clymer, "After the Vote, Margins Are Ignored, but Potential Divisions Are Serious," *New York Times*, January 14, 1991, sec. A.

67. Bush and Scowcroft, *World Transformed*, 452–53; Gordon and Trainor, *Generals' War*, 231–33.

68. Atkinson, *Crusade*, 118. See also Patrick E. Tyler, "U.S. Tells of Retaliation Plan That Israelis Abandoned," *New York Times*, March 7, 1991, sec. A.

69. Bush and Scowcroft, *World Transformed*, 456.

70. I have drawn on Gordon and Trainor, *Generals' War*, 235–36; Atkinson, *Crusade*, 130–32; Schwarzkopf, *It Doesn't Take*, 416–19; Bush and Scowcroft, *World Transformed*, 456.

71. Atkinson, *Crusade*, 278–81.

72. Gordon and Trainor, *Generals' War*, 307; Atkinson, *Crusade*, 270.

73. Gordon and Trainor, *Generals' War*, 307–8; Atkinson, *Crusade*, 271.

74. Baker, *Politics*, 402–8.

75. Gordon and Trainor, *Generals' War*, 332–34, 349; Powell, *American Journey*, 516–17, 536; Bush and Scowcroft, *World Transformed*, 474–79; Atkinson, *Crusade*, 347–51.

76. Gordon and Trainor, *Generals' War*, 349–50; Atkinson, *Crusade*, 351–52.

77. George H. W. Bush, "Address to the Nation on the Suspension of Allied Offensive Combat Operations in the Persian Gulf," February 27, 1991, *Weekly Compilation of Presidential Documents*, 27, no. 9 (March 4, 1991): 224. See also Bush and Scowcroft, *World Transformed*, 485–86; Powell, *American Journey*, 519–23; Andrew Rosenthal, "Bush Halts Offensive Combat," *New York Times*, February 28, 1991, sec. A; Rick Atkinson and Steve Coll, "Bush Orders Cease-Fire," *Washington Post*, February 28, 1991, sec. A.

78. "Excerpts from Schwarzkopf News Conference on Gulf War," *New York Times*, February 28, 1991, sec. A. See also Thomas E. Ricks, "Once 'Stormin Norman,' Gen. Schwarzkopf Is Skeptical about U.S. Action in Iraq," *Washington Post*, January 28, 2003, sec. C.

79. Gordon and Trainor, *Generals' War*, 418, 424.

80. Paul Wolfowitz, "The United States and Iraq," in *The Future of Iraq*, ed. John Calabrese (Washington, DC: Middle East Institute, 1997), 109.

81. Gordon and Trainor, *Generals' War*, 424; Mann, *Vulcans*, 193.

82. Gordon and Trainor, *Generals' War*, 423–24; Powell, *American Journey*, 522.

83. Gordon and Trainor, *Generals' War*, 424.

84. Ibid.; Powell, *American Journey*, 526.

85. Schwarzkopf, *It Doesn't Take*, 488–89; Gordon and Trainor, *Generals' War*, 446–47; Baker, *Politics*, 439–40.

86. Paul Wolfowitz, "Rising Up," *New Republic*, December 7, 1998, 12. See also Gordon and Trainor, *Generals' War*, 455.

87. Atkinson, *Crusade*, 490.

88. Powell, *American Journey*, 526; Gordon and Trainor, *Generals' War*, 456; Atkinson, *Crusade*, 490; Baker, *Politics*, 435, 440.

89. Gordon and Trainor, *Generals' War*, 454. See also Ann Devroy and Molly Moore, "U.S. Unprepared for Iraqi Retribution, Extent of Exodus in Conflict's Aftermath," *Washington Post*, April 14, 1991, sec. A; Ann Devroy and R. Jeffrey Smith, "Neutrality Reaffirmed by U.S.," *Washington Post*, March 27, 1991, sec. A.

90. George H. W. Bush, "News Conference of President Bush and Prime Minister Mulroney of Canada in Ottawa," March 13, 1991, *Weekly Compilation of Presidential Documents* 27, no. 11 (March 18, 1991): 304; "Statement by Press Secretary Fitzwater on Iraq: President Saddam Hussein's Use of Force Against the Iraqi People," March 13, 1991, *Weekly Compilation of Presidential Documents* 27, no. 11 (March 18, 1991): 308. See also Andrew Rosenthal, "Bush Accuses Iraq of Breaking Truce in Fighting Rebels," *New York Times*, March 14, 1991, sec. A; Patrick E. Tyler, "Copters a Threat, U.S. Warns Iraqis," *New York Times*, March 19, 1991, sec. A.

91. Bush and Scowcroft, *World Transformed*, 489; Powell, *American Journey*, 527; Baker, *Politics*, 441. See also Ann Devroy, "'Wait and See' on Iraq," *Washington Post*, March 29, 1991, sec. A; Andrew Rosenthal, "U.S., Fearing Iraqi Breakup, Is Termed Ready to Accept a Hussein Defeat of Rebels," *New York Times*, March 27, 1991, sec. A; Al Kamen and R. Jeffrey Smith, "U.S., Arabs Fear Breakup or Fundamentalist Takeover of Iraq," *Washington Post*, March 8, 1991, sec. A. However, on February 15, 1991, Bush called the Iraqi military and the Iraqi people to overthrow Saddam Hussein. George H. W. Bush, "Remarks to Raytheon Missile Systems Plant Employees in Andover, Massachusetts," February 15, 1991, *Weekly Compilation of Presidential Documents* 27, no. 7 (February 18, 1991): 177.

92. The March 1991 uprising is detailed in Marr, *Iraq*, 241–53. See also Charles Tripp, *A History of Iraq*, 2nd ed. (New York: Cambridge University Press, 2002), 255–59.

93. Marr, *Iraq*, 254–58.

94. Bush and Scowcroft, *World Transformed*, 432–33, 464, 489; Baker, *Politics*, 442.

95. Bush and Scowcroft, *World Transformed*, 489.

96. Paul Wolfowitz, "Victory Came Too Easily," *National Interest* 35 (Spring 1994): 91–92. See also Deputy Secretary of Defense Paul Wolfowitz, "Interview with Atlantic Monthly," January 2, 2002, *U.S. Department of Defense*, http://www.defenselink.mil/Transcripts/archive.aspx (accessed September 7, 2005).

97. Wolfowitz, "United States and Iraq," 109.

98. Wolfowitz, "Victory," 92.

99. Paul Wolfowitz, "They Must Be Equipped to Defend Themselves," *Wall Street Journal*, December 12, 1995, sec. A. See also Paul Wolfowitz and Douglas J. Feith, "The Argument Clinton Isn't Making on Bosnia," *Wall Street Journal*, November 28, 1995, sec. A; Paul D. Wolfowitz, "Prepared Statement," in *Situation In Bosnia*, Hearings before the Committee on Armed Services, United States Senate, 104th Cong., 1st sess., S. Hrg. 104-587, November 28, 1995, 268–70; Richard Perle and Paul Wolfowitz, "Bosnia: Before We Send in Peacemakers," *Washington Post*, October 24, 1995, sec. A; Paul Wolfowitz, "Testimony," in *United States Policy toward the Former Yugoslavia*, Committee on National Security, House of Representatives, 104th Cong., 1st and 2nd sess., H.N.S.C. No. 104-36, October 17, 1995, 90–96.

100. Paul Wolfowitz, "Clinton's Bay of Pigs," *Wall Street Journal*, September 27, 1996, sec. A.

101. Wolfowitz, "United States and Iraq," 112–13.

102. Zalmay M. Khalilzad and Paul Wolfowitz, "Overthrow Him," *Weekly Standard*, December 1, 1997, 14. See also Zalmay Khalilzad and Paul Wolfowitz, "We Must Lead the Way in Deposing Saddam," *Washington Post*, November 9, 1997, sec. C.

103. Letter to the Honorable William J. Clinton from the Project for the New American Century, January 26, 1998, *Project for the New American Century*, http://www.newamericancentury.org/iraqclintonletter.htm (accessed October 16, 2005). See also Thomas W. Lippman, "In U.S., Calls Grow Louder for Saddam Hussein's Removal," *Washington Post*, February 5, 1998, sec. A.

104. Open Letter to the President, February 19, 1998, *Iraq Watch*, http://www.iraqwatch.org/perspectives/rumsfeld-openletter.htm (accessed October 16, 2005).

105. *Iraq Liberation Act*, Public Law 105-338, *U.S. Code* 22 (1998), § 2151.

106. Paul Wolfowitz, "Rebuilding the Anti-Saddam Coalition," *Wall Street Journal*, November 18, 1997, sec. A; Paul Wolfowitz, "Statement," in *United States Policy Toward Iraq*, Committee on National Security, House of Representatives, 105th Cong., 2nd sess., H.N.S.C. No. 105-51, September 16, 1998, 77. See also James Mann, "Bush Wanted His Doctrine and the Allies, Too," *Washington Post*, March 16, 2003, sec. B.

CHAPTER 6. THE ROAD TO BAGHDAD, PART TWO: OPERATION ENDURING FREEDOM

1. Paul D. Wolfowitz, "Testimony," in *Nominations before the Senate Armed Services Committee*, Hearings before the Committee on Armed Services, United States Senate, 107th Cong., 1st sess., S. Hrg. 107-749, February 27, 2001, 223, 224. See also Jane Perlez, "Powell Goes on the Road and Scores Some Points," *New York Times*, March 2, 2001, sec. A; Jane Perlez, "Capital Hawks Seek Tougher Line on Iraq," *New York Times*, March 7, 2001, sec. A; Elaine Sciolino, "In a Humble World, Defense Deputy Stands Firm," *New York Times*, April 2, 2001, sec. A.

2. Bob Woodward and Vernon Loeb, "CIA's Covert War on Bin Laden," *Washington Post*, September 14, 2001, sec. A.

3. The 9/11 Commission Report, *Final Report of the National Commission on Terrorist Attacks upon the United States* (New York: W. W. Norton, 2004), 203.

4. Richard A. Clarke, *Against All Enemies: Inside America's War on Terror* (New York: Free Press, 2004), 231–32. See also p. 30.

5. *9/11 Commission Report*, 203. See also Steve Coll, *Ghost Wars: The Secret History of the CIA, Afghanistan and bin Laden from the Soviet Invasion to September 10, 2001* (New York: Penguin, 2004), 558–59.

6. Paul Wolfowitz, "Noble Work," Commencement Address at the U.S. Military Academy, West Point, New York, June 2, 2001, reprinted in *Vital Speeches of the Day* 67, no. 12 (July 15, 2001): 603–4.

7. The quotations are from *9/11 Commission Report*, 204-5, 510 n. 200, citing National Security Council memo Hadley to Armitage, Wolfowitz, McLaughlin, and O'Keefe, "Next Steps on al-Qaeda," June 7, 2001. See also Barton Gellman, "A Strategy's Cautious Evolution," *Washington Post*, January 20, 2002, sec. A.

8. *9/11 Commission Report*, 208.

9. Ibid., 206.

10. Ibid., 211–12.

11. Ibid., 214. See also Daniel Benjamin and Steven Simon, *The Age of Sacred Terror* (New York: Random House, 2002), 345–46; Coll, *Ghost Wars*, 573–74; Woodward, *Bush at War*, 35–36.

12. *9/11 Commission Report*, 214.

13. Wolfowitz, "Tanenhaus Interview."

14. Ibid.

15. Ibid.

16. Bob Woodward, *Plan of Attack* (New York: Simon and Schuster, 2004), 25.

17. *9/11 Commission Report*, 335.

18. Wolfowitz, "Tanenhaus Interview."

19. Ibid.

20. Fred Barnes, *Rebel-in-Chief: Inside the Bold and Controversial Presidency of George W. Bush* (New York: Crown Forum, 2006), 56, asserts that Bush crafted the new foreign and national-security policies mostly by himself and that it "was a Bush policy, not the work of his advisers . . . although Wolfowitz's vision of a democratic Middle East sharpened Bush's thinking" (60–61).

21. Jane Perlez, "The General Picks Up Where He Left Off," *New York Times*, January 28, 2001, sec. 4.

22. George W. Bush, "Address to the Nation on the Terrorist Attacks," September 11, 2001, *Weekly Compilation of Presidential Documents* 37, no. 37 (September 17, 2001): 1301.

23. *9/11 Commission Report*, 330, 558 n. 34, citing White House transcript, President Bush interview with Bob Woodward and Dan Balz, December 20, 2001. See also Woodward, *Bush at War*, 32–33; Dan Balz and Bob Woodward, "America's Chaotic Road to War," *Washington Post*, January 27, 2002, sec. 1.

24. Woodward, *Bush at War*, 49. In *Against All Enemies*, 32, Richard Clarke writes that on the night of September 12, he saw President Bush wandering alone around the White House Situation Room. According to Clarke, the president stopped and asked Clarke and a few aides to "go back over everything, everything. See if Saddam did this." Clarke replied, "But, Mr. President, al Qaeda did this." "I know, I know, but . . . see if Saddam was involved. Just look. I want any shred." After the president left, one of Clarke's aides said, "Wolfowitz got to him."

25. Woodward, *Bush at War*, 49.

26. Deputy Secretary of Defense Paul Wolfowitz, "Department of Defense Briefing," September 13, 2001, *U.S. Department of Defense*, http://www.defenselink.mil/Transcripts/archive.aspx (accessed September 7, 2005).

27. Deputy Secretary of Defense Paul Wolfowitz, "Interview, National Public Radio, All Things Considered," September 14, 2001, *U.S. Department of Defense*, http://www.defenselink.mil/Transcripts/archive.aspx (accessed September 7, 2005); Paul Wolfowitz, "Interview with Fox News," September 13, 2001, *U.S. Department of Defense*, http://www.defenselink.mil/Transcripts/archive.aspx (accessed September 7, 2005).

28. Wolfowitz, "Fox News Interview."

29. Woodward, *Bush at War*, 60.

30. Secretary of State Colin L. Powell, "On-the-Record Press Briefing," September 17, 2001, *U.S. Department of State*, http://www.state.gov/secretary/former/powell/

remarks/2001/4929.htm (accessed December 14, 2005). See also Patrick E. Tyler and Elaine Sciolino, "Bush's Advisers Split on Scope of Retaliation," *New York Times*, September 20, 2001, sec. A; R. W. Apple Jr., "Issue Now: Does U.S. Have a Plan?" *New York Times*, September 27, 2001, sec. A.

31. Alan Sipress, "U.S. Debating Whether to Overthrow Taliban," *Washington Post*, September 24, 2001, sec. A; Mike Allen and Alan Sipress, "High Stakes, Tension Magnify Differences among Members of Bush's 'War Cabinet,'" *Washington Post*, September 26, 2001.

32. Woodward, *Bush at War*, 61. See also Dan Balz, Bob Woodward, and Jeff Himmelman, "Afghan Campaign's Blueprint Emerges," *Washington Post*, January 29, 2002, sec. A.

33. For the Camp David meeting, I have drawn on Woodward, *Bush at War*, 74–91. See also Bob Woodward and Dan Balz, "At Camp David, Advise and Dissent," *Washington Post*, January 31, 2002, sec. A; Barton Gellman and Mike Allen, "President Sets Nation on New Course," *Washington Post*, September 23, 2001, sec. A.

34. *9/11 Commission Report*, 335, 559 n. 65, citing Department of Defense memo, Office of the Under Secretary of Defense for Policy, "War on Terrorism: Strategic Concept," September 14, 2001.

35. *9/11 Commission Report*, 332. See also Woodward, *Bush at War*, 75–78.

36. *9/11 Commission Report*, 333. See also Woodward, *Bush at War*, 79–80.

37. Woodward, *Bush at War*, 81–83.

38. Ibid., 83. See also Woodward, *Plan of Attack*, 26.

39. *9/11 Commission Report*, 335.

40. Woodward, *Bush at War*, 83.

41. Ibid.

42. Sam Tanenhaus, "Bush's Brain Trust," *Vanity Fair*, July 2003, 169. See also Elaine Sciolino and Patrick E. Tyler, "Some Pentagon Officials and Advisers Seek to Oust Iraq's Leader in War's Next Phase," *New York Times*, October 12, 2001, sec. B; Michael Dobbs, "Old Strategy on Iraq Sparks New Debate," *Washington Post*, December 27, 2001, sec. A.

43. Bowden, "Wolfowitz," 120.

44. Ibid.

45. Wolfowitz, "Tanenhaus Interview."

46. Woodward, *Bush at War*, 84.

47. Ibid.

48. Ibid., 84–85.

49. Ibid., 85.

50. The quotations in this paragraph are from ibid., 86–88.

51. Ibid., 88.

52. Ibid., 89–90.

53. Ibid., 91.

54. George W. Bush, "Remarks on Arrival at the White House and Exchange with Reporters," September 16, 2001, *Weekly Compilation of Presidential Documents* 37, no. 38 (September 24, 2001): 1323. See also R. W. Apple Jr., "A Clear Message: I Will Not Relent," *New York Times*, September 21, 2001, sec. A; Elisabeth Bumiller, "Bush Pledges Attack on Afghanistan Unless It Surrenders Bin Laden Now," *New York Times*, September 21, 2001, sec. A; John F. Harris and Mike Allen, "Bush Tells Nations to Take Sides as N.Y. Toll Climbs Past 6,000," *Washington Post*, September 21, 2001, sec. A; Dan Balz, "A Resolute and Focused Call to Arms," *Washington Post*, September 21, 2001, sec. A.

55. Jane Perlez, David E. Sanger, and Thom Shanker, "From Many Voices, One Battle Strategy," *New York Times*, September 23, 2001, sec. 1A.

56. *9/11 Commission Report*, 335.

57. Woodward, *Bush at War*, 99.

58. *9/11 Commission Report*, 335. See also Woodward, *Bush at War*, 99; Michael R. Gordon and Bernard E. Trainor, *COBRA II: The Inside Story of the Invasion and Occupation of Iraq* (New York: Random House, 2006), 17.

59. Bob Woodward and Dan Balz, "Combating Terrorism," *Washington Post*, February 1, 2002, sec. A.

60. *9/11 Commission Report*, 335–36, 559 n. 73, citing Department of Defense memo, Wolfowitz to Rumsfeld, "Preventing More Events," September 17, 2001.

61. *9/11 Commission Report*, 336, 559 n. 74, citing Department of Defense memo, Wolfowitz to Rumsfeld, "Were We Asleep?" September 18, 2001.

62. George W. Bush, "Address before a Joint Session of Congress on the United States Response to the Terrorist Attacks of September 11th," September 20, 2001, *Weekly Compilation of Presidential Documents* 37, no. 38 (September 24, 2001): 1348–49. See also Dan Balz and Bob Woodward, "A Presidency Defined in One Speech," *Washington Post*, February 2, 2002, sec. A.

63. Woodward, *Bush at War*, 107.

64. Deputy Secretary of Defense Paul Wolfowitz, "Press Conference in Brussels," September 26, 2001, *U.S. Department of Defense*, http://www.defenselink.mil/Transcripts/archive.aspx (accessed September 7, 2005).

65. Woodward, *Bush at War*, 167.

66. Ibid., 248.

67. Karen DeYoung and Rick Weiss, "U.S. Seeks to Ease Rhetoric on Iraq," *Washington Post*, October 24, 2001, sec. A.

68. Bowden, "Wolfowitz," 120.

69. General Tommy Franks, with Malcolm McConnell, provides an overview of the Afghan campaign in *American Soldier* (New York: Harper Collins, 2004): 283–315. See also David Rohde, with Eric Schmitt, "Taliban Give Way in Final Province Where They Ruled," *New York Times*, December 10, 2001, sec. A.

70. Bill Keller, "The Fighting Next Time," *New York Times Magazine*, March 10, 2002, 34. Albert Wohlstetter's impact on the technology-driven military strategy is summarized in Bacevich, *New American Militarism*, 158–63.

71. Deputy Secretary of Defense Paul Wolfowitz, "Interview with New York Times," January 7, 2002, *U.S. Department of Defense*, http://www.defenselink.mil/Transcripts/archive.aspx (accessed September 7, 2005).

72. Deputy Secretary of Defense Paul Wolfowitz, "Interview with Los Angeles Times," December 14, 2001, *U.S. Department of Defense*, http://www.defenselink.mil/Transcripts/archive.aspx (accessed September 7, 2005). See also Paul D. Wolfowitz, "Statement," in *Department of Defense Policies and Programs to Transform the Armed Forces to Meet the Challenges of the 21st Century*, Hearing before the Committee on Armed Services, United States Senate, 107th Cong., 2nd sess., April 8, 2002, 7, 13; Paul Wolfowitz, "The Greatest Deeds Are Yet To Be Done," *Naval War College Review* 57, no. 1 (Winter 2004): 17 (remarks to the Naval War College graduating class in June 2003); Paul Wolfowitz, "Thinking about the Imperatives of Defense Transformation," Heritage Lectures, no. 831, April 30, 2004, 3.

73. Wolfowitz, "Statement," in *Department of Defense Policies*, 8, 16.

74. George W. Bush, "Address to the United Nations General Assembly in New York City," November 10, 2001, *Weekly Compilation of Presidential Documents* 37, no. 46

(November 17, 2001): 1638. See also Elisabeth Bumiller, "All Must Fight against Terror, Bush Tells U.N.," *New York Times*, November 11, 2001, sec. 1; Karen De Young, "Bush Urges Coalition to Fulfill Its 'Duties,'" *Washington Post*, November 11, 2001, sec. A; Dan Balz, "In Role Reversal, War Criticism Is Mostly from Right," *Washington Post*, November 26, 2001, sec. A.

75. George W. Bush, "Remarks at a Welcoming Ceremony for Humanitarian Aid Workers Rescued from Afghanistan and an Exchange with Reporters," November 26, 2001, *Weekly Compilation of Presidential Documents* 37, no. 48 (December 3, 2001): 1713. See also Mike Allen, "Iraq's Weapons Could Make It a Target, Bush Says," *Washington Post*, November 27, 2001, sec. A.

76. Wolfowitz, "New York Times Interview." See also David B. Ottaway and Thomas E. Ricks, "Somalia Draws Anti-Terrorist Focus," *Washington Post*, November 4, 2001, sec. A; Thomas E. Ricks, "Pacific Plan Seeks Clues to Al Qaeda Contacts," *Washington Post*, November 4, 2001, sec. A; Karen De Young, "'Sleeper Cells' Of Al Qaeda Are Next Target," *Washington Post*, December 3, 2001, sec. A; Steve Vogel and Karl Vick, "Team in Somalia May Be Planning U.S. Strikes," *Washington Post*, December 11, 2001, sec. A; Steve Vogel and Molly Moore, "U.S. Warns Against Helping Bin Laden," *Washington Post*, December 19, 2001, sec. A; James Dao and Eric Schmitt, "U.S. Sees Battles in Lawless Areas after Afghan War," *New York Times*, January 8, 2002, sec. A.

77. Griff White, "Afghan Parliament Opens with Appeal by Karzai for Unity," *Washington Post*, December 20, 2005, sec. A; Carlotta Gall and Somini Sengupta, "Afghan Voters Take Next Step to Democracy," *New York Times*, September 19, 2005, sec. A.

78. Eric Schmitt, "Springtime for Killing in Afghanistan," *New York Times*, May 28, 2006, sec. 4, chronicles the resurgent Taliban attacks in the spring of 2006. See also Joel Hafvenstein, "Afghanistan's Drug Habit," *New York Times*, September 20, 2006, sec. A; Carlotta Gall, "Troops in Afghan District Find Anger at Lax Government," *New York Times*, September 18, 2006, sec, A; Pamela Constable, "Afghan Experiment Marked by Progress and Disillusionment," *Washington Post*, September 11, 2006, sec. A; Rachel Morarjee, "Doubts Intensify over Afghanistan's Future," *Christian Science Monitor*, September 11, 2006; Peter Bergen, "The Taliban Regrouped and Rearmed," *Washington Post*, September 10, 2006, sec. B; Carlotta Gall, "Nation Faltering, Afghans' Leader Draws Criticism," *New York Times*, August 23, 2006, sec. A; Pamela Constable, "Dozens Are Killed in Afghan Fighting," *Washington Post*, May 23, 2006, sec. A; Carlotta Gall, "Taliban Threat Is Said to Grow in Afghan South," *New York Times*, May 3, 2006, sec. A.

79. Todd S. Purdum, "Bush Makes His Mark," *New York Times*, March 17, 2005, sec. A.

80. David Frum, *The Right Man: The Surprise Presidency of George W. Bush* (New York: Random House, 2003), 196.

CHAPTER 7.   THE ROAD TO BAGHDAD, PART THREE: OPERATION IRAQI FREEDOM

1. I have drawn on Marr, *Iraq*, 13–15, 21–28; Tripp, *History*, 30–52. Elie Kedourie chronicles the history of Shiite-Sunni friction from 1921 to 1958 in *The Chatham House Version and Other Middle-Eastern Studies* (New York: Praeger, 1970), 236–82. British Military efforts in Iraq from 1920 to 1948 are summarized in Joel Rayburn, "The Last Exit from Iraq," *Foreign Affairs* 85, no. 2 (March/April 2006): 29–40.

2. Yitzhak Nakash, *The Shi'is of Iraq* (Princeton, NJ: Princeton University Press, 1994), 25–66.

3. Adeed Dawisha, "Democratic Attitudes and Practices in Iraq, 1921–1958," *Middle East Journal* 59, no. 1 (Winter 2005): 12, 29.

4. United Nations Security Council, S/Res/687 (1991), adopted April 3, 1991.

5. Tripp, *History*, 260–63; Marr, *Iraq*, 288–90.

6. United Nations Security Council, S/Res/1284 (1999), adopted December 17, 1999.

7. Tripp, *History*, 280.

8. United Nations Security Council, S/Res/986 (1995), adopted April 14, 1995.

9. Independent Inquiry Committee into the United Nations Oil-for-Food Programme, *Manipulation of the Oil-for-Food Programme by the Iraqi Regime*, October 27, 2005. See also Doreen Carvajal and Andrew Kramer, "Report on Oil-for-Food Scheme Gives Details of Bribes to Iraq," *New York Times*, October 28, 2005, sec. A.

10. Woodward, *Plan of Attack*, 15.

11. *Oil-for-Food Inquiry*.

12. Tripp, *History*, 278.

13. Ron Suskind, *The Price of Loyalty: George W. Bush, the White House, and the Education of Paul M. O'Neill* (New York: Simon and Schuster, 2004), 70–75.

14. Woodward, *Plan of Attack*, 13.

15. Ibid., 15.

16. Ibid., 19–20. For background on Chalabi, see George Packer, *The Assassins' Gate: America in Iraq* (New York: Farrar, Straus and Giroux, 2005), 75–78.

17. Gordon and Trainor, *COBRA II*, 14–15.

18. Woodward, *Plan of Attack*, 20–22.

19. Ibid., 21.

20. William Hamilton, "Bush Began to Plan War Three Months after 9/11," *Washington Post*, April 17, 2004, sec. A; Woodward, *Plan of Attack*, 22. Gordon and Trainor, *COBRA II*, 12, credits General Wayne Downing, the former head of the U.S. Special Operations Command with devising the enclave strategy. They also report on that September 13, 2001, Rumsfeld ordered the development of a military plan to seize a portion of southern Iraq (19–21). For a critique of the enclave strategy see Daniel Byman, Kenneth Pollack, and Gideon Rose, "The Rollback Fantasy," *Foreign Affairs* 78, no. 1 (January–February 1999): 24–41.

21. Hamilton, "Bush Began to Plan"; Woodward, *Plan of Attack*, 22. See also Glenn Kessler, "U.S. Decision on Iraq Has Puzzling Past," *Washington Post*, January 13, 2003, sec. A.

22. Bowden, "Wolfowitz," 118–19.

23. Woodward, *Plan of Attack*, 26. See also Kessler, "U.S. Decision on Iraq."

24. Christopher Marquis, "Bush Officials Differ on Way to Force Out Iraqi Leader," *New York Times*, June 19, 2002, sec. A. The various options are analyzed in Kenneth M. Pollack, *The Threatening Storm: The Case for Invading Iraq* (New York: Random House, 2002), 243–386.

25. Woodward, *Plan of Attack*, 1, 2, 30.

26. Gordon and Trainor, *COBRA II*, 21–23; Woodward, *Plan of Attack*, 31; Franks, *American Soldier*, 315. See also Hamilton, "Bush Began to Plan"; Thom Shanker and David E. Sanger, "U.S. Envisions Blueprint on Iraq Including Big Invasion Next Year," *New York Times*, April 28, 2002, sec. 1; William Arkin, "Planning an Iraq War but Not an Outcome," *Los Angeles Times*, May 5, 2002, sec. M.

27. The quotations are from Bob Woodward, *State of Denial: Bush at War, Part III* (New York: Simon and Schuster, 2006), 84–85.

28. Woodward, *Plan of Attack*, 80–82.

29. George W. Bush, "Address before a Joint Session of the Congress of the United States," January 29, 2002, *Weekly Compilation of Presidential Documents* 38, no. 5 (February 4, 2002): 135. See also Michael R. Gordon, "Broadening of 'Doctrine,'" *New York Times*, January 30, 2002, sec. A; David E. Sanger, "Bush, Focusing on Terrorism, Says Secure U.S. Is Top Priority," *New York Times*, January 30, 2002, sec. A; Karen DeYoung, "Bush Lays Down a Marker for 3 'Evil' States," *Washington Post*, January 30, 2002, sec. A; Elisabeth Bumiller, "Axis of Debate: Hawkish Words," *New York Times*, February 3, 2002, sec. 4. Frum, *Right Man*, 231–39, recounts how the "axis of evil" phrase entered the State of the Union address. He notes: "Together, the terror states and the terror organizations formed an axis of hatred against the United States. The United States could not wait for these dangerous regimes to get deadly weapons and attack us; the United States must strike first and protect the world from them" (236).

30. Ronald W. Reagan, "Remarks at the Annual Convention of National Association of Evangelicals," March 8, 1983, *Weekly Compilation of Presidential Documents* 19, no. 10 (March 14, 1983): 369. See also Paul Kengor, *God and Ronald Reagan: A Spiritual Life* (New York: Regan Books, 2004), 233–41, 245–49.

31. Bush, "2002 State of the Union Address," 135.

32. Woodward, *Plan of Attack*, 93.

33. Ibid., 94.

34. Mann, *Vulcans*, 320–21.

35. Bush, "2002 State of the Union Address," 138. In his 1999 campaign autobiography, *A Charge to Keep* (New York: William Morrow, 1999), George W. Bush states: "Our greatest export is freedom, and we have a moral obligation to champion it throughout the world" (240).

36. Woodward, *Plan of Attack*, 109.

37. Ibid., 108–9. See also Alan Sipress, "Bush Says U.S. Willing to Take Action against Iraq," *Washington Post*, February 14, 2002, sec. A; Bob Woodward, "With CIA Push, Movement to War Accelerated," *Washington Post*, April 19, 2004. sec. A. The CIA apparently recruited and trained an Iraqi paramilitary group, with the code name Scorpions, to foster rebellion, conduct sabotage, and ultimately help U.S. paramilitary forces. Dana Priest and Josh White, "Before the War, CIA Reportedly Trained a Team of Iraqis to Aid U.S.," *Washington Post*, August 3, 2005, sec. A; Risen, *State of War*, 138–39.

38. George W. Bush, "The President's News Conference with Prime Minister Tony Blair of the United Kingdom in Crawford, Texas," April 6, 2002, *Weekly Compilation of Presidential Documents* 38, no. 5 (April 15, 2002): 564.

39. George Bush, "2002 State of the Union Address," 135.

40. John Lewis Gaddis, *Surprise, Security, and the American Experience* (Cambridge, MA: Harvard University Press, 2004), 22. See also John Lewis Gaddis, "A Grand Strategy of Transformation," *Foreign Policy* 133 (November–December 2002): 50–57.

41. George W. Bush "Commencement Address at the United States Military Academy in West Point, New York," June 1, 2002, *Weekly Compilation of Presidential Documents* 38, no. 23 (June 10, 2002): 946. See also Elisabeth Bumiller, "U.S. Must Act First to Battle Terror, Bush Tells Cadets," *New York Times*, June 2, 2002, sec. 1; Mike Allen and Karen DeYoung, "Bush: U.S. Will Strike First at Enemies," *Washington Post*, June 2, 2002, sec. A.

42. George W. Bush "Commencement Address," 947.

43. Ibid.

44. Todd S. Purdum and Patrick E. Tyler, "Top Republicans Break with Bush on Iraq Strategy," *New York Times*, August 16, 2002, sec. A; Purdum, *Time of Our Choosing*, 34.

45. Woodward, *Plan of Attack*, 148–57.

46. Rupert Cornwell, "American Rattles Saddam's Cage Hoping He Will Lash Out in Anger," *Independent* (London), July 13, 2002.

47. Williamson Murray and Robert H. Scales Jr., *The Iraq War: A Military History* (Cambridge, MA: Harvard University Press, Belknap Press, 2003), 42–43.

48. Gordon and Trainor, *COBRA II*, 71–72. Woodward, *Plan of Attack*, 149–51.

49. Gordon and Trainor, *COBRA II*, 71. See also Bob Woodward, "Cheney Was Unwavering in Desire to Go to War," *Washington Post*, April 20, 2004, sec. A; Hamilton, "Bush Began to Plan"; Woodward, *Plan of Attack*, 150.

50. Woodward, *Plan of Attack.*, 154–57, 161.

51. Gordon and Trainor, *COBRA II*, 72–73.

52. Bob Woodward, "Cheney Was Unwavering." See also Woodward, *Plan of Attack*, 167, 174–76.

53. The quotations in this paragraph are from George W. Bush, "Address to United Nations General Assembly in New York City," September 12, 2002, *Weekly Compilation of Presidential Documents* 38, no. 37 (September 16, 2002): 1532. See also David E. Sanger and Elisabeth Bumiller, "Bush Presses U.N. to Act Quickly on Disarming Iraq," *New York Times*, September 13, 2002, sec. A; Karen DeYoung, "Bush Tells United Nations It Must Stand Up to Hussein, or U.S. Will," *Washington Post*, September 13, 2002, sec. A.

54. *The National Security Strategy of the United States of America*, September 2002, http://www.whitehouse.gov/nsc/nss.pdf. See also Judith Miller, "Keeping U.S. No. 1," *New York Times*, October 26, 2002, sec. B. For analyses of the NSS by proponents, see Gaddis, *Surprise*, 83–91 and Joshua Muravichik, "The Bush Manifesto," *Commentary*, December 2002, 23–30 and critiques by Francis Fukuyama, *America at the Crossroads: Democracy, Power, and The Neoconservative Legacy* (New Haven, CT: Yale University Press, 2006), 84–92; Francis Fukuyama, "The Bush Doctrine, Before and After," *Financial Times*, October 1, 2005; Robert Jervis, *American Foreign Policy in a New Era* (New York: Routledge, 2005), 79–101, 104–116. In March 2006, the Bush administration released an updated version of its national security strategy, backing the preventive attack on Iraq in 2003 and identifying Iran as the nation most likely to present the future greatest challenge to the U.S. White House, *The National Security Strategy of the United States of America*, March 2006, http://www.whitehouse.gov/nsc/nss/2006/. See also David E. Sanger, "Report Backs Iraq Strike and Cites Iran Peril," *New York Times*, March 16, 2006, sec. A; Peter Baker, "Bush to Restate Terror Strategy," *Washington Post*, March 16, 2006, sec. A.

55. *NSS 2002*, 6, 15.

56. Ibid., 30.

57. Ibid., iv, 3.

58. *Authorization for Use of Military Force against Iraq Resolution*, Public Law 107–243, enacted October 16, 2002.

59. *Congressional Record* 148 (October 10, 2002): H 7799 and (October 11, 2002): S 10342. See also Elizabeth Bumiller and Carl Hulse, "Threats and Responses: The Overview," *New York Times*, October 12, 2002, sec. A.

60. Woodward, *Plan of Attack*, 223–24.

61. Gordon and Trainor, *COBRA II*, 106–7.

62. United Nations Security Council, S/Res/1441 (2002), adopted November 8, 2002. See also Karen DeYoung, "For Powell, a Long Path to a Victory," *Washington Post*, November 10, 2002, sec. A; Tyler Marshall, Maggie Farley, and Doyle McManus, "A War of Words Led to Unanimous U.N. Vote," *Los Angeles Times*, November 10, 2002.

63. Woodward, *Plan of Attack*, 240, 296–97.

64. James Dao and Eric Schmitt, "U.S. Taking Steps to Lay Foundation for Action in Iraq," *New York Times*, November 18, 2002, sec. A; Michael R. Gordon, "Iraq's Neighbors Seem Ready to Support a War," *New York Times*, December 2, 2002, sec. A.

65. Eric Schmitt, "Buildup Leaves U.S. Nearly Set to Start Attack," *New York Times*, December 8, 2002, sec. 1. See also Woodward, *Plan of Attack*, 231–34.

66. Woodward, *Plan of Attack*, 246.

67. Michael Dobbs, "Lack of Hard Evidence Complicates U.S. Aims," *Washington Post*, December 8, 2002, sec. A.

68. Bob Woodward, "With CIA Push"; Hamilton, "Bush Began to Plan." See also Woodward, *Plan of Attack*, 247–50.

69. Deputy Secretary of Defense Paul Wolfowitz, "Speech on Iraq Disarmament," January 23, 2003, *U.S. Department of Defense*, http://www.defenselink.mil/Transcripts/archive.aspx (accessed September 4, 2005).

70. Woodward, "With CIA Push." See also Woodward, *Plan of Attack*, 289–90; Eric Schmitt, "Rumsfeld Says U.S. Has 'Bulletproof' Evidence of Iraq's Links to Al Qaeda," *New York Times*, September 28, 2002, sec. 4.

71. Paul Wolfowitz, "Why Saddam Is a Target in Our War on Terror," *Independent* (London), January 30, 2003.

72. George W. Bush, "Address before a Joint Session of the Congress on the State of the Union," January 28, 2003, *Weekly Compilation of Presidential Documents* 39, no. 51 (February 3, 2003): 115. See also Richard W. Stevenson and David E. Sanger, "Calling Iraq a Serious Threat, Bush Vows That He'll Disarm It, and Also Rebuild U.S. Economy," *New York Times*, January 29, 2003, sec. A; Michael Gordon, "Bush Enlarges Case for War by Linking Iraq with Terrorists," *New York Times*, January 29, 2003, sec. A; James Risen, "Bush's Speech Puts New Focus on State of Intelligence Data," *New York Times*, January 29, 2003, sec. A; Dana Milbank and Mike Allen, "Bush Stiffens Warning of War with Iraq, Says Hussein Missed His 'Final Chance,'" *Washington Post*, January 29, 2003, sec. A.

73. Secretary of State Colin L. Powell, "Remarks to the United Nations Security Council," February 5, 2003, *U.S. Department of State*, http://www.state.gov/secretary/former/powell/remarks/2003/17300.htm (accessed January 18, 2006). See also Steven R. Weisman, "Powell, in U.N. Speech, Presents Case to Show Iraq Has Not Disarmed," *New York Times*, February 6, 2003, sec. A; Patrick E. Tyler, "Intelligence Break Led U.S. to Tie Envoy Killing to Iraq Qaeda Cell," *New York Times*, February 6, 2003, sec. A; Karen DeYoung and Walter Pincus, "Satellite Images, Communication Intercepts and Defectors' Briefings," *Washington Post*, February 6, 2003, sec. A; Walter Pincus and Susan Schmidt, "Agency Coordination Helps Yield Details on Al Qaeda 'Associate,'" *Washington Post*, February 6, 2003, sec. A. Powell subsequently stated that his 2003 speech to the U.N. was "painful" for him and would serve as a permanent "blot" on his record. Steven R. Weisman, "Powell Calls His U.N. Speech a Lasting Blot on His Record," *New York Times*, September 9, 2005, sec. A.

74. Elisabeth Bumiller, "Just Another Monday, Except for Its Conclusion," *New York Times*, March 18, 2003, sec. A. During a January 31, 2003 meeting at the White House, Bush had made it clear to British Prime Minister Tony Blair that the U.S. would invade

Iraq without a second resolution. Don Van Natta Jr., "Bush Was Set on Path to War, Memo by British Adviser Says," *New York Times*, March 27, 2006, sec. A.

75. Woodward, *Plan of Attack*, 402.

76. Purdum, *Time of Our Choosing*, 100–101. Gordon and Trainor, *COBRA II*, 112–13, 115, details U.S. efforts to win over Turkey. See also Dexter Filkins, "Turkish Deputies Refuse to Accept American Troops," *New York Times*, February 25, 2003, sec. 1; David L. Phillips, *Losing Iraq: Inside the Postwar Reconstruction Fiasco* (Boulder, CO: Westview, 2005), 111–20.

77. The ground and air campaigns are detailed in Gordon and Trainor, *COBRA II*, 184–314, 318–43, 345–89, 391–433, 435–56; Murray and Scales, *Iraq War*, 88–233; Franks, *American Soldier*, 444–535; Anthony Cordesman, *The Iraq War: Strategy, Tactics, and Military Lessons* (Westport, CT: Praeger, 2003), 57–147.

78. George W. Bush, "Address to the Nation on Iraq from the U.S.S. Abraham Lincoln," May 1, 2003, *Weekly Compilation of Presidential Documents* 39, no. 18 (May 5, 2003): 516. See also David E. Sanger, "Bush Declares 'One Victory in a War on Terror,'" *New York Times*, May 2, 2003, sec. A; Elisabeth Bumiller, "Cold Truths behind Pomp," *New York Times*, May 2, 2003, sec. A; Karen DeYoung, "Bush Proclaims Victory in Iraq," *Washington Post*, May 2, 2003, sec. A.

79. Deputy Secretary of Defense Paul Wolfowitz, "Tanenhaus Interview." See also Paul D. Wolfowitz, "Statement," in *Iraq Stabilization and Reconstruction: U.S. Policy and Plans*, Hearing before Committee on Foreign Relations, United States Senate, 108th Cong., 1st sess., S. Hrg. 108-132, May 22, 2003, 16, 20, 21, 28, 29; Deputy Secretary of Defense Paul Wolfowitz, "Remarks at The IISS Asian Security Conference," May 31, 2003, *U.S. Department of Defense*, http://www.defenselink.mil/Transcripts/archive.aspx (accessed August 30, 2005); Deputy Secretary of Defense Paul Wolfowitz, "Briefing on His Recent Trip to Iraq," July 23, 2003, *U.S. Department of Defense*, http://www.defenselink.mil/Transcripts/archive.aspx (accessed August 30, 2005); Paul D. Wolfowitz, "Statement," in *Iraq: Status and Prospects for Reconstruction—Resources*, Hearing before Committee on Foreign Relations, United States Senate, 108th Cong., 1st sess., S. Hrg. 108-255, July 29, 2003, 23, 32.

80. Deputy Secretary of Defense, "Determination and Findings," December 5, 2003.

81. Thomas E. Ricks, "As Critics Zero In, Paul Wolfowitz Is Unflinching on Iraq Policy," *Washington Post*, December 23, 2003, sec. C.

82. Wolfowitz, "Statesmanship in the New Century," 323.

83. Packer, *Assassins' Gate*, 298–99. See also L. Paul Bremer III, with Malcolm McConnell, *My Year In Iraq: The Struggle to Build a Future of Hope* (New York: Simon and Schuster, 2006), 126–27.

CHAPTER 8.   THE AFTERMATH OF THE WAR AND THE QUEST FOR DEMOCRACY IN IRAQ AND ELSEWHERE IN THE MIDDLE EAST

1. I have drawn on Mark Fineman, Robin Wright, and Doyle McManus, "Preparing for War, Stumbling to Peace," *Los Angeles Times*, July 18, 2003, pt. 1; James Fallows, "Blind into Baghdad," *Atlantic Monthly*, January/February 2004, 56–58; Fallows, *Blind into Baghdad*, 52–59; Phillips, *Losing Iraq*, 35–39, 45–54, 77–87, 148–49, 150–64.

2. Bremer, *My Year in Iraq*, 25. See also Gordon and Trainor, *COBRA II*, 159, which states that the project "was of uneven quality. It offered a useful way to bring Iraqi exiles

together to discuss the problems of a new Iraq and proposed some good ideas but it was far short of a viable plan."

3. Reuel March Gerecht, "Now What?" *New York Times Book Review*, July 10, 2005, 9.

4. Michael E. O'Hanlon, "Iraq without a Plan," *Policy Review* 128 (December 2004–January 2005): 36.

5. Woodward, *Plan of Attack*, 133.

6. Paul D. Wolfowitz, "Statement," in *Iraq Stabilization and Reconstruction: U.S. Policy and Plans*, Hearing before the Committee on Foreign Relations, United States Senate, 108th Cong., 1st sess., S. Hrg. 108-132, May 22, 2003, 28.

7. Woodward, *Plan of Attack*, 148.

8. Franks, *American Soldier*, 393.

9. Ibid. Thomas E. Ricks, *Fiasco: The American Military Adventure in Iraq* (New York: Penguin Press, 2006), asserts that the Phase IV planning was "incoherent" (79) and lacking (109–10).

10. David Von Drehle, "Wrestling with History," *Washington Post Magazine*, November 13, 2005, 12, 14. Woodward, *Plan of Attack*, 206, lists some of Rumsfeld's concerns.

11. Woodward, *Plan of Attack*, 280–81.

12. Ibid.; Gordon and Trainor, *COBRA II*, 149; Woodward, *State of Denial*, 112. This decision was not modified until October 2003, when the White House, in an effort to extend its control over the running of Iraq, placed Rice in charge of a new Iraq Stabilization Group to improve interagency coordination and reassert civilian control over the reconstruction and transition. David E. Sanger, "White House to Overhaul Iraq and Afghan Missions," *New York Times*, October 6, 2003, sec. A; Woodward, *State of Denial*, 258. After the termination of the Coalition Provisional Authority, responsibility for Iraq transferred to the State Department. Woodward, *State of Denial*, 312. In December 2005, President Bush announced that the State Department would henceforth lead all U.S. postwar reconstruction efforts in Iraq and elsewhere. Steven R. Weisman, "Bush Gives State Dept. Priority in Helping Nations to Rebuild," *New York Times*, December 15, 2005, sec. A; Caroline Daniel and Guy Dinmore, "Pentagon Loses Responsibility for Rebuilding Iraq," *Financial Times*, December 15, 2005.

13. Gordon and Trainor, *COBRA II*, 147, 149. The Pentagon maintained that the traditional two lines of authority resulted in the State Department mishandling the Afghan reconstruction, particularly the lack of progress on the Kabul-to-Kandahar highway (147; Woodward, *State of Denial*, 111). See also Francis Fukuyama, "Nation-Building and the Failure of Institutional Memory," in *Nation-Building: Beyond Afghanistan and Iraq*, ed. Francis Fukuyama (Baltimore: Johns Hopkins University Press, 2006), 10.

14. Woodward, *Plan of Attack*, 283; Woodward, *State of Denial*, 112–13.

15. The responsibilities of ORHA and its postwar role are summarized by Paul D. Wolfowitz, "Concepts for Interim Government of Iraq," in *Military Implications of NATO Enlargement and Post-Conflict Iraq*, Hearing before Committee on Armed Services, United States Senate, 108th Cong., 1st sess., S. Hrg. 108-526, April 10, 2003, 42–44. See also Gordon and Trainor, *COBRA II*, 150; Woodward, *State of Denial*, 112–13; Risen, *State of War*, 134. For other views on ORHA, particularly the Pentagon's preventing Warrick from joining ORHA, see Fallows, "Blind into Baghdad," 72; Fallows, *Blind into Baghdad*, 95; Ricks, *Fiasco*, 102–4; Woodward, *State of Denial*, 126–29; Phillips, *Losing Iraq*, 126–28; David Rieff, "Blueprint for a Mess," *New York Times Magazine*, November 2, 2003, 32; Packer, *Assassins' Gate*, 124.

16. Wolfowitz, "Statement," in *Iraq Stabilization and Reconstruction*, 55, 73.

17. Scarborough, *Rumsfeld's War*, 54; Packer, *Assassins Gate*, 122–23. Woodward, *State of Denial*, 124–26, summarizes Garner's "rock drill" and a meeting on February 28, 2003 with the president and his war cabinet (131–34) where Garner indicated that defeating the terrorists and reshaping the Iraqi military and security forces were beyond his small team's capabilities.

18. Packer, *Assassins Gate*, 125–26.

19. Woodward, *Plan of Attack*, 328–29; Gordon and Trainor, *COBRA II*, 162. See also Michael R. Gordon, "Debate Lingering on Decision to Dissolve the Iraqi Military," *New York Times*, October 21, 2004, sec. A.

20. For the March 10 meeting, I have drawn on Woodward, *Plan of Attack*, 339–40; Gordon and Trainor, *COBRA II*, 107, 161–62; Risen, *State of War*, 133; Packer, *Assassins' Gate*, 128–29.

21. Woodward, *Plan of Attack*, 341–42.

22. Ibid., 342–43; Gordon and Trainor, *COBRA II*, 162.

23. Gordon and Trainor, *COBRA II*, 142.

24. Wolfowitz, "Statement," in *Iraq Stabilization and Reconstruction*, 18, 26, 68.

25. Franks, *American Soldier*, 419.

26. Paul Wolfowitz, *Operations and Reconstruction Efforts in Iraq*, Hearing before Committee on Armed Services, House of Representatives, 108th Cong., 2nd sess,, H.A.S.C. No. 108-28, June 22, 2004, 33, 98. See also Thom Shanker, "Wolfowitz Testifies Pentagon Misjudged Iraqi Insurgency," *New York Times*, June 23, 2004, sec. A. As early as July 2003, Wolfowitz alluded to threat from midlevel Baathists. Paul Wolfowitz, "Roots of Hope in a Realm of Fear," *Washington Post*, July 28, 2003, sec. A.

27. Andrew Rathmell et al, *Developing Iraq's Security Sector: The Coalition Provisional Authority's Experience* (Santa Monica, CA: RAND, 2005), 83.

28. Paul D. Wolfowitz, "Statement," in *Department of Defense Budget Priorities for Fiscal Year 2004*, Hearing before Committee on the Budget, House of Representatives, 108th Cong., 1st sess., Serial No. 108-6, February 27, 2003, 10. See also p. 18; Vernon Loeb, "Cost of War Remains Unanswered Question," *Washington Post*, March 1, 2003, sec. A.

29. Paul D. Wolfowitz, *Administration's FY 2003 Supplemental Budget Request*, Hearing before Defense Subcommittee, Appropriations Committee, House of Representatives, 108th Cong., 1st sess., March 27, 2003, http://web.lexis-nexis.com/ (accessed November 29, 2005). In contrast, a February 2003 report noted that "given the enormity of Iraq's reconstruction requirements and the size of its foreign debt, if the Bush Administration's goal is to turn Iraq into a stable, pro-US democracy, it would probably prove counterproductive to use Iraqi oil revenues to reimburse DoD for its costs." Steven M. Kosiak, "Potential Cost of a War with Iraq and Its Post-War Occupation," February 25, 2003, 6, *Center for Strategic and Budgetary Assessments*, http://www.csbaonline.org/4Publications/Archive/B.20030225.Potential_Costs_of/B.20030225.Potential_Costs_of.pdf (accessed January 19, 2007).

30. Deputy Secretary of Defense, Paul Wolfowitz, "Interview with 60 Minutes II," April 1, 2003, *U.S. Department of Defense*, http://www.defenselink.mil/Transcripts/archive.aspx (accessed August 31, 2005).

31. Deputy Secretary of Defense Paul Wolfowitz, "Briefing on His Recent Trip to Iraq," July 23, 2003, *U.S. Department of Defense*, http://www.defenselink.mil/Transcripts/archive.aspx (accessed August 30, 2005). See also Deputy Secretary of Defense Paul Wolfowitz, "Interview with the Los Angeles Times," *U.S. Department of Defense*, July 7, 2003, http://www.defenselink.mil/Transcripts/archive.aspx (accessed August 30, 2005);

Peter Slevin and Dana Priest, "Wolfowitz Concedes Iraq Errors," *Washington Post*, July 24, 2003, sec. A. By 2004, Woodward, *State of Denial*, reports that "Wolfowitz felt increasingly marginalized by Rumsfeld" (310).

32. Secretary of Defense Donald H. Rumsfeld, "DoD News Briefing—Secretary Rumsfeld and Ambassador Bremer," July 24, 2003, *U.S. Department of Defense*, http://www.dod.gov/transcripts/2003/tr20030724-secdef0452.html (accessed January 18, 2006). Ricks, *Fiasco*, 168–70, summarizes Rumsfeld's unwillingness to recognize the insurgency.

33. Bowden, "Wolfowitz," 115.

34. Donald H. Rumsfeld, "Transforming the Military," *Foreign Affairs* 81, no. 3 (May/June 2002): 20–32. George W. Bush, as a presidential candidate, in a speech at the Citadel in 2000 called for a "transformation" of the U.S. military, based on "a revolution in the technology of war." George W. Bush, "A Period of Consequences," September 23, 1999. Bacevich, *New American Militarism*, 165–74, provides background on the technological revolution in the Military Affairs Project, under Andrew Marshall, at the Pentagon. See also Doyle McManus, "Pentagon Reform Is His Battle Cry," *Los Angeles Times*, August 17, 2003, pt. 1.

35. Von Drehle, "Wrestling with History," 28–29.

36. Michael R. Gordon, "The Strategy to Secure Iraq Did Not Foresee a 2nd War," *New York Times*, October 19, 2004, sec. A, summarizes the troop-level debate. See also Packer, *Assassins' Gate*, 244–46.

37. Eric Shinseki provided this answer to a question in *Department of Defense Authorization for Appropriations for Fiscal Year 2004*, Hearings before the Committee on Armed Services, United States Senate, 108th Cong., 1st sess., S. Hrg. 108-241, pt. 1, February 25, 2003, 241.

38. Wolfowitz, "Statement," in *Department of Defense Budget Priorities for Fiscal Year 2004*, 8–10. See also Eric Schmitt, "Pentagon Contradicts General on Iraq Occupation Force's Size," *New York Times*, February 28, 2003, sec. A; Ricks, *Fiasco*, 96–100.

39. See, e.g., Secretary of Defense Donald H. Rumsfeld, "Beyond Nation Building," February 14, 2003, *U.S. Department of Defense*, http://www.defenselink.mil/Transcripts/archive.aspx (accessed April 30, 2006); Eric Schmitt, "Rumsfeld Says More G.I.'s Would Not Help U.S. in Iraq," *New York Times*, September 11, 2003, sec. A.

40. Bremer, *My Year in Iraq*, 106 (italics omitted). See also Packer, *Assassins' Gate*, 244.

41. I have drawn on Fineman, Wright, and McManus, "Preparing for War." See also Jonathan Weisman, "Iraq Chaos No Surprise but Too Few Troops to Quell It," *Washington Post*, April 14, 2003, sec. A; Peter Slavin and Vernon Loeb, "Plan to Secure Postwar Iraq Faulted," *Washington Post*, May 19, 2003, sec. A; Eric Schmitt and David E. Sanger, "Looting Disrupts Detailed U.S. Plan to Restore Iraq," *New York Times*, May 19, 2003, sec. A; Peter Slevin, "Wrong Turn at a Postwar Crossroads?" *Washington Post*, November 20, 2003, sec. A; Farnaz Fassihi et al, "Early U.S. Decisions on Iraq Now Haunt American Efforts," *Wall Street Journal*, April 19, 2004, sec. A.

42. Anthony Shadid, *Night Draws Near: Iraq's People in the Shadow of America's War* (New York: Henry Holt, 2005), 198. George Packer summarizes the looting and the impact of the failure to secure Baghdad after April 9 in *Assassins' Gate*, 137–39. See also Bremer, *My Year*, 18–19.

43. Rieff, "Blueprint for a Mess," 44.

44. Wolfowitz, "Statement," in *Iraq Stabilization and Reconstruction*, 16, 51.

45. O'Hanlon, "Iraq without a Plan," 39.

46. See, e.g., Shadid, *Night*, 157, 175, 212–13.

47. Bremer, *My Year*, 6–8, 11–13. See also Mike Allen, "Expert on Terrorism to Direct Rebuilding," *Washington Post*, May 2, 2003, sec. A; Mike Allen, "Bush Names Iraq Administrator," *Washington Post*, May 7, 2003, sec. A; James Dao and Eric Schmitt, "President Picks a Special Envoy to Rebuild Iraq," *New York Times*, May 7, 2003, sec. A; Karen DeYoung, "U.S. Sped Bremer to Iraq Post," *Washington Post*, May 23, 2003, sec. A.

48. Bremer, *My Year*, 17, 29, 32, 132.

49. Ibid., 12, 19. See also Patrick E. Tyler, "In Reversal, Plan for Iraq Self-Rule Has Been Put Off," *New York Times*, May 17, 2003, sec. A; Packer, *Assassins' Gate*, 133–34, 140.

50. Wolfowitz, "Statement," in *Military Implications of NATO Enlargement and Post-Conflict Iraq*, 11, 16–17.

51. *Coalition Provisional Authority Order Number 1, De-Ba'athification of Iraqi Society*, May 16, 2003, CPA/ORD/16 May 2003/01; Bremer, *My Year*, 39–42, 44–45. See also Phillips, *Losing Iraq*, 145–48; Ricks, *Fiasco*, 158–61; Woodward, *State of Denial*, 191, 193–94, 205.

52. Bremer, *My Year*, 261–62, 297. See also Packer, *Assassins' Gate*, 192.

53. Bremer, *My Year*, 343.

54. *Coalition Provisional Authority Order Number 2, Dissolution of Entities*, May 23, 2003, CPA/ORD/ 23 May 2003/02.

55. Bremer recounts the background of the order dissolving the Iraqi military in *My Year*, 53–57, 236. See Gordon and Trainor, *COBRA II*, 481–84, who maintain that the order "blindsided" the Joint Chiefs of Staff and top U.S. commanders in Iraq. Ricks, *Fiasco*, states, "Rumsfeld was surprised by Bremer's move" (163). See also Woodward, *State of Denial*, 198, 205.

56. Bremer, *My Year*, 26–27, 53, 55. See also Wolfowitz, "Statement," in *Iraq Stabilization and Reconstruction*, 68; Dan Senor and Walter Slocombe, "Too Few Good Men," *New York Times*, November 17, 2005, sec. A; Rathmell, *Developing*, 13. In contrast, Phillips, in *Losing Iraq*, sees the order as "one of the greatest errors in the history of U.S. warfare" (153). See also Michael R. Gordon, "Debate Lingering on Decision to Dissolve the Iraqi Military," *New York Times*, October 21, 2004, sec. A; Packer, *Assassins' Gate*, 193–95; Fallows, "Blind into Baghdad," 74; Fallows, *Blind into Baghdad*, 102–3, 159–61; Ricks, *Fiasco*, 163–64; Woodward, *State of Denial*, 194–96, 251.

57. Bremer, *My Year*, 58. See also Gordon and Trainor, *COBRA II*, 484. Woodward, *State of Denial*, 288, reports that Bremer "folded" on allowing the new Iraqi army's leadership to come from the old army's officers and noncommissioned officers. In November 2005, the Iraqi government called for the return of junior officers, up to the rank of major, from Saddam's disbanded army. Aimed at Sunni Arab officers eligible for reinstatement after a rigorous screening process, the policy officially recognized a practice under way for some time. Edward Wong, "Iraq Asks Return of Some Officers of Hussein Army," *New York Times*, November 3, 2005, sec. A.

58. United Nations Security Council, S/Res/1483 (2003), adopted May 22, 2003.

59. Ibid., parag. 8(c).

60. Bremer details the steps to the formation of the Governing Council in *My Year*, 78–103.

61. United Nations Security Council, S/Res/1500 (2003), adopted August 14, 2003.

62. The quotations from this meeting are from Bremer, *My Year*, 171 (italics omitted). See also p. 205.

63. The transfer of power to an interim government is summarized in Larry Diamond, "What Went Wrong and Right in Iraq," in Fukuyama, *Nation-Building*, 187–89. See also Packer, *Assassins' Gate*, 316–17, 321, 335–36.

64. Bremer recounts his struggles with Sisanti in *My Year*, 163–67, 190, 197–98, 201–2, 210–16, 224–27, 239–42, 272–73, 289, 302–4, 317–18. He outlined his seven-step process for the Governing Council to convene a Constitutional Convention in L. Paul Bremer III, "Iraq's Path to Sovereignty," *Washington Post*, September 8, 2003, sec. A. The seven-step plan was soon dropped. Ricks, *Fiasco*, 255. Reidar Visser, "Sistani, the United States and Politics in Iraq: From Quietism to Machiavellianism?" Norwegian Institute of International Affairs, Paper No. 700–2006, discusses Sistani's role in Iraqi politics. See also Woodward, *State of Denial*, 228–29, 263–64, 370.

65. United Nations Security Council, S/Res/1546 (2004), adopted June 8, 2004.

66. Bowden, "Wolfowitz," 120.

67. The provisions of the constitution as well as the negotiations leading up to its adoption by the Constitution Drafting Committee are summarized in Peter Galbraith, "Last Chance for Iraq," *New York Review of Books*, October 6, 2005, 20–22; Peter W. Galbraith, *The End of Iraq: How American Incompetence Created a War without End* (New York: Simon and Schuster, 2006), 169, 191–204.

68. Robert F. Worth, "Shiite-Kurd Bloc Falls Just Short in Iraqi Election," *New York Times*, January 21, 2006, sec. A; Neil King Jr. and Greg Jaffe, "Iraqi Shiites Win Just under Half of Parliamentary Seats," *Wall Street Journal*, January 21–22, 2006.

69. Dexter Filkins and Richard A. Oppel Jr., "Iraqis Form Government, with Crucial Posts Vacant," *New York Times*, May 21, 2006, sec. 1; Nelson Hernandez and Omar Fekeiki, "Iraqi Premier, Cabinet Sworn In," *Washington Post*, May 21, 2006, sec. A.

70. Edward Wong, "Doubts Increase about Strength of Iraq Premier," *New York Times*, September 20, 2006, sec. A; Sudarsan Raghavan, "Security Ring for Baghdad Underway," *Washington Post*, September 16, 2006, sec. A; Edward Wong and Paul von Zielbauer, "Iraq Stumbling in Bid to Purge Its Rogue Police," *New York Times*, September 17, 2006, sec. A; Michael Moss, David Rohde, and Kirk Sample, "How Iraq Police Reform Because Casualty of War," *New York Times*, May 22, 2006, sec. A.

71. The insurgency is traced by Joe Klein, "Saddam's Revenge," *Time*, September 26, 2005, 44–52.

72. Dexter Filkins, "Profusion of Rebel Groups Helps Them Survive in Iraq," *New York Times*, December 2, 2005, sec. A. See also Packer, *Assassins' Gate*, 301–3, 308, 310.

73. Paul D. Wolfowitz, "Statement," in *Iraq's Transition—The Way Ahead [Part I]*, Hearing before the Committee on Foreign Relations, United States Senate, 108th Cong., 2nd sess., S. Hrg. 108-645, May 18, 2004, 7. See also Thom Shanker, "Hussein's Agents behind Attacks, Pentagon Finds," *New York Times*, April 29, 2004, sec. A; Douglas Jehl, "U.S. Aides Say Kin of Hussein Aid Insurgency," *New York Times*, July 5, 2004, sec. A. Woodward, *State of Denial*, 184, summarizes a one-page, postwar directive issued by Saddam's intelligence service.

74. Bradley Graham, "Zarqawi 'Hijacked' Insurgency," *Washington Post*, September 28, 2005, sec. A; Dexter Filkins and David S. Cloud, "Defying U.S. Efforts, Guerrillas in Iraq Refocus and Strengthen," *New York Times*, July 24, 2005, sec. 1; Eric Schmitt, "U.S. and Allies Capture More Foreign Fighters, *New York Times*, June 19, 2005, sec. 1; Walter Pincus, "Zarqaqi Is Said to Swear Allegiance to Bin Laden," *Washington Post*, October 19, 2004, sec. A.

75. Jay Solomon, Yasmine El-Rashidi, and Glenn R. Simpson, "Radicals in Iraq Begin Exporting Violence, Mideast Neighbors Say," *Wall Street Journal*, October 7, 2005, sec. A; Michael Slackman and Scott Shane, "Terrorists Trained by Zarqawi Were Sent Abroad, Jordan Says," *New York Times*, June 11, 2006, sec. A.

76. Philip Shishkin and Yochi J. Dreazan, "Goal of Iraqi Unity Fades as Fissures Harden into Place," *Wall Street Journal*, March 14, 2006, sec. A.

77. Bill Marsh, "A Many-Headed Insurgency," *New York Times*, June 11, 2006, sec. 4. In *Insurgency and Counter-Insurgency in Iraq* (Ithaca, NY: Cornell University Press, 2006), Ahmed S. Hashim argues the insurgency is broadly based in the Sunni Arab community and draws strength from the tribal structure of Iraqi society.

78. John Ward Anderson, "Iraqi Tribes Strike Back at Insurgents," *Washington Post*, March 7, 2006, sec. A; Sabrina Tavernise and Dexter Filkins, "Local Insurgents Tell of Clashes with Al Qaeda's Forces in Iraq," *New York Times*, January 12, 2006, sec. A.

79. Sabrina Tavernise, "As Iraqi Shiites Police Sunnis, Rough Justice Feeds Bitterness," *New York Times*, February 6, 2006, sec. A; Sabrina Tavernise, "Many Iraqis See Sectarian Roots in New Killings," *New York Times*, May 27, 2005, sec. A.

80. Sabrina Tavernise, "Iraq Power Shift Widens a Gulf between Sects," *New York Times*, February 18, 2006, sec. A.

81. Sudaran Raghavan, "Distrust Breaks the Bonds of a Baghdad Neighborhood," *Washington Post*, September 27, 2006, sec. A; Damien Cave, "More Iraqis Fleeing Strife and Segregating by Sect," *New York Times*, July 21, 2006, sec. A; Sabrina Tavernise, "Alarmed by Raids, Neighbors Stand Guard in Iraq," *New York Times*, May 10, 2006, sec. A; Jonathan Finer, "Threat of Shiite Militias Now Seen as Iraq's Most Critical Challenge," *Washington Post*, April 8, 2006, sec. A; Ellen Knickermeyer, "Sectarian Fighting Changes Face of Conflict for Iraqis," *Washington Post*, March 13, 2006, sec. A.

82. Sabrina Tavernise, "Fear Invades a Once-Comfortable Iraqi Enclave," *New York Times*, June 24, 2006, sec. A; Sabrina Tavernise, "For Iraqis, Exodus to Syria and Jordan Continues," *New York Times*, June 14, 2006, sec. A; Sabrina Tavernise, "As Death Stalks Iraq, Middle-Class Exodus Begins," *New York Times*, May 19, 2006, sec. A; Doug Struck, "Professionals Fleeing Iraq as Violence, Threat Persist," *Washington Post*, January 23, 2006, sec. A. On balance, however, between April 2003 and December 2005, more than 1.2 million people returned to Iraq. Amir Taheri, "The Real Iraq," *Commentary*, June 2006, 22.

83. Richard A. Oppel, Jr., "Iraqi Official Reports Capture of Top Insurgent Leader Linked to Shrine Bombing," *New York Times*, September 4, 2006, sec. A; Amit R. Paley, "Iraq Cites Arrest of a Top Local Insurgent," *Washington Post*, September 4, 2006, sec. A; Edward Wong, "Iraqi Led Shrine Bombing that Sent Nation into Chaos," *New York Times*, June 29, 2006, sec. A; Joshua Partlow, "Iraqi Official Says Insurgent Cell Bombed Shiite Shrine," *Washington Post*, June 29, 2006, sec. A.

84. Special Inspector General for Iraq Reconstruction, *Report to Congress*, July 31, 2006, 5, 37–38. See also Robert F. Worth and James Glanz, "Oil Graft Fuels the Insurgency, Iraq and U.S. Say," *New York Times*, February 5, 2006, sec. A; Robert D. Novak, "Iraq's Oil Crisis," *Washington Post*, March 23, 2006, sec. A; Yochi J. Dreazen, "Audit of Iraq Reconstruction Finds Corruption Worsening," *Wall Street Journal*, August 2, 2006, sec. A. Fraud and price gouging also diverted reconstruction funds. Scott J. Paltrow, "Some Iraq Rebuilding Funds Go Untraced," *Wall Street Journal*, January 17, 2006, sec. A; James Glanz, "Audit Describes Misuse of Funds in Iraq Projects," *New York Times*, January 25, 2006, sec. A.

85. See, e.g., James Glanz, "Rebuilding of Iraqi Oil Pipeline as Disaster Waiting to Happen," *New York Times*, April 25, 2006, sec. A.

86. Special Inspector General for Iraq Reconstruction, *Report to Congress*, October 30, 2005, 18; T. Christian Miller, *Blood Money: Wasted Billions, Lost Lives, and Corporate Greed in Iraq* (New York: Little, Brown, 2006), 37, 96–97. See also Jeff Gerth, "Report Offered Bleak Outlook about Iraq Oil," *New York Times*, October 5, 2003, sec. 1, which critiqued

the assumptions about postwar Iraqi oil production and whether oil revenues could finance both routine government operations and some reconstruction.

87. For a list of attacks on Iraqi pipelines, oil installations, and oil personnel see "Iraq Pipeline Watch," www.iaqs.org/iraqpipelinewatch.htm (accessed April 3, 2006). See also Miller, *Blood Money*, 94.

88. The statistics in this paragraph are from Special Inspector General July 2006 *Report*, 29, 34; Special Inspector General for Iraq Reconstruction, *Report to Congress*, January 30, 2006, 20, table 2–4 ("Actual Oil Sector Production vs. U.S. Reconstruction Goals as of November 30, 2005"), 24, 27. See also Chip Cummins and Hassan Hafidh, "Fresh Woes Hinder Iraqi Oil Output," *Wall Street Journal*, February 21, 2006, sec. A; Ellen Knickmeyer and Salih Saif Aldin, "Attacks Halt Production at Iraq's Largest Refinery," *Washington Post*, December 30, 2005, sec. A; Kevin G. Hall, "Attacks Taking Heavy Oil Toll on Iraq," *Houston Chronicle*, November 18, 2005, sec. A; Miller, *Blood Money*, 93, 101, 290.

89. Special Inspector General, January 2006 *Report*, 26. See also Richard A. Oppel Jr., "In Iraq, Rich in Oil, Higher Gasoline Prices Anger Many," *New York Times*, December 31, 2005, sec. A.

90. International Monetary Fund, Staff Representatives for the 2005 Consultation with Iraq, *Staff Report for the 2005 Article IV Consultation*, IMF Country Report No. 05/294, August 2005, "Box 2. Iraq: Subsidies on Petroleum Products," 11.

91. Special Inspector General, January 2006 *Report*, 26; IMF Staff, *Report*, 10, 13, 25. See also Robert M. Kimmett, "Iraq's Post-Saddam Economy," *Wall Street Journal*, December 9, 2005, sec. A; Oppel, "In Iraq, Rich in Oil."

92. IMF Staff, *Report*, 7.

93. Special Inspector General, July 2006 *Report*, 19; Special Inspector General January 2006 *Report*, 16, table 2–1 ("Current Status of Electricity Reconstruction vs. Goals"). See also Ellen Knickermeyer, "U.S. Has End in Sight in Iraq Rebuilding," *Washington Post*, January 2, 2006, sec. A.

94. Special Inspector General, July 2006 *Report*, 19, table 204 ("Current Outcomes vs. Pre-War Levels and Goals"), 25; Special Inspector General, January 2006 *Report*, 17, table 2–2 ("Electricity Sector Outcomes").

95. National Security Council, "National Strategy for Victory in Iraq," November 24, 2005, 24; Special Inspector General, October 2005 *Report*, 19; Special Inspector General, January 2006 *Report*, 17–18. See also Miller, *Blood Money*, 275.

96. Office of the Special Inspector General for Iraq Reconstruction, "Challenges Faced in Carrying Out Iraq Relief and Reconstruction Fund Activities," January 26, 2006, SIGIR-05-029, 3; Special Inspector General, October 2005 *Report*, 3. See also Knickermeyer, "U.S. Has End in Sight"; Jonathan Finer, "Report Measures Shortfall in Iraq Goals," *Washington Post*, January 27, 2006, sec. A; Renae Merle and Griff Witte, "Security Costs Slow Iraq Reconstruction," *Washington Post*, July 29, 2005, sec. A. Some estimates placed the security and insurance outlays in the range from 30 to 50 percent of the total cost on reconstruction projects. IMF Staff, *Report*, 7.

97. IMF Staff, *Report*, 14 ("Box 3. Iraq: Trade and Investment Policies"), 18; National Security Council, "National Strategy," 23.

98. Amir Taheri, "Guess Who's Coming to Dinar," *Wall Street Journal*, September 14, 2005, sec. A; National Security Council, "National Strategy," 23.

99. Dan Murphy and Awadh Al-Taiee, "Iraqis Feel Weight of High Prices, Few Jobs," *Christian Science Monitor*, September 15, 2006: Damien Cave, "Weary Iraqis Face New Foe: Rising Prices," *New York Times*, August 26, 2006, sec. A.

100. Bowden, "Wolfowitz," 114. See also Austin Bay, "Nervous in Baghdad," *Weekly Standard*, June 25, 2005, 20–26.

101. See, e.g., George W. Bush, "Address to the Nation on the War on Terror," September 11, 2006, *Weekly Compilation of Presidential Documents* 42, no. 37 (September 18, 2006): 1599; George W. Bush, "Remarks to the Military Officers Association of America," September 5, 2006, *Weekly Compilation of Presidential Documents* 42, no. 36 (September 11, 2006): 1560; George W. Bush, "Remarks on the War on Terror in Annapolis, Maryland," November 30, 2005, *Weekly Compilation of Presidential Documents* 41, no. 48 (December 5, 2005): 1789. See also National Security Council, "National Strategy," 4; Karen DeYoung, "Spy Agencies Say Iraq War Hurting U.S. Terror Fight," *Washington Post*, September 24, 2006, sec. A.

102. George W. Bush, "Address to the Nation on Iraq and the War on Terror," December 18, 2005, *Weekly Compilation of Presidential Documents* 41, no. 51 (December 26, 2005): 1884.

103. The initial failures to train and equip Iraqi forces are detailed in Thom Shanker, "General Says Training of Iraqi Troops Suffered from Poor Planning and Staffing," *New York Times*, February 11, 2006, sec. A. According to Woodward, *State of Denial*, Wolfowitz indicated that "Rumsfeld had blocked efforts to get the training [of Iraqi security forces] up and running earlier" (309–10). See also Michael Moss and David Rohde, "Misjudgments Marred U.S. Plans for Iraqi Police," *New York Times*, May 21, 2006, sec. 1.

104. See, e.g., Dexter Filkins, "Iraq Set to Unify Security Forces to Battle Chaos," *New York Times*, May 11, 2006, sec. A.

105. Woodward, *Plan of Attack*, 426–27.

106. Deputy Secretary of Defense Paul Wolfowitz, "Tanenhaus Interview."

107. See *Comprehensive Report of the Special Advisor to the Director of Central Intelligence on Iraq's Weapons of Mass Destruction*, 3 vols. (Washington, DC: Superintendent of Documents, September 30, 2004, with March 2005 addendum). See also Douglas Jehl, "U.S. Report Finds Iraqis Eliminated Illicit Arms in 90's," *New York Times*, October 7, 2004, sec. A; Mike Allen and Dana Priest, "Report Discounts Iraqi Arms Threat," *Washington Post*, October 6, 2004, sec. A; Dana Priest and Walter Pincus, "U.S. 'Almost All Wrong' on Weapons," *Washington Post*, October 7, 2004, sec. A.

108. I have drawn on Charles Duelfer, Special Advisor to the Director of Central Intelligence, *Comprehensive Report*, 1:7, 9, and 29; "Regime Strategic Intent," 1:1; "Delivery Systems, in *Comprehensive Report*, 2:2; "Nuclear," 2:1–2; "Iraq's Chemical War Program," in *Comprehensive Report*, 3:1–3; "Biological Warfare," 3:103. See also Gordon and Trainor, *COBRA II*, 65.

109. "Saddam and WMD: Russia's Role," *Investor's Business Daily*, March 7, 2006, sec. A. See also Georges Sada, with Jim Nelson Black, *Saddam's Secrets: How An Iraqi General Defied and Survived Saddam Hussein* (Brentwood, TN: Integrity Publishers, 2006), 251–64; "'Bush Was Right,'" *Investor's Business Daily*, February 22, 2006, sec. A; "Saddam Had WMD," *Investor's Business Daily*, February 27, 2006, sec. A; "Saddam Had WMD (Cont'd)," *Investor's Business Daily*, February 28, 2006, sec. A.

110. Deputy Secretary of Defense Paul Wolfowitz, "On MSNBC Hardball," June 23, 2004, *U.S. Department of Defense*, http://www.defenselink.mil/Transcripts/archive.aspx (accessed August 24, 2005). See also Paul Wolfowitz, President, the World Bank Group, "Trade—The Missing Link," December 7, 2005, *World Bank*, http://web.world bank.org (accessed December 15, 2005).

111. Bowden, "Wolfowitz," 114.

112. Ibid.

113. *9/11 Commission Report*, 66. Two top senior al Qaeda members denied the existence of any ties between Iraq and al Qaeda (470 n. 76). After the 2003 war, according to a Senate report, the U.S. intelligence community concluded that there were no prewar links between Saddam Hussein and Osama bin Laden or Abu Musab al-Zarqawi. *Report of the U.S. Senate Select Committee on Intelligence on Postwar Findings about Iraq's WMD Programs and Links to Terrorism and How They Compare with Prewar Assessments*, 109th Cong., 2nd sess., September 8, 2006, 67–69, 71–75, 90–94, 100–101. See also Mark Mazzetti, "C.I.A. Said to Find No Hussein Link to Terror Chief," *New York Times*, September 9, 2006, sec. A; Jonathan Weisman, "Iraq's Alleged Al-Qaeda Ties Were Disputed before War," *Washington Post*, September 9, 2006, sec. A. Stephen F. Hayes, "How Bad Is the Senate Intelligence Report?" *Weekly Standard*, September 25, 2006, 18–23, provides a critique of the Senate report.

114. Wolfowitz, *Operations and Reconstruction Efforts In Iraq*, 90.

115. Stephen F. Hayes and Thomas Joscelyn, "The Mother of All Connections," *Weekly Standard*, July 17, 2005, 21–33. See also Dan Darling, "The Al-Douri Factor," *Daily Standard*, July 19, 2005, http:www//weeklystandard.com (accessed July 13, 2006), which analyzes the coordination between one of Saddam's closest Baath party officials and al Qaeda groups. For a detailed analysis by a proponent of the Iraq-al Qaeda link see Stephen F. Hayes, *The Connection: How al Qaeda's Collaboration with Saddam Hussein Has Endangered America* (New York: HarperCollins, 2004); Richard Miniter, "Proof of Al-Qaida's Links to Iraq Just Too Strong to Be Dismissed," *Investor's Business Daily*, May 22, 2006, sec. A. See also "Iraq and Terror," *Investor's Business Daily*, March 23, 2006, sec, A; "Don't Hold Back," *Investor's Business Daily*, March 22, 2006, sec. A.

116. Stephen F. Hayes, "Saddam's Terror Training Camps," *Weekly Standard*, January 16, 2006, 22.

117. Stephen F. Hayes, "Saddam's Philippines Terror Connection," *Weekly Standard*, March 27, 2006, 14–17.

118. Woodward, *Plan of Attack*, 427.

119. Deputy Secretary of Defense Paul Wolfowitz and Vice Chairman of the Joint Chiefs of Staff General Peter Pace, "NBC 'Meet the Press,'" April 6, 2003, *U.S. Department of Defense*, http://www.defenselink.mil/Transcripts/archive.aspx (accessed August 31, 2005). See also Edward Walsh and Peter Slevin, "U.N. Role in Postwar Government Debated," *Washington Post*, April 7, 2003, sec. A.

120. Purdum, *Time of Our Choosing*, 274. See also Paul Wolfowitz, "Live from Baghdad," *American Spectator*, August/September 2003, 32–33; Eric Schmitt, "Wolfowitz Sees Challenges, and Vindication, in Iraq," *New York Times*, July 22, 2003, sec. A.

121. Deputy Secretary of Defense Paul Wolfowitz, "Interview with the Jerusalem Post," September 22, 2003, *U.S. Department of Defense*, http://www.defenselink.mil/Transcripts/archive.aspx (accessed August 30, 2005).

122. George W. Bush, "Inaugural Address," January 20, 2005, *Weekly Compilation of Presidential Documents* 41, no. 3 (January 24, 2005): 74, 75. See also Todd S. Purdum, "Focus on Ideals, Not the Details," *New York Times*, January 21, 2005, sec. A; Peter Baker and Michael A. Fletcher, "Bush Pledges to Spread Freedom," *Washington Post*, January 21, 2005, sec. A.

123. The quotations in this paragraph are from Secretary of State Condoleezza Rice, "Remarks at the American University in Cairo," June 20, 2005, *U.S. Department of State*, http://www.state.gov/secretary/ rm/2005/48328.htm (accessed December 4, 2005). See also Condoleezza Rice, "The Promise of Democratic Peace," *Washington Post*, December 11, 2005, sec. B; Steven R. Weisman, "Rice Urges Egyptians and Saudis to Democratize,"

New York Times, June 21, 2005, sec. A; Glenn Kessler, "Rice Criticizes Allies in Call for Democracy," *Washington Post*, June 21, 2005, sec. A.

124. Bush's worldwide efforts are summarized in Peter Baker, "The Realities of Exporting Democracy," *Washington Post*, January 25, 2006, sec. A. For a negative assessment of the prospects for democratization in the Middle East see Hassan M. Fattah, "Arab Democracy, a U.S. Goal, Falters," *New York Times*, April 10, 2006, sec. A. See also Glenn Kessler, "Oil Wealth Colors the U.S. Push for Democracy," *Washington Post*, May 14, 2006, sec. A; Neil King Jr. and Yasmine el-Rashidi, "In Volatile Mideast, U.S. Finds a Use for Old Autocrats," *Wall Street Journal*, August 8, 2006, sec. A.

125. For political developments in Egypt, I have drawn on Michael Slackman, "Egypt, Defying West, Jails Hundreds at Rally," *New York Times*, May 19, 2006, sec. A; Michael Slackman and Mona El-Naggar, "Police Beat Crowds Backing Egypt's Judges," *New York Times*, May 12, 2006, sec. A; Daniel Williams, "Egypt Extends 25-Year-Old Emergency Law," *Washington Post*, May 1, 2006, sec. A; Michael Slackman, "Egypt Renews Emergency Detention Law, *New York Times*, May 1, 2006, sec. A; Karby Leggett and Yasmine El-Rashidi, "Blasts Muddle Cairo's Mission," *Wall Street Journal*, April 26, 2006, sec. A; Michael Slackman, "Egypt's Leader Moves to Delay Elections," *New York Times*, February 14, 2006, sec. A; Daniel Williams, "Banned Islamic Movement Now the Main Opposition in Egypt," *Washington Post*, December 10, 2005, A13; Yasime El-Rashidi, "Islamists Gain in Egypt's Elections," *Wall Street Journal*, December 7, 2005, sec. A; Michael Slackman, "Egyptian Vote Is Again Marred by Attacks on Opposition," *New York Times*, December 2, 2005, sec. A; Michael Slackman, "In Egypt, a Vote More for Change than Faith," *New York Times*, November 29, 2005, sec. A; Michael Slackman, "Under Duress, Egypt's Islamist Party Still Surges at Polls," *New York Times*, November 28, 2005, sec. A; Daniel Williams, "New Tests for Egypt's Opposition," *Washington Post*, September 24, 2005, sec. A; Daniel Williams, "Mubarak Wins Easily, but Vote Fails to Engage Egypt," *Washington Post*, September 10, 2005, sec. A; Michael Slackman, "Mubarak's Victory Orderly, but Opposition Is Still Angry," *New York Times*, September 10, 2005, sec. A; Michael Slackman, "Egypt's Metamorphosis," *New York Times*, September 9, 2005, sec. A; Michael Slackman, "Egypt Holds a Multi-Choice Vote, but the Answer Is Mubarak," *New York Times*, September 8, 2005, sec. A.

126. Scott Wilson, "Some Palestinians See End of Secular Dream," *Washington Post*, January 29, 2006, sec. A; John Kifner, "How Hamas Rose from Wild Card to Power," *New York Times*, January 20, 2006, sec. 4; Scott Wilson, "Hamas Sweeps Palestinian Elections, Complicating Peace Efforts in Mideast," *Washington Post*, January 27, 2006, sec. A.

127. Strategies to promote democracy are discussed in David Adesnik and Michael McFaul, "Engaging Autocratic Allies to Promote Democracy," *Washington Quarterly* 29, no. 2 (Spring 2006): 7–26. John Mueller, *Capitalism, Democracy, and Ralph's Pretty Good Grocery* (Princeton, NJ: Princeton University Press, 1999), argues that democracy will flourish in the absence of imposed obstacles, when people are free to complain and to organize those who complain.

128. See Irving Louis Horowitz, "Democracy's Visions and Divisions," *Chronicle of Higher Education*, February 24, 2006, sec. B.

129. Robert A. Dahl, "What Political Institutions Does Large-Scale Democracy Require?" *Political Science Quarterly* 120, no. 2 (Summer 2005): 187–97, sets forth a political theory of democracy, focusing on elected representatives; free, fair, and frequent elections; freedom of expression; alternative information; associational autonomy; and inclusive citizenship. See also White House, *National Security Strategy*, March 2006, 4–5.

130. In *Foreign Policy in a New Era* (New York: Routledge, 2005), 129–34, Robert Jarvis provides a critique of democracy as the answer, in the context of poverty, militaristic institutions, cultural (deep religious and/or ethnic) divisions, a lack of a democratic tradition, and a commitment to individualism.

131. Amartya Sen offers a critique of cultural determination in "Democracy Isn't 'Western'," *Wall Street Journal*, March 24, 2006, sec. A.

132. Edward D. Mansfield and Jack Snyder, *Electing to Fight: Why Emerging Democracies Go to War* (Cambridge, MA: MIT Press, 2005), argues that nations undergoing a transition to democracy generally are not pacifistic. See also Randall Schweller, "Democracy and the post–Cold War Era," in *The New World Order: Contrasting Theories*, ed. Birthe Hansen and Bertel Heurlin (New York: St. Martin's Press, 2000).

133. See, e.g., Morton H. Halperin, Joseph T. Siegle, and Michael M. Weinstein, *The Democracy Advantage: How Democracies Promote Prosperity and Peace* (New York: Routledge, 2004), 93–114; R. J. Rummel, "Democracies ARE Less Warlike than Other Regimes," *European Journal of International Relations* 1, no. 4 (1995): 459–79. Miriam Fendius Elman, ed., *Paths to Peace: Is Democracy the Answer?* (Cambridge, MA: MIT Press, 1997), presents case studies to test the democratic-peace thesis.

134. George W. Bush, "Inaugural Address," 74. See also 2006 *National Security Strategy*, 10–11. Gregory Gause III, "Can Democracy Stop Terrorism?" *Foreign Affairs* 84, no. 5 (September/October 2005): 62–76, concludes, however, that the available evidence does not support the proposition that democracy reduces or prevents terrorism. See also Dimitri K. Simes, "America's Imperial Dilemma," *Foreign Affairs* 82, no. 6 (November/December 2003): 91–102.

135. Wolfowitz, "Statesmanship in the New Century," 320–21.

136. Seymour Martin Lipset, "Some Social Requisites of Democracy: Economic Development and Political Legitimacy," *American Political Science Review* 53, no. 1 (March 1959): 75–85.

CHAPTER 9.   WOLFOWITZ AT THE WORLD BANK

1. Nancy Birdsall et al., "The Hardest Job in the World: Five Crucial Tasks For the New President of the World Bank," June 1, 2005, *Center for Global Development*, http://www.cgdev.org/content/publications/detail/2868 (accessed January 20, 2007).

2. Bowden, "Wolfowitz," 118.

3. I have drawn on the World Bank, *The World Bank Annual Report 2006*, 8, http://treasury.worldbank.org/web/AnnualReport2006.pdf (accessed January 20, 2007); "A Regime Changes—Paul Wolfowitz at the World Bank," *Economist*, June 4, 2005, 65–67.

4. "Operational Summary/Fiscal 2006," *World Bank Annual Report*. See also pp. 8, 58.

5. "Operational Summary/Fiscal 2006," *World Bank Annual Report*. See also pp. 8, 61.

6. *World Bank Annual Report*, 9.

7. Ibid., 10.

8. Ibid.

9. Eric Schmitt, "The World Is His Stage," *New York Times*, March 17, 2005, sec. A.

10. Quoted in Bradley Graham, "Tsunami Tour Said to Spur Wolfowitz Move," *Washington Post*, March 17, 2005, sec. A.

11. President George W. Bush, "The President's News Conference," March 16, 2005, *Weekly Compilation of Presidential Documents* 41, no. 11 (March 21, 2005): 447. See also Paul Blustein and Peter Baker, "Wolfowitz Picked for World Bank," *Washington Post*,

March 17, 2005, sec. A; Elizabeth Becker and David E. Sanger, "Wolfowitz Gets Bush Nomination for World Banker," *New York Times*, March 17, 2005, sec. A.

12. Keith B. Richburg and Glenn Frankel, "Nomination Shocks, Worries Europeans," *Washington Post*, March 17, 2005, sec. A.

13. Ann Gerhart, "World Bank's Loan Ranger," *Washington Post*, June 9, 2005, sec. C.

14. Elizabeth Becker, "New World Bank Chief Says Aiding Africa Is His Top Goal," *New York Times*, June 1, 2005, sec. C; Gerhart, "World Bank's."

15. I have drawn on Elizabeth Becker, "World Bank Vote Confirms Wolfowitz Unanimously," *New York Times*, April 1, 2005, sec. A; Greg Hitt, "Wolfowitz Sees 'Noble Mission' for World Bank," *Wall Street Journal*, March 31, 2005, sec. A; Elaine Sciolino, "Europe on Wolfowitz as Banker," *New York Times*, March 31, 2005, sec. A; Paul Blustein, "Wolfowitz Draws Nearer to World Bank Post," *Washington Post*, March 24, 2005, sec. A; Paul Blustein, "Wolfowitz Closing In on Bank Post," *Washington Post*, March 22, 2005, sec. E.

16. Sciolino, "Europe on Wolfowitz."

17. "Statements on Confirmation of Paul Wolfowitz as Tenth World Bank President," Washington, D.C., March 31, 2005, *World Bank*, http://web.worldbank.org (accessed June 3, 2005).

18. Quoted in Gerhart, "World Bank's."

19. Paul Blustein, "All Eyes on Wolfowitz as He Ascends at World Bank," *Washington Post*, June 1, 2005, sec. D.

20. International Bank for Reconstruction and Development (IBRD), Articles of Agreement, Article V, Section 5.

21. Edward Alden and Andrew Balls, "Wolfowitz Anti-graft Mission Triggers World Bank Strife," *Financial Times* (London), January 23, 2006; Andrew Balls, "Wolfowitz Aides Spark World Bank Dispute," *Financial Times* (London), January 31, 2006; Paul Blustein, "Muttering at the World Bank," *Washington Post*, February 8, 2006, sec. D.

22. Quoted in Paul Blustein, "World Bank Staffers Protest Appointments," *Washington Post*, January 24, 2006, sec. D. See also Blustein, "Muttering."

23. "World Bank President Announces Appointment of Managing Directors," April 21, 2006, *World Bank*, http://web.worldbank.org (accessed April 23, 2006) and "President Wolfowitz Announces the Appointment of Ana Palacio as Senior Vice President and World Bank Group General Counsel," June 16, 2006, *World Bank*, http://web.worldbank. org (accessed July 3, 2006). See also Paul Blustein, "Wolfowitz Turns Outside for World Bank Picks," *Washington Post*, April 20, 2006, sec. D.

24. Blustein, "Muttering."

25. IBRD Articles of Agreement, Article IV, Section 10; International Development Association, Articles of Agreement, Article V, Section 6.

26. "Annual Meetings Address by James D. Wolfensohn," Washington, D.C., October 1, 1996, *World Bank*, http://web.worldbank.org (accessed November 1, 2005). See also Sebastian Mallaby, *The World's Banker: A Story of Failed States, Financial Crises, and the Wealth and Poverty of Nations* (New York: Penguin Press, 2004), 176.

27. "Interview, Bank Anti-corruption Chief Maarten de Jong," *Development Today* (Norway), no. 12 (2005): 7.

28. World Bank, *World Development Report 1997: The State in a Changing World* (New York: Oxford University Press, 1997), 99–109.

29. World Bank, Public Sector Group, Poverty Reduction and Economic Management (PREM) Network, *Reforming Public Institutions and Strengthening Governance: A World Bank Strategy* (Washington, DC: World Bank, 2000).

30. *World Bank Annual Report*, 58.

31. Report from the Executive Directors of the International Development Association to the Board of Governors, "Addition to IDA Resources: Fourteenth Replenishment: Working Together to Achieve the Millennium Development Goals," March 10, 2005, "Annex 1: Summary of the Performance-Based Allocation System for IDA-14."

32. Press Release, "World Bank President Paul Wolfowitz to Visit Four African Countries during June," June 7, 2005, Press Release No. 2005/504/S, *World Bank*, http://web.worldbank.org (accessed April 16, 2006). See also Tony Allen-Mills, "Wolfowitz the Hawk Turns African Dove," *Sunday Times* (London), June 12, 2005.

33. Press Release, "New World Bank President Paul Wolfowitz Takes Office," June 1, 2005, Press Release No. 2005/495/S, *World Bank*, http://web.worldbank.org (accessed November 2, 2005). See also Becker, "New World Bank Chief"; Andrew Balls, "Loan Wolf," *Financial Times*, September 24–25, 2005, Weekend sec.; Edward T. Pound and Danielle Knight, "On Top of the World," *U.S. News & World Report*, April 3, 2006, 28.

34. World Bank, Africa Region, "Meeting the Challenge of Africa's Development: A World Bank Group Action Plan," September 7, 2005, updated as of September 26, 2005. See also Gobind Nankani, Vice President, Africa Region, World Bank Group, "The Africa Action Plan—Time for Action," September 21, 2005, *World Bank*, http://web.worldbank.org (accessed September 26, 2005); "2006 Annual Meetings Address by Paul Wolfowitz," September 19, 2006, *World Bank*, http://web.worldbank.org (accessed September 25, 2006); *World Bank Annual Report*, 16.

35. Mallaby, *World's Banker*, 104–8, 112, 114–15, 248.

36. "G8 Finance Ministers' Conclusions on Development," London, June 10–11, 2005, *G8 Gleneagles 2005*, http://www.g8.gov.uk (accessed October 31, 2005). See also Alan Cowell, "Finance Chiefs Cancel Debt of 18 Nations," *New York Times*, June 12, 2005, sec. 1; Paul Blustein, "Debt Cut Is Set for Poorest Nations," *Washington Post*, June 12, 2005, sec. A.

37. "Chair's Summary: Gleneagles Summit," July 8, 2005, *G8 Gleneagles 2005*, http://www.g8.gov.uk (accessed December 4, 2005).

38. International Development Association, "The G8 Debt Relief Proposal: Assessment of Costs, Implementation Issues, and Financial Options," September 1, 2005, *World Bank*, http://siteresources.worldbank.org/IDA/Resources/G8DebtPaperSept05.pdf (accessed January 20, 2007).

39. Letter to the President of the World Bank from the G8 Finance Ministers on the G8 Debt Proposal, 23 September 2005. See also Edmund L. Andrews, "Rich Nations Reach Deal to Drop Debt of Poor Ones," *New York Times*, September 25, 2005, sec. 1; Andrew Balls and Chris Giles, "Doubters Assent to Details of Debt Relief Plan," *Financial Times*, September 26, 2005; Michael M. Phillips, "Debt-Relief Plan Gains Key Support at World Bank, IMF," *Wall Street Journal*, September 26, 2005, sec. A.

40. Press Release, "World Bank Approves US$37 Billion for Multilateral Debt Relief Initiative," March 28, 2006, Press Release No. 2006/327/PREM, *World Bank*, http://web.worldbank.org (accessed April 9, 2006); Press Release, "World Bank: Full Debt Cancellation Approved for Some of the World's Poorest Countries," April 21, 2006, Press Release No. 2006/370/PREM, *World Bank*, http://web.worldbank.org (accessed April 23, 2006); Press Release, "World Bank Implements Multilateral Debt Relief Initiative," June 29, 2006, Press Release No. 2006/504/WB, *World Bank*, http://web.worldbank.org (accessed July 3, 2006). The eighteenth nation, Mauritania, will qualify for debt relief after implementing public expenditure management reforms (ibid).

41. Philip Thornton, "Wolfowitz Demands Crackdown on Third World Corruption," *Independent* (London), June 11, 2005.

42. "Chair's Summary: Gleneagles Summit." See also Jim VandeHei and Paul Blustein, "African Aid Is Doubled by G-8," *Washington Post*, July 9, 2005, sec. A; Richard W. Stevenson, "8 Leaders Hail Steps on Africa and Warming," *New York Times*, July 9, 2005, sec. A.

43. Balls, "Loan Wolf."

44. See, e.g., Celia W. Dugger, "Some Rich Nations Slow with Pledged Aid," *New York Times*, June 9, 2006, sec. A.

45. Paul Wolfowitz, "Everyone Must Do More for Doha to Succeed," *Financial Times*, October 24, 2005; Paul Wolfowitz, "Free Trade for a Better Future," *Los Angeles Times*, December 13, 2005, sec. B.

46. Agence France Presse English Wire, "Africa Has 'Real Chance' to Turn Corner with Spotlight on: World Bank Chief," July 6, 2005, 7/6/05 AGFFRP 19:12:00, http://www.westlaw.com/. See also *Agricultural Trade Reform and the Doha Development Agenda*, ed. Kym Anderson and Will Martin (New York: Palgrave Macmillan, 2006).

47. Wolfowitz, "Everyone Must Do More." See also Wolfowitz, "Free Trade." However, Margaret McMillan, Alix Peterson Zwane, and Nava Ashraf, "My Policies or Yours: Does OECD Support for Agriculture Increase Poverty in Developing Countries?" October 2005, *National Bureau of Economic Research*, http://www.nber.org/books/glob-pov/mcmillan-et-al10-19-05.pdf, concludes that agricultural support for farmers in industrialized nations boosted the per capita income of two-thirds of seventy-seven developing nations, including most of the poorest countries. See also Eduardo Porter, "Ending Aid to Rich Farmers May Hurt the Poor Ones," *New York Times*, December 18, 2005, Week in Review sec.

48. The proposals by the United States are summarized in Rob Portman, "America's Proposal to Kick-start Doha Trade Talks," *Financial Times*, October 10, 2005. See also David E. Sanger, "Trade Chief Makes Offer to Reduce Crop Subsidies," *New York Times*, October 10, 2005, sec. A; Scott Miller and Greg Hitt, "U.S. Prepares to Compromise on Farm Tariffs," *Wall Street Journal*, October 10, 2005, sec. A; Alexei Barrionuevo and Tom Wright, "Europe Entertains an American Offer to Cut Farm Aid," *New York Times*, October 11, 2005, sec. C; Tom Wright, "Trade Talks Are Hung Up on Subsidies to Farmers," *New York Times*, October 13, 2005, sec. C.

49. The EU proposals are summarized in Paul Blustein, "Chirac's Concerns Could Threaten Trade Deal," *Washington Post*, October 28, 2005, sec. D; Scott Miller, Juliane von Reppert-Bismarck, and Greg Hitt, "EU Proposes Cuts in Tariffs Protecting Farmers," *Wall Street Journal*, October 29, 2005, sec. A; Raphael Minder and Alan Beattie, "EU Farm Offer Helps Keep Doha Round Alive," *Financial Times*, November 1, 2005; James Kanter, "Trade Leader for Europe Refuses to Cut Farm Tariffs," *New York Times*, December 1, 2005, sec. C; Edward Alden, "EU 'Cannot Cut Farm Tariffs Further,'" *Financial Times*, December 8, 2005.

50. The attempts to bridge the differences and reach a compromise are summarized to Greg Hitt and Scott Miller, "Trade Talks Yield Few Winners," *Wall Street Journal*, December 20, 2005, sec. A; Keith Bradsher, "Orthodoxies on Trade Worn Down in Marathon," *New York Times*, December 20, 2005, sec. C; Guy de Jonquières, "Tentative Steps Forward Seen as Better than None at All," *Financial Times*, December 19, 2005; Paul Blustein, "WTO Keeps Talks Alive with Deals on Some Trade Barriers," *Washington Post*, December 19, 2005, sec. A.

51. Steven R. Weisman, "World Bank Chief Urges Trade Concession," *New York Times*, July 10, 2006, sec. A. See also Paul Wolfowitz, "Doha's Last Chance," *Wall Street*

Journal, July 1–2, 2006, sec. A; Tom Wright and Steven R. Weisman, "Trade Talks Fail over an Impasse on Farm Tariffs," *New York Times,* July 25, 2006, sec. A; Paul Blustein, "Trade Talks Fail after Stalemate over Farm Issues," *Washington Post,* July 25, 2006, sec. D; Steven R. Weissman and Alexei Barrionuevo, "Failure of Global Trade Talks Is Traced to the Power of Farmers," *New York Times,* July 27, 2006, sec. C; Larry Rohter, "Agriculture Discord Stymies World Trade Talks' Revival," *New York Times,* September 11, 2006, sec. A.

52. Thornton, "Wolfowitz Demands."

53. Becker, "New World Bank Chief." See also Paul Wolfowitz, "Good Governance and Development: A Time for Action," Jakarta, Indonesia, April 11, 2006, *World Bank,* http://web.worldbank.org (accessed April 12, 2006).

54. Elizabeth Becker, "For McNamara and Wolfowitz, a War and Then the World Bank," *New York Times,* March 22, 2005, sec. C.

55. Alan Sipress and Ellen Nakashima, "Jakarta Tenure Offers Glimpse of Wolfowitz, *Washington Post,* March 28, 2005, sec. A. See also Wolfowitz, "Good Governance and Development."

56. Quoted in Becker and Sanger, "Wolfowitz Gets Bush Nomination."

57. Paul Wolfowitz, "Charting a Way Ahead: The Results Agenda, 2005 Annual Meetings Address," Washington, D.C., September 24, 2005, *World Bank,* http://web.worldbank.org (accessed December 20, 2005). See also Andrew Balls and Chris Giles, "Leadership Key in Poor Nations, Says Wolfowitz," *Financial Times* (London), September 26, 2005.

58. "Media Roundtable with World Bank President Paul Wolfowitz," Washington, DC, July 5, 2005, *World Bank,* http://web.worldbank.org (accessed September 25, 2005). See also Alan Freeman, "World Bank Chief Urges Integrated Approach to Aid," *Globe and Mail* (Toronto), July 6, 2005, sec. A. A study by Harvard University economist Benjamin A. Olken, "Monitoring Corruption: Evidence from a Field Experiment in Indonesia," National Bureau of Economic Research, NBER Working Paper no. 11753, October 2005, found that the threat of central government audits reduced mission expenditures by eight percentage points; while more intensive community monitors only reduced missing wages, but not missing materials expenditures.

59. Pound and Knight, "On Top of the World."

60. I have drawn on Edward T. Pound, Danielle Knight, and Jennifer Jack, "Cleaning Up the World Bank," *U.S. News & World Report,* April 3, 2006, 43–44, 48, 50; "The World Bank Just Saying No," *Economist,* March 4, 2006, 69; Sebastian Mallaby, "Wolfowitz's Corruption Agenda," *Washington Post,* February 20, 2006, sec. A. The Bank subsequently approved projects for India's health sector. Press Release, "World Bank Supports India's Health Sector," August 22, 2006, Press Release No. 2007/55/SAR, *World Bank,* http:web.worldbank.org (accessed September 5, 2006). Sources dealing with Wolfowitz's action regarding Chad include Lydia Polgreen, "Chad Backs Out of Pledge to Use Oil Wealth to Reduce Poverty," *New York Times,* December 13, 2005, sec A; Paul Blustein, "Chad May Alter Its Pledge on Oil Funds," *Washington Post,* December 27, 2005, sec. D; Paul Blustein, "World Bank Cuts Off Aid to Chad in Oil Dispute," *Washington Post,* January 7, 2006, sec. D; Celia W. Dugger, "World Bank Suspends Loans to Chad over Use of Oil Money," *New York Times,* January 7, 2006, sec. A; David White, "Chad Defies World Bank over Use of Oil Revenues," *Financial Time* (London), January 13, 2006. Pursuant to an April 2006 three-month interim agreement, Chad agreed to spend 70 percent of its oil revenues on priority poverty sectors and to improve its public finances, including stricter audits of its oil revenues; in turn, the bank began to disperse loan funds and part of the accumulated oil revenues. Paul Blustein, "Chad May Soon Regain Access to Its Oil Funds," *Washington Post,* April 27, 2006, sec. D. Then, under a July 2006 arrangement, Chad agreed to allocate

70 percent of its budget, including all of its oil-related revenues, to poverty-reduction programs. Press Release, "World Bank, Gov't of Chad Sign Memorandum of Understanding on Poverty Reduction," July 14, 2006, Press Release No. 2007/19/EXC, *World Bank*, http://web.worldbank.org (accessed July 23, 2006). See also Paul Blustein, "Chad, World Bank Settle Dispute over Oil Money," *Washington Post*, July 15, 2006, sec. D; Lydia Polgreen, "World Bank Reaches Pact with Chad over Use of Oil Profits," *New York Times*, July 15, 2006, sec. A. Mallaby, *World's Banker*, 342–56, 369–73, traces the history of the bank's involvement in the controversial Chad-Cameroon oil pipeline under Wolfensohn.

61. Blustein, "World Bank Staffers Protest Appointments."

62. Wolfowitz, "Good Governance and Development." See also Celia W. Dugger, "World Bank Chief Outlines a War on Fraud," *New York Times*, April 12, 2006, sec. A; Paul Blustein, "World Bank Strategy Targets Corruption," *Washington Post*, April 12, 2006, sec. D.

63. Dugger, "World Bank Chief Outlines"; Chris Giles and Krishna Guha, "Wolfowitz Pledges to Develop Formal Framework to Help Tackle Corruption," *Financial Times* (London), April 24, 2006.

64. Development Committee Communiqué, Joint Ministerial Committee of the Boards of Governors of the Bank and the Fund on the Transfer of Real Resources to Developing Countries, September 18, 2006. See also "President Paul Wolfowitz—Remarks to the Development Committee," September 18, 2006, *World Bank*, http://web.worldbank.org (accessed September 18, 2006); Steven R. Weisman, "I.M.F. Votes to Enhance Power of China and Others," *New York Times*, September 19, 2006, sec. C; Chris Giles and Krishna Guha, "Blow to Wolfowitz as Governments Insist on Final Say over Corruption," *Financial Times* (London), September 19, 2006; Steven R. Weisman, "Wolfowitz Corruption Drive Rattles World Bankers," *New York Times*, September 14, 2006, sec. C.

65. Becker, "New World Bank Chief."

66. David Dollar and Lant Pritchett, *Assessing Aid: What Works, What Doesn't, and Why* (New York: Oxford University Press, 1998). See also Mallaby, *World's Banker*, 175, 202–3, 222–30, 233.

67. Mallaby, *World's Banker*, 254, 259.

68. Birdsall et al., "Hardest Job," 8, fig. 1.

69. Adam Lerrick, "Why Is the World Bank Still Lending?" *Wall Street Journal*, October 28, 2005, sec. A.

70. Christopher Swann, "Wolfowitz Avoids Rocking Boat," *Financial Times* (London), June 2, 2005.

71. Richard McGregor, "Bank President Defends Loans for China," *Financial Times* (London), October 18, 2005. See also "Press Conference with Paul Wolfowitz," Tokyo, Japan, October 9, 2005, *World Bank*, http://web.worldbank.org (accessed October 19, 2005). Desmond Lachman, "The World Bank's business Is Aid Not Commerce," *Financial Times*, November 4, 2005, critiques continued bank loans to China.

72. "Remarks by President Wolfowitz on the Graduation of the Czech Republic from World Bank Group," Prague, Czech Republic, February 28, 2006, *World Bank*, http:// web. worldbank.org (accessed March 26, 2006).

73. Ibid.

74. Birdsall et al., "Hardest Job," 11, fig. 2.

75. Blustein, "All Eyes."

76. Bloomberg News Service, "Paul Wolfowitz to Be Nominated as Next World Bank President," March 16, 2005, http://www.bloomberg.com/ (accessed November 1, 2005); Don D'Crug, "Back to Basics at the Bank," *Australian*, June 3, 2005.

77. World Bank, *The World Bank Annual Report 2004*, vol. 1, *Year in Review*, 104, table 5.2, *World Bank*, http://www.worldbank.org/html/extpb/2004/.

78. World Bank Operations Evaluation Department, *2004 Annual Review of Development Effectiveness: The World Bank's Contributions to Poverty Reduction* (Washington, DC: World Bank, 2005), xiv, 51.

79. Blustein, "All Eyes."

80. Wolfowitz, "Charting a Way Ahead."

81. Becker, "New World Bank Chief."

82. See, e.g., William Easterly, *The White Man's Burden: Why the West's Efforts to Aid the Rest Have Done So Much Ill and So Little Good* (New York: Penguin Press, 2006).

83. "Annual Meetings 2005 Opening Press Conference with Paul Wolfowitz," Washington, DC, September 22, 2005, *World Bank*, http://www.worldbank.org (accessed April 16, 2006). See also "Interview with New World Bank President Paul Wolfowitz," June 4, 2005, *World Bank*, http://web.worldbank.org (accessed September 25, 2005); "Press Conference with World Bank President Paul Wolfowitz," Washington, DC, June 7, 2005, *World Bank*, http://web.worldbank.org (accessed June 23, 2005).

84. Greg Hitt, "A Kinder, Gentler Wolfowitz at World Bank?" *Wall Street Journal*, September 22, 2005, sec. A; Paul A. Gigot, "Dr. Wolfowitz, I Presume," *Wall Street Journal*, September 24–25, 2005, sec. A.

85. Wolfowitz, "Charting a Way Ahead."

86. Lewis D. Solomon, "Human Reconstruction in America's Inner Cities: A Legal and Policy Analysis," *Harvard Journal of Law and Public Policy* 15, no. 1 (Winter 1992): 191–221. See also Brigit Helms, *Access for All: Building Inclusive Financial Systems* (Washington, DC: World Bank, 2006), which describes how micro-finance can help the poor to become part of the financial mainstream.

87. The World Bank, "2005 Celebrating the Year of Microcredit," September 11, 2005, *World Bank*, http://web.worldbank.org (accessed April 16, 2006).

88. Cris Prystay, "With Loans, Poor South Asian Women Turn Entrepreneurial," *Wall Street Journal*, May 25, 2005, sec. B. See also C. K. Prahalad, *The Fortune at the Bottom of the Pyramid* (Upper Saddle River, NJ: Wharton School Publishing, 2005), 207–35; John Lancaster, "Building Wealth by the Penny," *Washington Post*, March 14, 2004, sec. A; S. Dinakar, "A Penny a Packet," *Forbes*, November 28, 2005, 186, 188; C. K. Prahalad, "Aid Is Not the Answer," *Wall Street Journal*, August 31, 2005, sec. A; David Ignatius, "Profits, A Penny at a Time," *Washington Post*, July 6, 2005, sec. A.

89. "Opening Remarks by Paul Wolfowitz at High-Level Consultation: Promoting the Gender Equality MDG [Millennium Development Goal]," Washington, DC, February 16, 2006, *World Bank*, http://web.worldbank.org (accessed March 26, 2006).

90. "Press Conference with World Bank President Paul Wolfowitz at the Conclusion of a Meeting of Women's Groups," Hyderabad, India, August 18, 2005, *World Bank*, http://web.worldbank.org (accessed September 25, 2005). See also World Bank Group, "Women of Andhra Pradesh and Their Life beyond Poverty," August 18, 2005, *World Bank*, http://web.worldbank.org (accessed September 25, 2005).

91. Associated Press, "Wolfowitz in Talks with Finance Minister," August 19, 2005, Story no. 459230, http://www.aparchive.com (accessed April 10, 2006). See also Hindu Business Line (Internet Edition), "Andhra Predesh Women Self-help Groups' Success 'Remarkable,' Says Wolfowitz," August 19, 2005, www.blonnet.com/2005/08/19/stories/20050819028,0900.htm (accessed January 10, 2006).

Selected Bibliography

BOOKS

Bacevich, Andrew J. *The New American Militarism: How Americans Are Seduced by War*. New York: Oxford University Press, 2005.

Bremer, L. Paul, III, with Malcolm McConnell. *My Year In Iraq: The Struggle to Build a Future of Hope*. New York: Simon and Schuster, 2006.

Cordesman, Anthony. *The Iraq War: Strategy, Tactics, and Military Lessons*. Westport, CT: Praeger, 2003.

Fallows, James. *Blind into Baghdad: America's War in Iraq*. New York: Vintage, 2006.

Galbraith, Peter W. *The End of Iraq: How American Incompetence Created a War without End*. New York: Simon and Schuster, 2006.

Gaddis, John Lewis. *Surprise, Security, and the American Experience*. Cambridge, MA: Harvard University Press, 2004.

Easterly, William. *The White Man's Burden: Why the West's Efforts to Aid the Rest Have Done So Much Ill and So Little Good*. New York: Penguin Press, 2006.

Gordon, Michael R., and Bernard E. Trainor. *COBRA II: The Inside Story of the Invasion and Occupation of Iraq*. New York: Pantheon, 2006.

———. *The Generals' War: The Inside Story of the Conflict in the Gulf*. Boston: Little, Brown, 1995.

Mallaby, Sebastian. *The World's Banker: A Story of Failed States, Financial Crises, and the Wealth and Poverty of Nations*. New York: Penguin Press, 2004.

Mann, James. *About Face: A History of America's Curious Relationship with China, from Nixon to Clinton*. New York: Alfred A. Knopf, 1999.

———. *Rise of the Vulcans: The History of Bush's War Cabinet*. New York: Viking, 2004.

Packer, George. *The Assassins' Gate: America in Iraq*. New York: Farrar, Straus and Giroux, 2005.

Ricks, Thomas E. *Fiasco: The American Military Adventure in Iraq*. New York: Penguin, 2006.

Risen, James. *State of War: The Secret History of the CIA and the Bush Administration*. New York: Free Press, 2006.

Woodward, Bob. *Bush at War*. New York: Simon and Schuster, 2002.

————. *The Commanders*. New York: Simon and Schuster, 1991.

————. *Plan of Attack*. New York: Simon and Schuster, 2004.

————. *State of Denial: Bush at War, Part III*. New York: Simon and Schuster, 2006.

ARTICLES

Bowden, Mark. "Wolfowitz: The Exit Interviews." *Atlantic Monthly*, July–August 2005, 110–22.

Dudley, David. "Paul's Choice." *Cornell Alumni Magazine*, July–August 2004, 48–57.

Keller, Bill. "The Sunshine Warrior." *New York Times Magazine*, September 22, 2002, 48.

Podhoretz, Norman. "World War IV: How It Started, What It Means, and Why We Have to Win." *Commentary*, September 2004, 17–54.

Sen, Amartya. "Democracy Isn't 'Western.'" *Wall Street Journal*, March 24, 2006.

Tanenhaus, Sam. "Bush's Brain Trust." *Vanity Fair*, July 2003, 114.

Index

About the Author

LEWIS D. SOLOMON is Van Vleck Research Professor of Law at the George Washington University Law School. He is the author of numerous books, among them *From Athens to America: Virtues and the Formulation of Public Policy* (2006), *The Quest for Human Longevity* (2006), and *In God We Trust? Faith-based Organizations and the Quest to Solve America's Social Ills* (2003).

www.ingramcontent.com/pod-product-compliance
Lightning Source LLC
Chambersburg PA
CBHW070446100426
42812CB00004B/1217